Visual QuickStart Guide
## Internet Explorer 5 For Windows
Steve Schwartz

## Peachpit Press
1249 Eighth Street
Berkeley, CA 94710
510/524-2178
800/283-9444
510/524-2221 (fax)

Find us on the World Wide Web at http://www.peachpit.com

Peachpit Press is a division of Addison Wesley Longman.

Editor: Corbin Collins
Production Coordinator: Amy Changar
Compositor: Maureen Forys, Happenstance Type-O-Rama
Indexer: Emily Glossbrenner
Cover Design: The Visual Group

ISBN 0-201-35444-6

9 8 7 6 5 4 3 2 1

Printed and bound in the United States of America

♻ Printed on recycled paper

## About the author

Steve Schwartz began writing professionally in 1978 as a contributing editor for *Nibble*, a popular Apple II magazine. In the past 20 years, he's written hundreds of reviews and computer-related articles, in addition to almost 40 books. He was also the chief methodologist and a founding editor for Software Digest, Business Applications Editor for MACazine, and Technical Services Director for Funk Software. He has a Ph.D. in Psychology and lives in the fictional town of Lizard Spit, Arizona.

**Special thanks to**
Corbin Collins of Peachpit Press for his kind
assistance and support, and to Amy Changar
and Maureen Forys for their excellent
production work.

# TABLE OF CONTENTS

TABLE OF CONTENTS

TABLE OF CONTENTS

# INTRODUCTION

Welcome to *Internet Explorer 5 for Windows: Visual QuickStart Guide*!

## About this book

The intent of this book (and every other title in the *Visual QuickStart* series) is to get you up and running as quickly as possible. This book makes only a few assumptions about you:

◆ You understand the fundamentals of using a computer, such as how to use a mouse and how to choose menu commands. You do not have to be an expert computer user or an Internet maven.

◆ You have some form of Internet access. It doesn't matter whether you use an ISP (Internet Service Provider), a major information service such as America Online, or if you connect via your office's network.

◆ You have or can obtain a copy of Microsoft Internet Explorer 5 (called IE5 throughout this book).

   If you don't already have a copy of the program, you can download it from Microsoft's Web site at:

   http://www.microsoft.com/windows/ie/

## The philosophy of this book

Internet Explorer is a special breed of software. It is a full-featured suite of Internet programs. Like many current programs, though, Internet Explorer does not include a manual. Although extensive help files are provided, you'll find that many of your questions and problems are not addressed.

The purpose of this book is to provide you with answers to those questions—in the succinct, step-by-step, visually rich style for which the *Visual QuickStart* series is known.

## Parts of the book

This book is divided into three parts, each corresponding to a logical component of the Internet Explorer package:

- *Internet Explorer.* The Web browser itself.

- *Outlook Express.* The email program and Usenet newsgroup reader.

- *Appendixes.* If you stumble across a term that you don't understand, look in the Glossary (Appendix A) for a definition. You can find keyboard shortcuts for the programs in Appendices B through D. And for tips on installing the downloadable version of IE5, see Appendix E.

## Feedback

You can send comments and suggestions to ie5vqs@hotmail.com.

# PART 1

# THE BROWSER

# THE ACTIVE DESKTOP

Introduced in Internet Explorer 4 and included as an integral part of Windows 98, *Active Desktop* integrates Internet functions into Windows. With Active Desktop, you can:

◆ Visit Web sites by choosing them from the Start > Favorites menu.

◆ Perform advanced Find commands.

◆ Add favorite programs and documents to the taskbar, making them available at a click.

◆ Browse files on hard disks using the same commands and interface you use to browse the Web.

◆ Customize folders by using a picture or a Web page as the background.

◆ Launch programs and open documents with a single click, rather than a double-click.

◆ Customize your desktop by placing Web pages or other Internet components on it.

## ✔ Important Note

■ Active Desktop is *not* a component of IE5. Only users that previously installed IE4 or use Windows 98 will be able to use the features described in this chapter. If you are running Windows 95, and have not previously installed IE4, to use Active Desktop you must install IE4 and enable Active Desktop before installing IE5.

# The New Start Menu

With Active Desktop installed and enabled, the Start menu has three new features:

◆ A Favorites folder that contains copies of your IE5 favorite sites, enabling you to go directly to Web sites of interest.

◆ An enhanced Find command.

◆ An Active Desktop command in the Settings menu.

## The Start menu's Favorites folder

*Favorites* (see Chapter 4) are Web pages that you've asked IE5 to remember for you, so you can easily visit them again without having to type their addresses. With Active Desktop, you can simultaneously launch IE5 and visit a specific Web page by selecting the page from the Favorites folder on the Start menu. You can reorganize pages in the Favorites folder by dragging them to new positions.

### To open IE5 to a given Web page:

1. Click the Start button on the task bar, choose Favorites, and choose the desired Web page (**Figure 1.1**).

2. Release the mouse button.

If IE5 is already running, the chosen page is fetched and displayed. If IE5 is not running, IE5 launches and then fetches the chosen page.

### To reorganize favorites in the Favorites folder:

1. Click the Start button on the task bar, choose Favorites, and highlight the Web page or folder you want to move.

2. Drag the favorite or folder to a new position in the menu (indicated by a black horizontal bar, as shown in **Figure 1.2**) and release the mouse button.

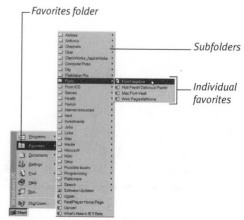

Favorites folder — Subfolders — Individual favorites

**Figure 1.1** The Favorites menu.

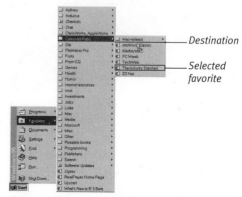

Destination — Selected favorite

**Figure 1.2** Click and drag to change a page's position in the Favorites menu.

**Figure 1.3** The Find menu.

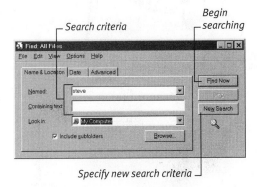

*Search criteria*

*Begin searching*

*Specify new search criteria*

**Figure 1.4** The Find: All Files dialog box.

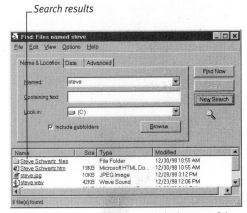

*Search results*

**Figure 1.5** Search results appear at the bottom of the dialog box.

## Enhanced Find command

If you click Start > Find, you'll see that the Find menu has new commands (**Figure 1.3**). Now you can use it to search for files and folders on your hard disk, people in your address book or on the Internet, and Web sites.

## To find files or folders on your computer:

1. Choose Start > Find > Files or Folders.

   The Find: All Files dialog box appears (**Figure 1.4**). Specify your search criteria by completing any of Steps 2–6.

2. In the Named box, type all or part of the filename or folder name sought.

3. In the Containing text box, type a text string that is contained within the file. (For example, if you know that a text file contains the phrase "Simi Valley Bond" but don't know the file's name, you can use this option to search for this text *within* files.)

4. In the Look in box, select the drive or folder in which to search. (Click Browse if you want to search in a folder that is not listed in the drop-down list.) To also search all folders within the chosen drive or folder, click the option to Include subfolders.

5. Click the Date tab to search for files or folders based on their creation, modification, or last access date.

6. Click the Advanced tab to search for files or folders based on their type or size.

7. To begin the search, click Find Now. Results are shown in a scrolling list at the bottom of the dialog box (**Figure 1.5**).

8. To open a found file, folder, or program, double-click its name in the list.

9. To conduct another search, click New Search. Otherwise, click the close box (*x*) to dismiss the Find dialog box.

## To find people in Address Book:

1. Choose Start > Find > People.

   The Find People dialog box appears (**Figure 1.6**).

2. From the Look in drop-down list, choose Contacts to search your Address Book.

3. Enter search strings in the Name, E-mail, Address, Phone, and/or Other fields.

   Enter as much or as little information as you want. Search strings can be partial or complete words.

4. Click the Find Now button.

   Results of the search are shown in the bottom of the window.

5. *Optional:* To determine whether you've found the correct person, select his or her name and click Properties.

6. *Optional:* To perform an action on a found person (such as sending him/her an email message), right-click the name and choose the desired action (**Figure 1.7**).

7. When you are finished, click Close to dismiss the dialog box.

## To find people on the Internet:

1. Choose Start > Find > People.

   The Find People dialog box appears.

2. From the Look in drop-down list, choose an Internet search site.

3. Enter a name and/or email address for which to search.

   *or*

   Click the Advanced tab to enter more specific search criteria (**Figure 1.8**). Define each criterion by choosing options from the drop-down lists and typing one or more keywords. Click Add after defining each new criterion. To remove a criterion, select it and click Remove.

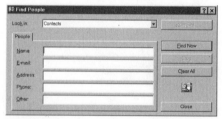

**Figure 1.6** The Find People dialog box looks like this when searching for someone in your Windows Address Book.

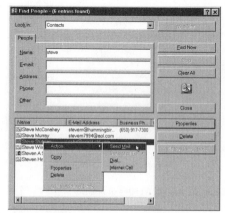

**Figure 1.7** Right-click a possible match and choose Action, followed by the action you want performed.

*Specify criteria here* ___ *Criteria list*

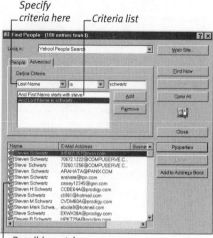

*Possible matches*

**Figure 1.8** You can specify multiple search criteria in the Advanced section of the Find People dialog box.

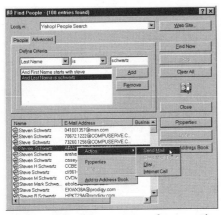

**Figure 1.9** Right-click a name to perform an action on the found person.

*Search Assistant*

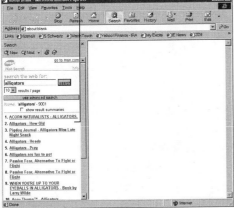

**Figure 1.10** The Search Assistant appears in the left side of the IE5 window. This is the same as clicking IE5's Search button.

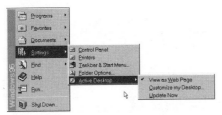

**Figure 1.11** Use the Settings › Active Desktop menu to configure Active Desktop.

4. To begin the search, click Find Now. Results of the search are shown in the bottom of the window.

5. To determine whether you've found the correct person, select his/her name and click Properties.

6. *Optional:* To perform an action on a found person (such as sending an email message or adding the person to your Address Book), right-click the name and choose Action, followed by the desired action (**Figure 1.9**).

7. *Optional:* To perform the same search using a different search engine, select the new site from the Look in list and click Find Now.

8. When you are done, click Close to dismiss the Find People dialog box.

## To find Web sites on the Internet:

1. Choose Start > Find > On the Internet. IE5 launches (if it's not already running), and a blank page containing the Search Assistant appears (**Figure 1.10**).

2. Follow the instructions in Chapter 5 for using the Search Assistant.

## The Active Desktop menu

When you choose the Start > Settings menu, you'll find a new Active Desktop submenu (**Figure 1.11**) with the following commands: View as Web Page, Customize My Desktop, and Update Now.

Choose *View as Web Page* to turn Active Desktop off or on. (When View as Web Page is checked, Active Desktop is on.)

Choose *Customize My Desktop* to add or remove custom Internet components from your desktop. A modified version of the Display control panel (**Figure 1.12**) appears, open to the new Web section. (See "Customizing Active Desktop," later in this chapter, for details.)

Choose *Update Now* to download new information for all your Active Desktop items.

## ✔ Tips

- Other programs installed on your computer (**Figure 1.13**) sometimes add their own commands to the Find menu.

- You can visit the Web site of any of the people-search engines by clicking the Web Site button in the Find People dialog box.

- Disconnect from the Internet before dialing the phone number of a person found with the Find People command.

- You can also access the Settings > Active Desktop menu by right-clicking the desktop.

- If you have multiple Active Desktop items, you can update them individually by clicking the tiny down arrow in the upper left-hand corner of the item and choosing Synchronize (**Figure 1.14**). For more information on adding and managing Active Desktop items, see "Active Desktop Items," later in this chapter.

Active Desktop items

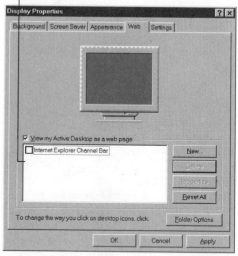

**Figure 1.12** You use the Web section of the Display control panel to add, remove, or edit Active Desktop items.

Find using Microsoft Outlook

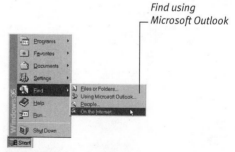

**Figure 1.13** If you use Microsoft Outlook rather than Outlook Express, you'll see an additional command in the Find menu.

**Figure 1.14** Click the down arrow in the area at the top of any desktop item to reveal a command menu.

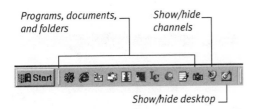

**Figure 1.15** Icons immediately to the right of the Start button represent programs, documents, and folders that you can launch with a single click.

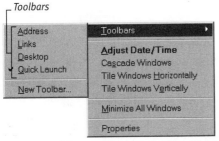

**Figure 1.16** Adding a toolbar to the taskbar. (Checked toolbars are already enabled.)

# The Taskbar

Active Desktop enhances the Windows taskbar with these new features:

◆ You can add favorite program, document, and folder shortcuts to the taskbar.

◆ You can customize the taskbar by adding Web-related toolbars, such as Links.

## Adding a shortcut to the taskbar:

1. Right-click a blank spot in the taskbar and be sure that Toolbars > Quick Launch is checked.

2. Drag a shortcut icon for a program, document, or folder onto the taskbar (**Figure 1.15**).
   A dark, vertical bar indicates the item's placement.

3. When the item is properly positioned, release the mouse button.

## Launching an item on the taskbar:

◆ To open a program, document, or folder, click its icon on the taskbar.

   *or*

◆ To open a document with a program that is on the taskbar, drag the document icon onto the program's icon on the taskbar.

## Adding toolbars to the Taskbar

Right-click any blank spot in the taskbar and choose Toolbars, followed by the name of the toolbar (**Figure 1.16**). Choose an unchecked toolbar to add it to the taskbar. Choose a checked toolbar to remove it from the taskbar.

## ✔ Tips

■ You can create a toolbar that represents a Web site or any folder on your hard disk by choosing New Toolbar (see **Figure 1.16**).

■ You can move the taskbar to a different edge of the screen by clicking on it and dragging.

THE TASKBAR

# Windows Explorer Windows

With Active Desktop installed and enabled, browser and folder windows are interchangeable. You can use either type of window to open programs or files on a local hard disk, as well as visit Web sites. IE5 recognizes whether you are currently exploring your hard disk or the Web and changes the window's toolbars as appropriate (**Figure 1.17**).

To visit a Web page from a folder, you can:

◆ Type the page's URL in the Address box and then press (Enter) or click Go.

◆ Click a Links button.

◆ Select a page from the Favorites menu.

◆ Choose View > Explorer Bar, followed by Search, Favorites, or History.

To work with items on disk from within an IE5 window, you can:

◆ Type the path for the folder, file, or program in the Address box, such as C:\Temp\winlogo.jpg.

◆ Choose File > Open and type the path for a folder, file, or program. (You can also click Browse to select a file to open or a program to launch.)

◆ Transform a browser window or any open folder window into Windows Explorer by choosing View > Explorer Bar > Folders.

## Folder navigation

With the new folder window toolbar, you can navigate your computer's drives in much the same way as you navigate the Web. After opening any folder, you can open folders that are nested inside the current folder or click the Up button to go to the next higher folder or drive in the path hierarchy. Click the Back button to go the previously opened folder or Web page.

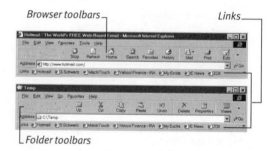

*Browser toolbars* — *Links* —

*Folder toolbars*

**Figure 1.17** Browser toolbars (top) and folder toolbars (bottom) share many of the same features.

—Thumbnail

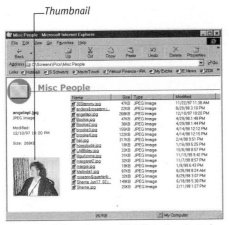

**Figure 1.18** When View > as Web Page is selected, thumbnail images are automatically generated for certain types of graphic files.

**Figure 1.19** This is the default page used in Web view. To see the available and used space on one of your hard disks, open My Computer and highlight a drive.

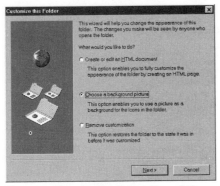

**Figure 1.20** This wizard walks you through the process of creating a custom folder background.

## Viewing graphics

If you highlight the name of a GIF, JPEG, or Windows bitmap (BMP) graphics file in an open folder, you're shown a thumbnail image of the graphic (**Figure 1.18**). If you *don't* see a thumbnail, be sure View > as Web Page is selected.

## Customizing folders

If you're tired of the staid, old Windows folders, Active Desktop offers some surprising folder enhancements. You can:

◆ Display folders as Web pages or with a picture background.

◆ Display graphic files as thumbnails.

◆ Set default folder options.

### To display a folder as a Web page:

1. Open the folder.

2. Choose View > as Web Page.

   View > as Web Page is a toggle command. When checked, the folder uses a Web page as the background (**Figure 1.19**). When unchecked, the standard blank background is used.

### To create a custom background for a folder:

1. Open the folder.

2. Choose View > Customize this Folder or right-click a blank spot inside the folder and choose Customize this Folder.

   The Customize this Folder wizard appears (**Figure 1.20**).

3. To edit the current Web page background in your default editor (such as Notepad), click *Create or edit an HTML document* and then click Next. Go to Step 7.

4. To choose a background picture for the folder, click *Choose a background picture* and then click Next.

5. Select a BMP, JPEG, or GIF file to serve as a background picture (**Figure 1.21**).

   *or*

   Specify a background color by clicking the Background checkbox and choosing a color (**Figure 1.21**).

6. *Optional*: Choose a text color by clicking the large colored block.

7. Click Finish. **Figure 1.22** shows an example of a custom folder background.

## Displaying file icons as graphic thumbnails

As previously mentioned, when you open a folder and run the cursor over the name or icon of a graphic file, a thumbnail of the graphic is automatically created and displayed. Optionally, you can simultaneously display *all* graphic file icons in a given folder as thumbnails.

## To turn on thumbnail view for a folder:

1. Open the folder.

2. Right-click in a blank area of the folder and choose Properties.

   The *Filename* Properties dialog box appears (**Figure 1.23**).

3. Click the checkbox for Enable thumbnail view.

4. Click OK to dismiss the dialog box.

   If the graphic files are not automatically shown as thumbnails, right-click in the folder and choose Refresh.

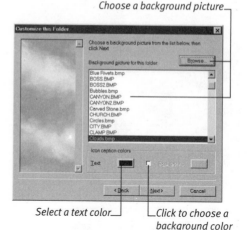

*Choose a background picture*

*Select a text color* — *Click to choose a background color*

**Figure 1.21** Folders can have a background picture or a solid background color. Choose a picture from the list presented or by clicking the Browse button.

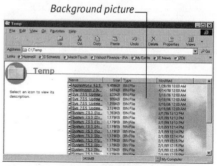

*Background picture*

**Figure 1.22** Clouds.bmp (the Windows startup picture) makes a nice folder background, too.

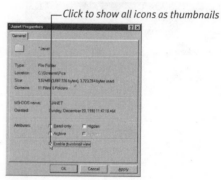

*Click to show all icons as thumbnails*

**Figure 1.23** The Properties dialog box for a folder.

**Figure 1.24** The Toolbars submenu.

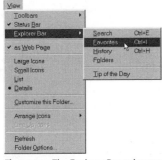

**Figure 1.25** The Explorer Bar submenu.

# Default folder and system options

Active Desktop has several customization options that affect the appearance of folders and the manner in which you interact with the computer. You can:

◆ Specify which components, such as toolbars, are displayed in all folders.

◆ Set your computer to act in Web fashion, standard Windows fashion, or a combination of the two styles.

◆ Designate a standard folder style, so all folder windows look alike.

## To specify default folder window components:

1. Open any folder on your hard disk.

2. Choose View > Toolbars and then choose a toolbar to show or hide (**Figure 1.24**). (Visible toolbars are preceded by a checkmark in the Toolbars menu.)
   The toolbar is shown or hidden.

3. Choose View > Explorer Bar, and then choose an Explorer bar to display (**Figure 1.25**). (A visible Explorer bar is preceded by a checkmark in the menu. Only one Explorer bar can be enabled at a time.)
   The Explorer bar appears on the left side of the window. Like the View > Toolbars command, this command works as a toggle. To remove the current Explorer bar, choose the same command again or click the Explorer bar's close box (the tiny *x*).

4. To show or hide the status bar at the bottom of the window, choose View > Status Bar.

**WINDOWS EXPLORER WINDOWS**

## To specify default system behaviors:

1. Choose Start > Settings > Folder Options or choose View > Folder Options in any folder window.

   The Folder Options dialog box appears (**Figure 1.26**).

2. On the General tab, specify the manner in which your computer will operate:

   ◆ *Web style*. The desktop and folders act like Web pages. You use single clicks to launch programs and open documents.

   ◆ *Classic style*. The computer will operate in normal Windows fashion.

   ◆ *Custom*. If you want to mix and match Web and classic features, choose this option and click the Settings button (**Figure 1.27**).

3. Click OK to close the dialog box.

*Custom settings*

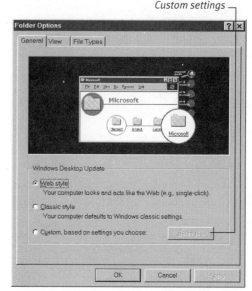

**Figure 1.26** Choose system style settings in the General section of the Folder Options dialog box.

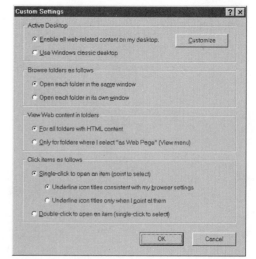

**Figure 1.27** Specify custom settings, mixing Active Desktop and classic Windows settings as you like.

*Set all folders to match current folder*

*Reset all folders to the default settings*

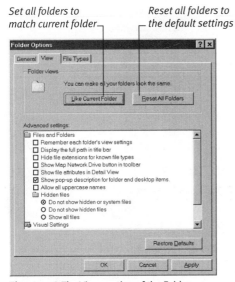

**Figure 1.28** The View section of the Folder Options dialog box.

## Single-Click Mode

When Folder Options are set for *Web style*, you interact with files using single clicks rather than double clicks. Although this takes some getting used to, it is easier if you keep the following facts in mind:

◆ Single-click any program on the desktop, taskbar, or in a folder to launch it.

◆ Single-click any document icon on the desktop, taskbar, or in a folder to open it with the appropriate program.

◆ To select an item on the desktop or in a folder, move the cursor over it; do *not* click it.

◆ To select multiple items on the desktop, click and drag a rectangle around them. Then right-click any one of the selected items to choose a command.

◆ To choose the default command in any file dialog box (when opening a file, for example), you must still double-click the filename.

## To make all folders the same:

1. Open the folder on which you want to standardize. Make any changes that you like, such as choosing toolbars and a display mode (Details or Large Icons, for example).

2. Choose View > Folder Options.
   The Folder Options dialog box appears (refer to **Figure 1.26**).

3. Click the View tab (**Figure 1.28**).

4. Click the Like Current Folder button.

5. Click OK.
   To restore all folders to their original, unmodified state, click Reset All Folders in Step 4.

## ✔ Tips

■ To reset the background for the current folder to its most recent state, choose View > Customize this Folder and then click *Remove customization*.

■ When picking a folder background, be sure that the file and folder names can still easily be read. If not, try a less complex picture.

# Active Desktop Items

If your computer is usually connected to the Internet or a company Intranet, you may want to take advantage of Active Desktop's ability to display live Internet items on the desktop, such as Web pages and Java applets. With an open Internet/Intranet connection, these items can automatically update themselves, presenting you with the latest stock quotes, sports scores, or company sales figures, for example. Items can also contain links that—when clicked—launch IE5 and display the destination Web page.

## Adding items to the Active Desktop

You can add new Active Desktop items to the desktop by dragging Web page links from IE5 onto the desktop, or by choosing them from Microsoft's Web site or your Favorites folder.

### To create an Active Desktop item from a Web page or a link:

1.  Launch IE5 and visit the Web page that you want to make into a desktop item.

    Note that you can create an item from any *link* on a Web page, as well as from the page itself.

2.  In the Address box, right-click the Web page icon or right-click a link on the Web page, and drag it onto the desktop.

    When you release the mouse button, a pop-up menu appears (**Figure 1.29**).

3.  Choose Create Active Desktop Item(s) Here.

    A dialog box appears, asking if you want to add the item to the desktop.

4.  Click Yes.

    The Add Item to Active Desktop dialog box appears (**Figure 1.30**).

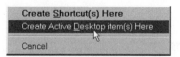

**Figure 1.29** When you create an Active Desktop item by right-dragging a Web page URL or link to the desktop, this menu appears.

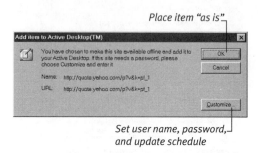

*Place item "as is"*

*Set user name, password, and update schedule*

**Figure 1.30** You can quickly create a desktop item by clicking OK in this dialog box. To set a user name, password, and/or update schedule, click Customize.

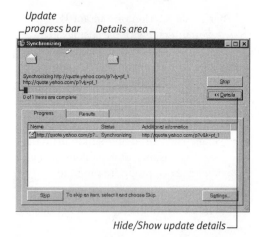

*Update progress bar*  *Details area*

*Hide/Show update details*

**Figure 1.31** The Synchronizing dialog box shows the update progress as new data is downloaded from the Internet.

Add a new item

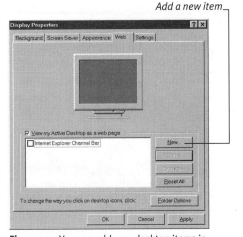

**Figure 1.32** You can add new desktop items in the Display Properties dialog box.

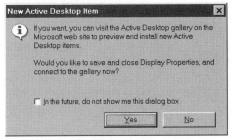

**Figure 1.33** Create a new desktop item by choosing it from Microsoft's Active Desktop Gallery or use a wizard to select one.

Stock ticker

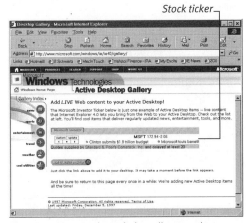

**Figure 1.34** Browse through the gallery to select Active Desktop items, such as this stock price and business news ticker.

**5.** If manual updates are satisfactory, and a user name/password are not required, click OK. If the item requires you to enter a user name and password, or if you want to specify a schedule on which automatic updates will occur, click Customize. Use the Online Favorite wizard to specify an update schedule and/or a user name/password combination. When you return to the Add Item to Active Desktop dialog box, click OK.

**6.** The Synchronizing dialog box appears (**Figure 1.31**), current data for the item is downloaded from the Internet, and the item appears on your desktop.

The item can be resized by dragging any edge or corner. You can change an item's position by clicking in its gray title bar and dragging.

## To create an Active Desktop item from a Favorite:

**1.** Right-click the desktop and choose Active Desktop > Customize My Desktop or click Start > Settings > Active Desktop > Customize My Desktop.

The Display Properties dialog box appears (**Figure 1.32**).

**2.** Click the New button.

The New Active Desktop Item dialog box appears (**Figure 1.33**).

**3.** To add a desktop item from Microsoft's Web site, click Yes and follow the instructions on the Web page that appears (**Figure 1.34**). Go to Step 7.

ACTIVE DESKTOP ITEMS

**4.** Click No to add an item from another source (such as a Web page from your Favorites list or an HTML page or Web shortcut stored on your hard disk).

The New Active Desktop Item dialog box appears (**Figure 1.35**).

**5.** Type or paste the address of the Web page you want to install as a desktop item. Or click Browse to select a Web page from your Favorites folder or elsewhere on your hard disk.

**6.** Click OK.

The Add item to Active Desktop dialog box appears (refer to **Figure 1.30**).

**7.** If manual updates are satisfactory and a user name/password are not required, click OK.

*or*

If the item requires you to enter a user name and password or if you want to specify a schedule on which automatic updates will occur, click Customize. Use the Online Favorite Wizard to specify an update schedule (**Figure 1.36**) and/or a user name/password combination (**Figure 1.37**). When you return to the Add Item to Active Desktop dialog box, click OK.

**8.** The Synchronizing dialog box appears (refer to **Figure 1.31**), current data for the item is downloaded from the Internet, and the item appears on your desktop.

Address

**Figure 1.35** Type or paste the address of a Web page in the Location box or click Browse to locate the address among your Favorites.

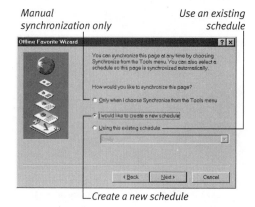

Manual synchronization only

Use an existing schedule

Create a new schedule

**Figure 1.36** Select a schedule on which updates will occur.

**Figure 1.37** Specify a user name and password (if the Web site requires you to log-on).

## ✔ Tips

- Occasionally, the Active Desktop gets trashed (typically after a crash or serious system error). To restore your desktop, click the Restore link text in the white desktop background that appears.

- If you ever want to return to the black Internet Explorer wallpaper that is installed with Active Desktop, open the Display control panel, click the Background tab, and choose the `wallpapr` HTML document.

### Drag-and-Drop

With Active Desktop installed, there are many ways you can use drag-and-drop to make your computing sessions more productive:

- Drag key program, document, or folder icons onto the taskbar to make them easily accessible and eliminate desktop clutter.

- Open a document in a specific program by dragging the document's icon onto a program icon in the taskbar.

- Remove icons from the taskbar by dragging them back onto the desktop.

- To quickly create a shortcut for a Web page that you're viewing in IE5, drag its document icon from the Address bar onto the desktop. You can also drag Outlook Express email and newsgroup messages onto the desktop.

- Designate a new home page by dragging the page's icon from the Address bar, the Favorites menu or bar, or the desktop onto IE5's Home button. Create a new Links button in the same manner.

Because drag-and-drop is so extensively implemented in IE5 and Active desktop, you should try it anywhere it makes sense to you. It will probably work!

# Managing Active Desktop Items

To make sure that you're viewing the most current information for any components or Web pages that you have added to the Active Desktop, you can manually update them as a group or individually, or you can have them automatically update on a schedule. You can also enable, disable, or permanently delete Active Desktop items as necessary.

To manually update a single desktop item, click the tiny down-arrow in the upper-left corner of the component and choose Synchronize.

To manually update all desktop items, right-click the desktop and choose Active Desktop > Update Now, or click Start > Settings > Active Desktop > Update Now (**Figure 1.38**).

## To update desktop items on a schedule:

1. When adding the item to the desktop, click Customize in the Add Item to Active Desktop dialog box (**Figure 1.39**). The Online Favorite Wizard appears.

2. Click Next.

3. To create a new schedule, choose *I would like to create a new schedule.*

   *or*

   To use a currently defined schedule, choose *Use this existing schedule.*

4. Click Next.

5. If accessing the item requires you to enter a user name/password, click *Yes, my user name and password are* and enter them in the appropriate boxes.

6. Click Finish to dismiss the wizard.

7. Click OK to add the component to your desktop.

**Figure 1.38** Updating Active Desktop.

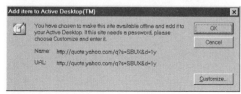

**Figure 1.39** Adding an item to Active Desktop.

Disabled
item

Delete
selected item

Reset all
items to their
default state

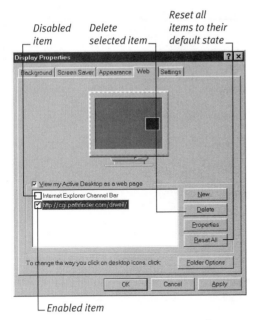

Enabled item

**Figure 1.40** You can enable, disable, and delete items in the Display Properties dialog box.

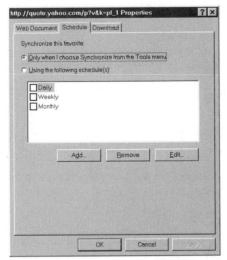

**Figure 1.41** Click the Schedule tab to set an update schedule for a desktop item.

## To disable, enable, delete, or reset Active Desktop items:

1. Click Start > Settings > Active Desktop > Customize My Desktop or right-click the desktop and choose Active Desktop > Customize My Desktop.

   The Display Properties dialog box appears, open to the Web tab (**Figure 1.40**).

2. To temporarily disable an item, click to remove the checkmark in front of its name.

   The item is removed from the desktop, but can later be enabled using this same control panel.

3. To enable an item that is currently disabled, click to add a checkmark in front of its name. The item is added to the desktop.

4. To delete an item, select it and click Delete.

   The item is deleted. If the item was on the desktop, it is also removed.

5. To reset the Web section of the Display Properties dialog box to its original settings, click Reset All.

6. Click OK to accept all changes, or click Cancel to ignore your changes.

## ✔ Tips

■ If you need to update a desktop item several times per day, set it for manual updates. The most frequent automatic update schedule for user-created items is "Daily."

■ To assign an update schedule to a desktop item that doesn't have one or to change an existing schedule for an existing item, click the tiny down-arrow in the upper-left corner of the component, choose Properties and click the Schedule tab (**Figure 1.41**).

■ You can also disable a desktop item by clicking its close box (the tiny *x* in the upper-right corner of the item).

**MANAGING ACTIVE DESKTOP ITEMS**

# BROWSER BASICS

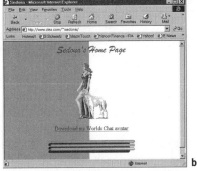

**Figure 2.1** When viewed in a browser, this HTML code (a) generates this Web page (b).

**Figure 2.2** When you download most types of audio or video clips or streaming media, Windows Media Player automatically opens.

As you almost surely know, a *browser*, such as Internet Explorer 5 (IE5), is an application used to view and experience the text, graphic, audio, and video content of the World Wide Web. Each document (or *page*) on the Web is created with a computer language called HTML (*Hypertext Markup Language*). **Figures 2.1a-b** show how HTML is used to create a Web page.

Unlike most languages, HTML was designed to work on multiple computer platforms. It doesn't matter whether a particular Web page is created or viewed on a PC or a Mac. The page will display the same information and will still be presentable regardless of platform.

The capabilities of your browser, though, *do* have an impact on how some advanced page elements are handled. Whether you can hear an audio clip, view a movie (**Figure 2.2**), or run a Java-based chat program depends on whether your browser supports these options— either via built-in capabilities or helper applications. Some browsers can only display text, for instance. Any graphic, audio, or video elements are simply ignored.

These aren't issues for your chosen browser, though. IE5 is a state-of-the-art browser, capable of presenting graphics, frames, movie clips, sound effects, music, and Java applets.

# About Browsing

The process of using a browser to view and interact with pages on the World Wide Web is commonly referred to as *browsing*. The "surfing" aspect of using the Internet comes largely from the way a browser is often used to jump from page to page—much like using a TV remote control to channel surf.

Web pages usually contain *links*—either text or graphics—that tie the current page to other Web pages. When you click a link, you are instructing the browser to go to the Web page that is represented by the link (**Figure 2.3**). If you like, you can jump from link to link, viewing a seemingly endless series of pages devoted to almost any topic under the sun.

Some Web pages also contain *forms*, such as the one shown in **Figure 2.4**. By filling in the blanks and clicking the Submit button, you can apply for a password to a Web site; order a book, program, or pizza; check out the holdings in your stock portfolio; or log onto an Internet dating service.

The Internet is also a great source of software. Shareware, freeware, and program updates are readily available, for example. Using your browser, you can download all the data files and programs you want. In fact, if you are still using an earlier version of Internet Explorer or another browser, you can download version 5 from:

```
http://www.microsoft.com/windows/ie
```

Graphic link      Text links

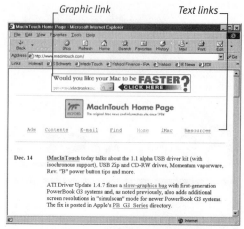

**Figure 2.3** Text links are usually underlined. Graphics, such as pictures and buttons, can also be links.

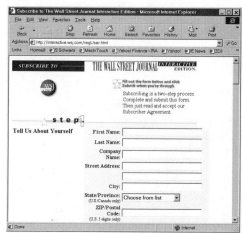

**Figure 2.4** Fill-in-the-blank forms require an advanced browser, such as IE5. The form shown here is used to register for a subscription provided by the site.

**Figure 2.5** Launching IE5 from the Start button.

**Figure 2.6** You can simultaneously launch IE5 and go directly to a specific Web page by choosing it from the Favorites menu.

_Dial whenever a network connection is not present_

**Figure 2.7** If you launch IE5 when you aren't connected to the Internet, and you have set the option to Dial whenever a network connection is not present, a connection will automatically be made for you.

# Launching the Browser

To begin a browsing session, all you need to do is connect to the Internet (via a modem or local area network) and launch IE5. A connection method can be defined by running the Connection Wizard, a component of IE5.

## To launch Internet Explorer 5:

◆ Click the Start button on the taskbar, and choose Internet Explorer (**Figure 2.5**).

◆ Click a desktop shortcut for the browser or for a Web page.

◆ Click the Internet Explorer icon in the taskbar (if Active Desktop is installed).

◆ Click the Start button, and choose a Web site from the Favorites menu (**Figure 2.6**).

    _or_

◆ In Outlook Express, click any Web address (such as http://www.microsoft.com) contained in an email message or newsgroup post.

## ✔ Tips

■ To combine the process of connecting to the Internet and launching the browser into one step, choose Tools > Internet Options, click the Connections tab, and click the option to Dial whenever a network connection is not present (**Figure 2.7**). When you launch IE5, an Internet connection is automatically made if one isn't already active.

■ Once you have an open connection, you can run any Internet program—regardless of whether it is a component of IE5. And like other Windows programs, you can run several Internet programs at the same time. You might, for instance, have IE5, Outlook Express, and a chat program open.

# The Browser Window

The browser window is divided into three parts (**Figure 2.8**). The toolbars have buttons for performing basic browsing commands and quickly reaching favorite Web sites. Page addresses (called *URLs*) can be typed in the Address box, enabling you to visit any page of interest. The icons below the Address box are called Links (formerly known as Quick Links). Clicking any of these links instantly transports you to the Web page it represents.

The document area displays the contents of each Web page. As shown in **Figure 2.8**, pages often combine text and graphics. Other elements can include hypertext or graphic links to other pages, buttons, frames (dividing the window into multiple sections), tables, and fill-in-the-blank forms. Some elements, such as audio and video players, may appear in their own windows rather than as part of the browser.

The status bar (**Figure 2.9**) is at the bottom of the window. Messages appear in the status bar. You may note that a particular Web or FTP (*File Transfer Protocol*) site is being sought or that a graphic is loading, for example.

## ✔ Tips

■ You can have multiple browser documents open simultaneously—to view another site while waiting for a slow-loading page to appear, for example. To create another window, choose File > New > Window (or press ⟨Ctrl⟩+⟨N⟩).

■ As in most other programs, you can change the onscreen position or the size of the browser window (**Figure 2.10**). To move it to a new location, click and drag in the title bar. To change its size, click and drag the lower-right corner of the window, click in the Maximize/Restore box, or choose View > Full screen (or press ⟨F11⟩).

Toolbars    Address box    Document area

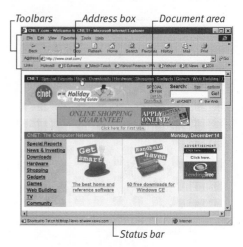

Status bar

**Figure 2.8** The three parts of the browser window.

**Figure 2.9** Keep an eye on the status bar, and you can always tell what's happening.

Click and drag to change the window's location    Maximize/Restore box

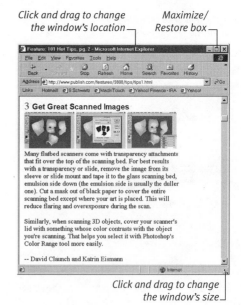

Click and drag to change the window's size

**Figure 2.10** You can change the size and location of the browser window.

Buttons

**Figure 2.11** Click the toolbar buttons to perform common browser functions. The Explorer icon at the right side of the toolbar shows whether the current page is still loading (active) or is fully displayed (inactive).

**Figure 2.12** Click the Back and Forward buttons to move through pages already visited during the current session.

**Figure 2.13** To go directly to a page visited during this session, click the down arrow beside the Back or Next button.

**Figure 2.14** Click the Stop button to tell IE5 to halt the present action, such as downloading graphics for the current page.

# The Toolbar Buttons

The buttons on the top row of the toolbar (**Figure 2.11**) provide convenient access to basic browser functions. Clicking the appropriate button during an on-line session accomplishes the tasks described below.

## To move backward and forward:

Click the Back and Forward buttons (**Figure 2.12**), choose the Back and Forward commands in the View > Go to menu, or press Alt+← and Alt+→ to move backward and forward through the pages viewed during the session. Each click of the Back button moves you back one page. When the Back button is inactive, it means that you are at the first page visited during the session.

Click the Forward button to move forward through the pages you've viewed during the session. When the Forward button is inactive, you are already on the last page visited during the session.

To jump directly to a Web page viewed during the session, click the tiny arrow beside the Back or Forward button. A menu of visited pages appears (**Figure 2.13**).

## To stop a page from loading:

Click the Stop button (**Figure 2.14**), choose the View > Stop command, or press Esc to stop the current page from loading or finishing loading. (Note that as long as the Explorer icon at the end of the toolbar is in motion, elements of the page are still loading.)

There are many instances when you will not want a page to load, such as:

◆ A page is loading slowly, and you don't want to wait for it to finish.

◆ You discover that the *wrong* page is loading.

◆ The information needed from the page (such as a link or company phone number) is already visible, so there is no reason to wait for the rest of the elements to appear.

**Figure 2.15** Click the Refresh button to reload the current Web page.

### ✔ Tip

■ If you want to go immediately to a site represented by a link on a page that is still loading, you don't have to click Stop before clicking the link—just click it. This is true for all types of links, such as those for viewing a full-size image of a thumbnail graphic, downloading a file, and so on.

**Figure 2.16** Click the Home button to return to your *start page* (the page that you automatically go to at the start of each normal browser session).

### To refresh the current page:

Click the Refresh button (**Figure 2.15**), choose View > Refresh, or press F5 to force the current page to reload. Here are two reasons why you might want to refresh a page:

◆ You believe that the information on the page has been updated. (Clicking Refresh automatically displays the most current information for a page.)

◆ The page is displaying incorrectly or is incomplete.

### To go to your home page:

At the start of every Explorer session, your *home page* automatically loads. You can return to the home page at any time during a session by clicking the Home button (**Figure 2.16**) or choosing View > Go to > Home Page.

The Microsoft Web site is the default home page, but you can change it to another page.

_Set a home page_

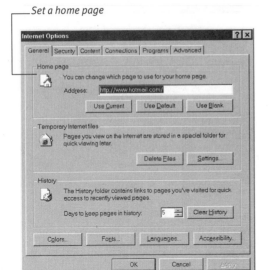

**Figure 2.17** You can specify a new home page in this part of the Internet Options dialog box.

**Figure 2.18** When changing your home page by dragging a link onto the Home button, this dialog box appears. Click Yes to make this your new home page.

## To set a new home page:

1. Go to the page that you intend to make your new home page (by typing its URL in the Address box or selecting the page from the Favorites menu, for example).

   _or_

   Make a note of the URL of the page that you intend to make the new home page.

2. Choose Tools > Internet Options.

   The Internet Options dialog box appears (**Figure 2.17**).

3. In the Home section of the General tab, do one of the following:

   ◆ Click Use Current to make the current Web page your home page.

   ◆ If you want to use a different page, type or paste its URL into the Address box.

   ◆ Click Use Default to reset the home page to Microsoft's site.

   ◆ Click Use Blank if you do not want to designate a home page.

4. Click OK.

## ✔ Tip

■ You can also set a new home page using drag-and-drop. Drag the icon for the page from the desktop, the Favorites folder, or the Address box onto the Home button in the browser toolbar. Click Yes to confirm this change (**Figure 2.18**).

**THE TOOLBAR BUTTONS**

## To use the Search Assistant:

When you click the Search button, choose View > Explorer Bar > Search, or press Ctrl+E, the Search Assistant opens in the left side of the browser window (**Figure 2.19**). You can use the Search Assistant to search Web pages or newsgroups for topic-specific material (all mentions of the words Congress, for example); company Web sites; maps; or someone's phone number, address, and email address.

The Search Assistant lets you quickly switch among several *search engines* (such as Alta-Vista, Excite, Lycos, and Yahoo!) and view the proposed hits without constantly having to click the Back button. For more on the Search Assistant, see Chapter 5.

## To display the Favorites list:

Click the Favorites button, choose View > Explorer Bar > Favorites, or press Ctrl+I to display the Favorites bar—a folder-based list of all Web page addresses that you've stored (**Figure 2.20**). Favorite sites can be revisited by choosing them from this list. You can also visit your favorite sites by opening the Favorites menu—either from within IE5 or by choosing it from the Start menu on the Windows taskbar.

To close the Favorites bar, click the Favorites button again or click the tiny *x* in the Favorites Bar. For more information on adding and managing Favorites, see Chapter 4.

## Working with the history list

IE5 maintains a History folder with the addresses of pages that you've recently viewed. The History folder can store information on many days' sessions, depending on how your preferences have been set (see Chapter 11).

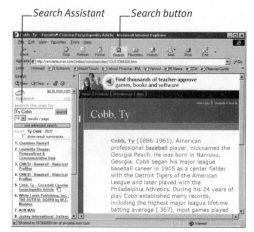

_Search Assistant          _Search button

**Figure 2.19** When you click the Search button, the Search Assistant appears in a separate pane on the left side of the browser window. Click links in the Search Assistant to view the resulting Web pages in the right side of the window.

_Favorites bar

**Figure 2.20** Click the Favorites button to display the Favorites bar, enabling you to choose a Web page to revisit.

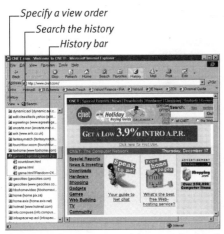

Specify a view order
Search the history
History bar

**Figure 2.21** If you want to revisit a recently visited site, you'll find it listed in the History bar.

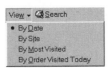

**Figure 2.22** You can change the order in which history items are listed by choosing an option from the History bar's View menu.

Search keywords
Search results appear here

**Figure 2.23** If you can't find a given history item, try a keyword search.

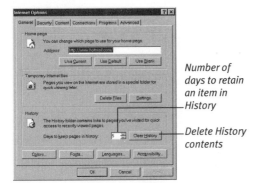

Number of days to retain an item in History
Delete History contents

**Figure 2.24** Choose Tools > Internet Options to change the history settings.

## To go to a history page:

1. Open the History bar (**Figure 2.21**) by clicking the History button, choosing View > Explorer Bar > History, or pressing Ctrl+H.

2. In the History bar, click View to choose a sort order for displaying the history list (**Figure 2.22**).

3. Click the page you want to revisit, opening folders as necessary.

4. When you're finished, close the History bar by clicking the History button or the tiny *x* in the History Bar.

## ✔ Tips

■ You can search the history for a particular Web page by clicking Search and entering one or more keywords (**Figure 2.23**).

■ To delete an entry in the History bar, right-click it and choose Delete.

■ The length of time an entry remains in the History folder depends on the settings in Internet Options (**Figure 2.24**). For information on altering this and other history settings, see Chapter 11.

THE TOOLBAR BUTTONS

## Working with email and Usenet newsgroups

In IE5, email and newsgroup support are both available in a program called Outlook Express. In addition to using Outlook Express directly to work with mail and newsgroups, you can send email messages and links to Web pages from within the browser.

Click the Mail button to reveal a pop-up menu of email and newsgroup commands (**Figure 2.25**). The commands are as follows:

**Figure 2.25** Click the Mail button to send messages and links via email or to read newsgroup posts.

- ◆ *Read Mail.* Use this command to open (or switch to) Outlook Express and display the messages that are in your Inbox.

- ◆ *New Message.* This command opens a New Message window (**Figure 2.26**), enabling you to compose and send email to an individual.

- ◆ *Send a Link.* This command sends a URL shortcut for the current Web page as email.

- ◆ *Send Page.* Rather than sending a Web page address (as the Send a Link command does), choose this command to send the Web page itself.

- ◆ *Read News.* Open Outlook Express and view newsgroup messages.

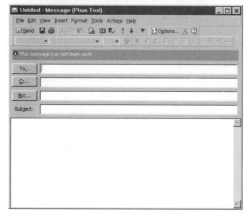

**Figure 2.26** Choose the New Message command to open a blank message form in your email program.

## ✔ Tips

- ■ The Mail button commands can also be found in the Tools > Mail and News menu.

- ■ You can also send a URL by right-clicking a desktop shortcut and choosing Send To > Mail Recipient. This same technique can be used to email other types of files, such as pictures and word processing documents. The files are sent as email attachments.

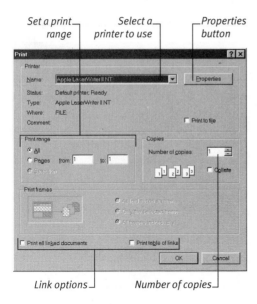

Set a print range — Select a printer to use — Properties button

Link options — Number of copies

**Figure 2.27** The Print dialog box.

## Printing Web pages

Using the printers you've defined for Windows 95, 98, or NT, you can print the current Web page, selected frames on a page, all linked pages, or a list of URLs referenced on a page.

Note that there is no length limit imposed on Web pages. A single Web page can be one or many printed pages in length.

## To print a Web page:

1. Display the Web page that you want to print.

2. Click the Print button, choose File > Print, or press Ctrl+P.
   The Print dialog box appears (**Figure 2.27**).

3. Select a printer to use from the list of currently installed printers.
   *Optional:* To specify properties for this print job, such as the type and size of paper, graphics quality, and so on, click the Properties button.

4. Set a print range by clicking All or by entering numbers in the From and To boxes.
   Note that the From/To range refers to the number of pieces of paper to print rather than to the number of Web pages. "All" prints the entire Web page, regardless of the number of sheets of paper needed.

5. Specify the number of copies to be printed.
   *Optional:* If you're printing several copies, you can automatically collate the copies by clicking the Collate checkbox.
   *Optional:* To print the addresses of all hypertext and graphic links embedded in the Web page, click the Print table of links checkbox.
   *Optional:* To also print Web pages that are referenced by the links embedded in the current page, click the Print all linked documents checkbox.

**THE TOOLBAR BUTTONS**

**6.** Click OK to begin printing.

If the page you are printing contains separate areas called *frames*, the printing procedure differs slightly. You can print the entire page (as you would if it did *not* have frames), only the currently selected frame, or each frame individually.

## To print a Web page with frames:

**1.** To print a specific frame, right-click within the frame and choose Print from the menu that appears.

*or*

To print the entire page or create a separate printout for each frame, click Print, choose File > Print, or press Ctrl + P.
The Print dialog box appears (**Figure 2.28**).

**2.** Set print options as specified in Steps 3–5 of "To print a Web page" above.

**3.** Choose a frame printing option:
  ◆ *As laid out on screen* prints the entire Web page.
  ◆ *Only the selected frame* treats the selected frame as a separate page for printing.
  ◆ *All frames individually* generates a separate printout for each frame.

**4.** Click OK to begin printing.

For more on printing, see Chapter 9.

## ✔ Tips

■ If you want to set other print options (such as orientation, margins, and header or footer text), choose File > Page Setup.

■ Printing a selected frame makes most sense when you are only interested in the material in a particular frame. In most cases, you will not want to print a menu frame, for example.

*Frame printing options*

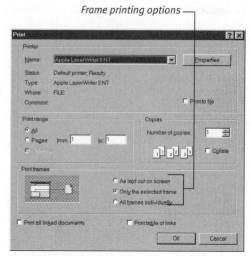

**Figure 2.28** When a page contains frames, this modified version of the Print dialog box appears. Specify the frames to be printed and how they will be printed.

*Print backgrounds*

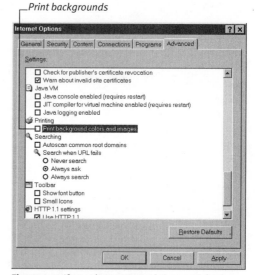

**Figure 2.29** If you also want to print a page's background picture or background color, be sure to set this option.

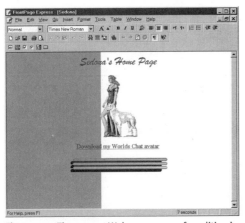

**Figure 2.30** The current Web page opens for editing in FrontPage Express.

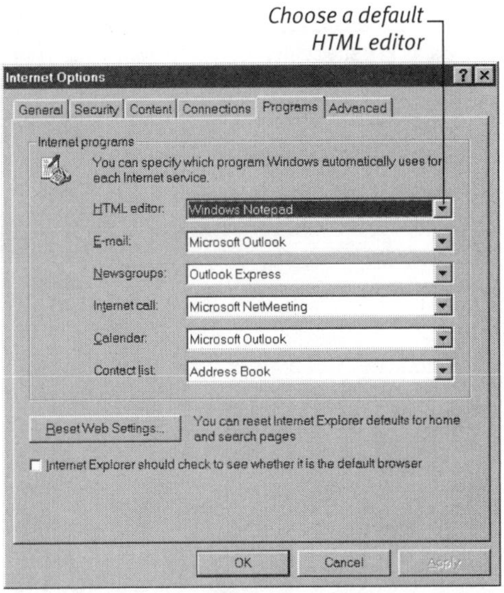

*Choose a default HTML editor*

**Figure 2.31** Set a default editor in the Programs section of the Internet Options dialog box. This editor is automatically used if you click the Edit button, rather than pick an editor from the Edit button's drop-down menu.

■ Electing the option to Print all linked documents can occasionally generate massive printouts. This option makes more sense when there are a limited number of linked pages.

■ By default, a Web page's background color or picture (if either has been set) is *not* printed. To include them in your printouts, choose Tools > Internet Options, click the Advanced tab in the dialog box appears, and check the option to Print background colors and images (**Figure 2.29**).

## Editing Web pages

If you have HTML programming skills or simply want to learn more about how other people create Web pages, you can open the source code for any page that you visit.

## To view or edit a page's code:

1. Click the Edit button to open the current page in the default editor.

   *or*

   Click the arrow beside the Edit button to choose a specific editor, such as Windows Notepad or FrontPage Editor (a component that can be downloaded as part of IE5).

   The current Web page opens in the chosen editor (**Figure 2.30**).

2. View and/or edit the page as desired.

## ✔ Tips

■ To quickly open the code in Windows Notepad, choose View > Source.

■ You can specify a default HTML editor by choosing Tools > Internet Options and then clicking the Programs tab in the dialog box that appears (**Figure 2.31**).

# More About the Toolbar

The toolbar contains two other important sections that you will frequently use: the Address box and the Links buttons.

## The Address box

The Address box (**Figure 2.32**) displays the address of the current Web page. You can also type or paste addresses into the Address box to visit pages. Examples of addresses include:

♦ http://www.tips.com

[the home page for a Web site]

♦ http://www.tips.com/list.html or http://www.tips.com/list.htm

[a specific page within a Web site (typically having an .html or .htm file extension)]

♦ ftp://aclu.org/pub/

[the public directory of an FTP site (**Figure 2.33**)]

♦ c:\graphics\fish.jpg

[a graphics file on your own hard disk]

To the right of the Address box is the Go button, a new feature in Internet Explorer 5. To visit a URL that you have typed or pasted into the Address box, you can now complete a URL by clicking Go or pressing (Enter).

## ✔ Tips

■ Although you can type an address from scratch or edit the current one, you can also enter simplified URLs. You don't have to type http:// as the prefix, for example. If the prefix is omitted, it is filled in for you.

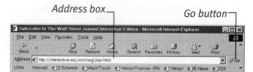

Address box⎯⎜              Go button⎯⎤

**Figure 2.32** Type or paste URLs into the Address box.

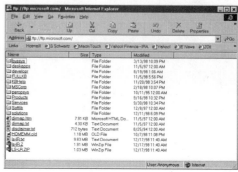

**Figure 2.33** FTP site contents are displayed in the same manner as files or folders on your own hard disk.

Click to view the address history list

**Figure 2.34** Any URL that you have recently typed into the Address box can be selected from this list.

Links

**Figure 2.35** The Links buttons represent special Web sites that you like to visit frequently.

- Click the tiny arrow at the right end of the Address box to view and select from a list of all links you have previously typed into the Address box (**Figure 2.34**).

- IE5 has a related feature called *Auto-complete* that makes it easy to re-enter URLs. If the URL you are typing appears to match one that you previously typed, a drop-down list of potential matches appears. Select one to go to that Web page or, if there are no matches, continue typing as you normally would.

## The Links buttons

The buttons in the Links section of the toolbar make it easy to get to important or favorite Web pages. Click any button to go to the page it represents (**Figure 2.35**).

Although the links are preset for Microsoft sites, you can change them so they'll go to other pages. For information on how to change the links, as well as storing and organizing your other favorite Web pages, see Chapter 4.

### ✔ Tips

- If the links aren't visible in the toolbar, click the word Links and drag downward.

- Links can contain pages from your Favorites list and vice versa. Similarly, you can also create desktop shortcuts to them. Place copies of your favorite links wherever it is most convenient for you.

---

### More about Autocomplete

Autocomplete can also be used to help you fill in forms or enter log-on information for chat sites and other subscription services. It can optionally record any information that you enter on a Web page and then recall it for you the next time you visit the page. For more on using Autocomplete, see Chapter 11.

**MORE ABOUT THE TOOLBAR**

# Customizing the Toolbar

IE5's toolbar is highly customizable. You can add or remove buttons, change the five Links buttons (as explained in Chapter 4), and reorganize or selectively hide the toolbar parts.

## To change the toolbar buttons:

1. Choose View > Toolbars > Customize (or right-click to the right of the last button and choose Customize).

   The Customize Toolbar dialog box appears (**Figure 2.36**). You can now perform any of the following actions:

   ◆ To change the way button labels are displayed, choose an option from the Text options drop-down menu.

   ◆ To change the size of the buttons, choose an option from the Icon options drop-down menu.

   ◆ To remove a button, select it in the Current toolbar buttons list and click Remove.

   ◆ To add a new button, select it in the Available toolbar buttons list and click Add.

   ◆ To alter the position of a button in the toolbar, select it in the Current toolbar buttons list and click Move Up or Move Down until the position is correct.

   ◆ To reset the toolbar back to its default settings, click Reset.

2. When you are done making changes, click Close (**Figure 2.37**).

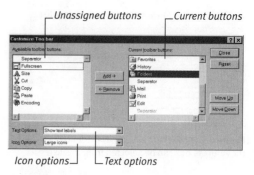

*Unassigned buttons*   *Current buttons*

*Icon options*   *Text options*

**Figure 2.36** The Customize Toolbar dialog box.

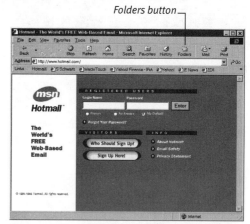

*Folders button*

**Figure 2.37** The toolbar has been altered by adding a Folders button to display the folders on my hard disk and removing the Edit button.

CUSTOMIZING THE TOOLBAR

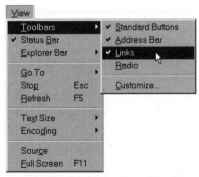

**Figure 2.38** To hide or reveal a section of the toolbar, choose the appropriate command from the View > Toolbars menu.

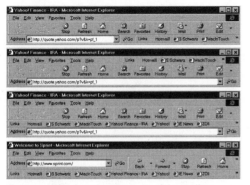

**Figure 2.39** By dragging the parts of the toolbar, you can create a variety of useful and pleasing arrangements.

You can also make the following changes to the toolbar and the status bar.

◆ **Hide one or more sections of the toolbar.**

To hide a section of the toolbar, choose View > Toolbars, followed by the section you want to hide (Standard Buttons, Address Bar, Links, or Radio), as shown in **Figure 2.38**. Choose the same command again to reveal the formerly hidden section.

◆ **Reorganize the toolbar sections.**

You can drag the toolbar sections to the left, right, up, or down in order to change their position. (Click and drag the section names or the divider bars.) **Figure 2.39** shows several possible arrangements.

◆ **Hide or display the Go button.**

To hide the Go button, right-click it and choose Go Button to remove the checkmark. Repeat this command to restore the Go button.

◆ **Hide or display the status bar.**

To hide the status bar, choose View > Status Bar to remove the checkmark. Repeat this command to restore the status bar.

## ✔ Tips

■ If two toolbar sections are in the same row, you can expose the hidden one by clicking and dragging its name.

■ You can customize many additional display options, such as the default text font, size, and color. See Chapter 11 for more information.

# NAVIGATING THE WEB

**3**

Moving from one Web site or page to another is an important part of almost every browser session. In this chapter, you will learn how to use Internet Explorer to navigate (or *surf*) the World Wide Web.

# Entering a URL

One of the most common ways to visit a Web page is by typing its *URL* (Uniform Resource Locator) into the Address box and then pressing [Enter] or clicking the Go button (**Figure 3.1**). As an alternative, choose File > Open (or press [Ctrl]+[O]), type the address (such as http://www.adobe.com) in the Open dialog box, and click OK (**Figure 3.2**).

## ✔ Tips

- IE5 intelligently handles typed Web addresses. You don't need to include the http://.

- It's often faster to edit the current URL than to type one from scratch. Addresses frequently start with http://www., for instance, so you can replace everything from there on.

- IE5 has a feature called *Autocomplete* that can help you re-enter any URL you've recently typed in the Address box. Soon after you begin typing, Autocomplete displays a drop-down list of potential matches. Choose one, or—if there are no matches—continue typing.

- If you recently typed a URL for a Web page into the Address box, you can easily return to that page by clicking the arrow at the end of the Address box and choosing the URL from the list that appears. (Typed URLs are automatically recorded in this drop-down list and remain there until IE5's History is cleared.)

- You can copy and paste a URL from an email message into the Address box. In Outlook Express, Outlook, and Eudora, all URLs are hypertext links (**Figure 3.3**). Clicking one of these links launches IE5 and fetches the Web page.

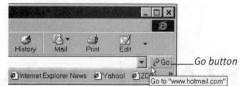

**Figure 3.1** You can click the Go button to complete any URL that you type or paste into the Address box.

**Figure 3.2** You can use the Open dialog box to type, paste, or choose the URL of a Web page you'd like to visit.

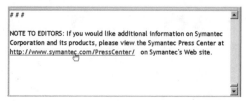

**Figure 3.3** In many current email programs and newsgroup readers, clicking any valid URL opens that Web page in IE5.

text link   graphic link

**Figure 3.4** A link in a Web page can be a text string or a graphic.

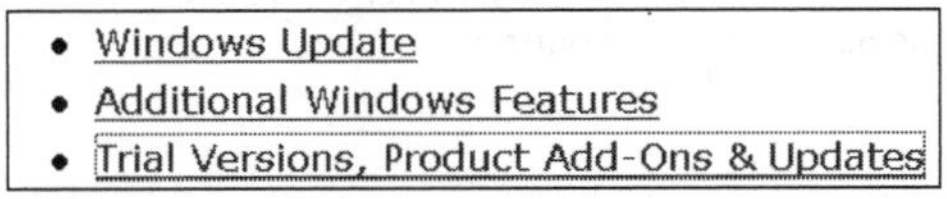

- Windows Update
- Additional Windows Features
- Trial Versions, Product Add-Ons & Updates

**Figure 3.5** A link selected by Tabbing is shown surrounded by a dotted rectangle.

Click to see additional links

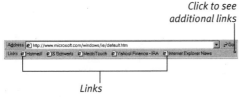

Links

**Figure 3.6** Links in the Links bar are handy shortcuts to your favorite Web pages.

# Clicking Links

When you're viewing a Web page, you can go to any link that is referenced in the page by clicking the hypertext or link object. Depending on the purpose of the link, you may be taken to a spot on the same page, another page in the same Web site, or a different Web site.

Text links are usually underlined (**Figure 3.4**). Graphics, such as the ones shown in **Figure 3.4**, can also be links. When you click a graphic link, the same thing happens as when you click a text link—you are taken to the page referred to by the link .

## ✔ Tips

- You can easily tell which text strings and graphics are links. Just move the pointer over them. When moved over a link, the pointer changes to a pointing hand, and the link information (a URL or page reference) is shown in the status bar (**Figure 3.4**).

- You can keep your hands on the keyboard while Web surfing by pressing (Tab) and (Shift)+(Tab) to move from one link to another. The currently selected link is surrounded by a dotted line (**Figure 3.5**). Press (Enter) to go to the chosen link.

- Tiny graphic images (called *thumbnails*) are often used as links to larger versions of the same pictures.

- You can create desktop shortcuts for important links (as described in Chapter 5). Click the shortcut to go to the Web page it represents.

- You can go directly to any page listed in the Links bar by clicking the link's name (**Figure 3.6**). If there are more links than can be displayed, click the right arrow at the end of the Links bar to display the additional links.

CLICKING LINKS

# Revisiting a Web Page

IE5 provides several ways for you to return to previously visited Web pages: the Back and Forward buttons, the History bar, and the Favorites menu and bar.

## The Back and Forward buttons

Click these toolbar buttons to flip through pages you've viewed during the current on-line session. Each time you click the Back or Forward button (**Figure 3.7**), you move one Web page in the direction indicated.

## To move between viewed pages:

- To view the last Web page visited, click Back or press (Backspace) or (Alt)+(←).

- To view the next Web page, click Forward or press (Shift)+(Backspace) or (Alt)+(→) arrow.

- To display a menu of the last ten pages visited in this session, choose View > Go To.

## ✔ Tips

- You can only go forward if you have previously clicked the Back button; that is, you must be somewhere in the middle of the pages viewed during the session. If you can't move in a particular direction, the appropriate button is disabled.

- You can quickly go straight to specific pages visited in the current session. Click the down arrow beside the Back or Forward button and then choose the page name from the list that appears (**Figure 3.8**).

**Figure 3.7** Click the Back and Forward buttons to revisit pages viewed during the current browsing session.

**Figure 3.8** To revisit a specific page viewed during this session, click the down arrow beside the Back or Forward button.

*Click View to specify a
display method*

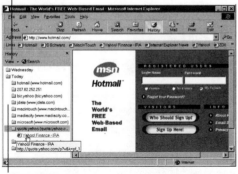

*History bar*

**Figure 3.9** The History bar lists all Web pages that
you've recently viewed. Click any entry to revisit
that page.

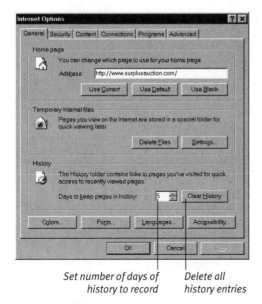

*Set number of days of          Delete all
history to record               history entries*

**Figure 3.10** Choose Tools > Internet Options to erase
the current history entries or specify the number of
days of history you'd like to track.

## Using the History Bar

IE5 maintains a History folder with the
names and addresses of Web pages that
you've recently viewed. (All viewed pages
are tracked, even if they're not "favorites.")
Unlike the way the Back and Forward buttons work, the History folder's contents
can—and usually do—encompass *multiple*
on-line sessions.

## To go to a History page:

◆ Click the arrow beside the Back or
Forward button to go to a page visited
during the current session. Only pages
viewed during the current session are
listed in the menu that appears.

◆ Open the History bar (**Figure 3.9**) by
clicking the History button. Click the
View button to choose a display method
for the page list. Click the page you want
to revisit.

*or*

◆ Click the arrow at the end of the Address
box, and choose a page. (Only URLs that
you recently typed into the Address box
are listed.)

## ✔ Tip

■ The length of time an entry remains in
the History folder depends on the options
you've set (**Figure 3.10**). For information
on altering this and other History settings, see Chapter 11.

**REVISITING A WEB PAGE**

## Going to a Favorite page

You can store the addresses of important Web pages in the Favorites folder (as described in Chapter 4) and go to those pages whenever you wish.

You can choose a page to visit from the Favorites menu or, if you prefer, you can click the Favorites button to display the Favorites bar (**Figure 3.11**) and then choose a page.

### ✔ Tip

■ You can also reach the Favorites menu by clicking the Start button on the Windows taskbar. If IE5 isn't currently running, choosing a Web page from this menu will launch the browser and take you directly to the chosen page.

*Favorites bar*

**Figure 3.11** The Favorites bar provides a convenient way to choose sites to visit.

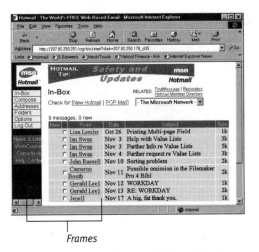

Frames

**Figure 3.12** Frames are often used to separate an index area from the content area of a Web site.

Scroll toward beginning

Scroll box

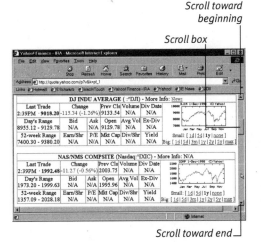

Scroll toward end

**Figure 3.13** You can click and drag in the scroll bars to change your location in a page.

# Navigating within a Page

Not all Web pages can fit on one screen. In fact, there is no established length limit for Web pages. A page can sometimes span dozens of screens, for example.

## To move within a Web page:

◆ To scroll to the top or bottom of the current page, press (Home) or (End), respectively.

◆ To move up or down one screen of information, press (Pg Up) or (Pg Dn), respectively.

◆ To scroll one line up or down, press (↑) or (↓), respectively.

◆ To move from link to link in the current page, press (Tab) to move forward or press (Shift)+(Tab) to move backward. The screen scrolls automatically, as necessary.

◆ To switch from one frame on the current page to the next frame on the same page, press (Ctrl)+(Tab). **Figure 3.12** shows an example of a page with frames. (You can also make any frame the current one by simply clicking in it.)

## ✔ Tips

■ You can also navigate within a page by using the scroll bars. To move a small distance, click an arrow button on the scroll bar. To scroll continuously in a direction, click an arrow button and hold down the mouse button. To move a greater distance, drag the scroll box or click in the blank area of the scroll bar (**Figure 3.13**).

■ Some Web pages contain text or graphic links that, when clicked, take you to another part of the same page, such as the top, bottom, or a named section.

NAVIGATING WITHIN A PAGE

# WORKING
# WITH FAVORITES

**Figure 4.1a** Choose favorite sites to visit from the Favorites menu.

Whether you jump from one link to the next or spend your on-line time roaming aimlessly around the Web, you're certain to find sites that you'd like to visit again. IE5 calls such sites *favorites* and provides tools for recording and organizing them. After you've saved a site as a favorite, you can easily return to it by choosing its name from the Favorites menu or the Favorites bar (**Figures 4.1a–c**).

As the figures show, you can choose a favorite site to visit by doing any of the following:

◆ Open IE5's Favorites menu (**Figure 4.1a**).

◆ Click the Favorites button to display the Favorites bar (**Figure 4.1b**).

◆ Click the Start button on the taskbar and open the Favorites menu (**Figure 4.1c**).

All three methods provide identical results. After you choose a favorite, its Web page is displayed.

## ✔ Tips

■ If IE5 isn't already running, use the Start button method to open directly to the site of interest, rather than to your home page.

■ To close the Favorites bar, click the tiny *x* or click the Favorites button again.

■ If you find a useful Web site and want to quickly find other sites that are similar, choose Tools > Show Related Links.

*Add the current site as a new favorite*   *Close the Favorites bar*   *Display or remove the Favorites bar*

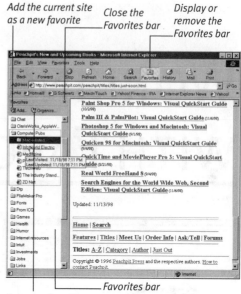

*Organize favorites*   *Favorites bar*

**Figure 4.1b** With the Favorites bar open, it is easy to visit a series of favorite sites.

*Favorites menu*

*Start button*

**Figure 4.1c** To simultaneously launch IE5 and go to a particular Web site, click the Start button and choose the site from the Favorites folder.

Name box    Show/hide folder list

**Figure 4.2** Use the Add Favorite dialog box to specify a name and folder to use for a new favorite.

Create a new folder within
the selected folder

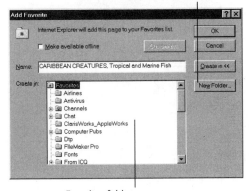

Favorites folders

**Figure 4.3** The expanded Add Favorite dialog box.

Drag this icon...    ...onto the Favorites button

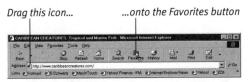

**Figure 4.4** Adding the current page as a new favorite.

# Adding Favorites

The easiest way to create a favorite is to go to the Web page and then add the page to the Favorites menu.

## To add a page as a favorite:

1. Display the page that you want to make into a favorite. (It doesn't matter whether you reach the page by typing its URL in the Address box or by clicking a link.)

2. Choose Favorites > Add to Favorites.

    The Add Favorite dialog box appears (**Figure 4.2**). The name for the Web page is shown in the Name box. You can edit the proposed name if you like.

3. The favorite can be added to the top level of the Favorites menu or stored in a folder within the Favorites menu.

    To save the favorite in the top level of the Favorites menu, click OK.

    *or*

    To save the favorite inside a folder, click Create in. The dialog box expands to show the folder list (**Figure 4.3**). Select a folder in which to place the new favorite and then click OK. If the folder doesn't already exist, click New Folder, name the folder, and then click OK to save the favorite in the folder.

## ✔ Tips

■ To quickly add the current page as a new favorite, drag the Web page icon in the left corner of the title bar onto the Favorites button (**Figure 4.4**).

■ When you create a new favorite, you can optionally mark the page to be automatically downloaded to your hard disk at regular intervals, enabling you to view the material offline. See Chapter 6 for details.

- New folders for favorites can be nested within other folders. As shown previously in **Figure 4.1c**, the Computer Pubs folder contains a folder named Mac-related.

- You don't have to save a site's main page as a favorite. If there's a page in the site that interests you more, save it instead.

- You don't have to organize a favorite the moment it's created. If you're in a hurry, choose Favorites > Add to Favorites and click OK. When time permits, you can rename the favorite and move it into a folder (see the next section, "Organizing Favorites," for details).

- Your *home page* is a special type of favorite. When you launch Internet Explorer, your home page is automatically loaded and displayed. To learn how to designate a home page, see Chapter 11.

- Web pages in the Links bar are a special type of favorite. Any page in the Links bar can be displayed by merely clicking a button. To learn about the Links bar, see "Defining and Organizing Links" later in this chapter.

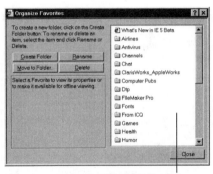

*The Favorites list*

**Figure 4.5** The Organize Favorites dialog box.

**Figure 4.6** The Browse for Folder dialog box.

---

## Why Make Folders for Favorites?

When you first start using Internet Explorer, it may not be obvious why you'd want to bother making folders for favorites. However, if you save all your favorites at the top level (that is, store them loose in the Favorites folder), finding a favorite will become progressively harder. Folders enable you to *organize* your favorites in a way that makes sense to you.

Using folders, you can group favorites by subject matter or create folders for special projects, such as a particular business topic or a new disease. At the end of the project, you can simultaneously delete all these favorites by deleting the folder in which they're stored.

---

# Organizing Favorites

As I mentioned earlier in this chapter, favorites can be organized in folders, making it easier for you to find them. IE5 also has commands for renaming and deleting favorites.

## To create a new favorites folder:

1. Choose Favorites > Organize Favorites (or, in the Favorites bar, click Organize).
   The Organize Favorites dialog box appears (**Figure 4.5**).

2. To create a new top-level folder, click the Create Folder button.
   *or*
   To create a folder within another folder, select the containing folder and then click Create Folder.
   In either case, an empty folder named New Folder is created.

3. Type a name for the folder.

4. Press (Enter) or click the Close button.

## To move a favorite:

1. Choose Favorites > Organize Favorites (or, in the Favorites bar, click Organize).
   The Organize Favorites dialog box appears.

2. Select the favorite(s) you want to move, opening folders as necessary.

3. Click the Move to Folder button. The Browse for Folder dialog box appears (**Figure 4.6**).

4. Select a destination folder for the favorite, opening folders as necessary. (To store the favorite at the top level of the Favorites menu, select the Favorites folder.)

5. Click OK to complete the move or click Cancel if you change your mind.

## To rename a favorite or folder:

1. Choose Favorites > Organize Favorites (or, in the Favorites bar, click Organize). The Organize Favorites dialog box appears, as shown previously in **Figure 4.5**.

2. Select a favorite or folder to rename.

3. Click the Rename button.

4. Edit the name.

5. To accept the new name, press (Enter) or click the Close button.

## To delete a favorite or folder:

1. Choose Favorites > Organize Favorites (or, in the Favorites bar, click Organize). The Organize Favorites dialog box appears, as shown previously in **Figure 4.5**.

2. Select a favorite or folder to delete.

3. Click the Delete button or press (Del). The selected favorite or folder is deleted.

## ✔ Tips

■ Because each favorite is an actual file, and the favorite folders are real folders, you can manipulate favorites and favorite folders with Windows Explorer (**Figure 4.7**). For example, you can easily move favorites from one folder to another, create new folders, and rename or delete favorites.

■ You can move favorites by dragging them to different folders in the Organize Favorites dialog box. You can also rearrange favorites by opening the Favorites menu (either from the Start button or within IE5) and then dragging favorites or folders.

■ You can perform many actions on favorites by right-clicking them in the Organize Favorites dialog box or the Favorites bar and then choosing menu commands (**Figure 4.8**).

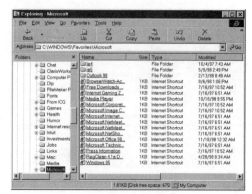

**Figure 4.7** Favorites and Favorites folders can also be renamed, moved, or deleted using Windows Explorer.

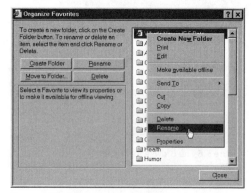

**Figure 4.8** Another way to modify a favorite is to right-click it and then choose a menu command.

*Links bar*

**Figure 4.9** Frequently visited pages can be added to the Links bar.

**Figure 4.10** To delete or rename a link, right-click it and then choose the appropriate command from the menu that appears.

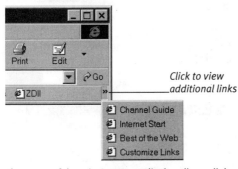

*Click to view additional links*

**Figure 4.11** If there isn't room to display all your links, click the » button to see the others.

# Defining and Organizing Links

If you examine the IE5 toolbar (**Figure 4.9**), you'll note a row of buttons labeled *Links*. Click any link button to visit the Web page it represents. You can freely modify the Links list as you see fit.

◆ To add a new link, go to the desired Web page and drag its icon from the title bar or the Address box into the Links toolbar. Alternatively, you can create a new link by storing it as a favorite in the Links folder.

◆ To delete a link, right-click its name and choose Delete from the menu that appears (**Figure 4.10**).

◆ To change the position of a link, drag it to a new location in the list.

◆ To rename a link, right-click its name and choose Rename from the menu that appears.

## ✔ Tips

■ At times, there may not be room to display all the links you've created. To see or select the remaining links, click the » button at the right end of the Links bar. A menu of the additional links appears (**Figure 4.11**).

■ Any link found on a Web page can be added to the Links bar by dragging it into position in the Links bar.

# Creating a Web Page Shortcut

Some Web pages are more important than others. To avoid having to hunt for an important page in the Favorites menu, you may prefer to create a desktop shortcut for it. When you want to go to the page, you can just click its shortcut.

## To create a shortcut for a page:

1. In IE5, go to the Web page for which you want to create a shortcut.

   After the page loads, its URL is displayed in the Address box (**Figure 4.12**). The URL is saved as part of the shortcut's definition.

2. Choose File > Send > Shortcut to Desktop (**Figure 4.13**).

   A shortcut to the page's URL appears on the desktop.

## ✔ Tips

- You can examine and modify a shortcut's properties (**Figure 4.14**) by right-clicking the shortcut icon and choosing Properties from the menu that appears.

- You can create a shortcut for any link found on a Web page by dragging the link text or object onto the desktop or into a folder.

- You can create a shortcut for the current page by dragging the Web page icon in the left corner of the IE5 title bar onto the desktop.

*URL appears here*

**Figure 4.12** The URL for the current Web page is shown in the Address box.

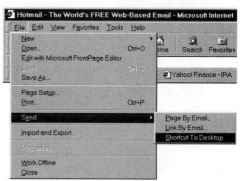

**Figure 4.13** Creating a desktop shortcut for the current Web page.

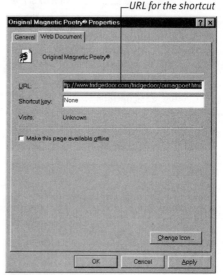

*URL for the shortcut*

**Figure 4.14** Properties for any Web page shortcut include its URL, an optional shortcut keystroke, and whether the page will be tracked for offline viewing.

# Visiting a Favorite Page

There are several ways to go to a favorite Web page. After launching Internet Explorer, you can do any of the following:

- Choose the Web page from the Favorites menu (in IE5 or by clicking the Start button).

- Click the Favorites button to reveal the Favorites bar and then—opening folders as necessary—choose the Web page.

- If there is a desktop shortcut for a favorite, click (or double-click) it.

- Click a button in the Links bar to go to the page that it represents.

## ✔ Tip

- The same folders and commands appear regardless of whether you pull down the Favorites menu, click the Favorites button, or display the Favorites menu by clicking the Start button. Use whichever method is most convenient.

# Importing and Exporting Favorites

IE5 enables you to exchange favorites among friends, different computers, and browsers. Using the Import/Export Wizard (**Figure 4.15**), you can:

◆ Add favorites from another browser that you previously used (such as Netscape Navigator) or from another computer (whether yours or someone else's). This process is called *importing*.

◆ Save your favorites to a file that can be read by other computers and browsers. This is called *exporting*.

## To import a list of favorites:

1. Choose File > Import and Export.
   The Import/Export Wizard appears.

2. Click Next to continue.

3. Select Import Favorites (**Figure 4.16**) and click Next.

4. If the favorites are stored as part of another program installed on your computer, click Import from an Application and choose the program.

   *or*

   If the favorites are in an HTML file (such as the type of file that IE5 exports), click Import from a File or Address (**Figure 4.17**), enter the path and name of the file (or click Browse to select it visually), and click Next.

5. Select a destination folder for the imported favorites (**Figure 4.18**) and click Next.

6. Click Finish.

**Figure 4.15** The Import/Export Wizard presents a series of dialog boxes, such as this one.

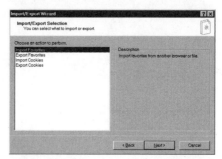

**Figure 4.16** Choose an import or export option to perform.

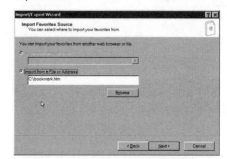

**Figure 4.17** Favorites can be imported from another program or from an HTML file.

**Figure 4.18** Choose a folder in which to store the imported favorites.

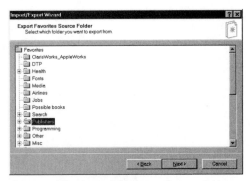

**Figure 4.19** The chosen folder, as well as any folders nested inside it, will be exported.

**Figure 4.20** If you aren't comfortable typing the DOS path to where the export file will be saved, you can choose the folder in the Select Bookmark File dialog box.

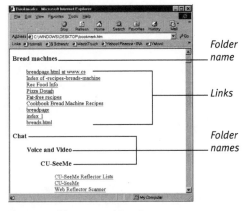

**Figure 4.21** The exported favorites are saved as an HTML file. Folder names are displayed as bold headings and favorites are clickable text links.

## To export a list of favorites:

1. Choose File > Import and Export.
   The Import/Export Wizard appears.

2. Click Next to continue.

3. Select Export Favorites, and click Next.

4. Select the folder of favorites that you want to export (**Figure 4.19**), and click Next. To export a list of *all* favorites, select the Favorites folder.

5. Type a directory path and name for the export file, or click Browse to visually select the destination for the file (**Figure 4.20**). Click Next to continue.

6. Click Finish.
   The selected favorites are exported as an HTML file that can be opened with any browser's File > Open command. Each favorite is a clickable link (**Figure 4.21**).

## ✔ Tips

- If Netscape Navigator is installed on your computer, its *bookmarks* (Netscape's term for *favorites*) are automatically copied into the Imported Bookmarks folder when you install IE5.

- In addition to sharing favorites with others, it's sometimes useful to export them strictly for your own use. You can use the Export procedure to create a list of sites that are relevant to a particular project or to generate a site list to use while traveling on business.

**IMPORTING AND EXPORTING FAVORITES**

# SEARCHING THE WEB

**Figure 5.1** Yahoo! (`http://www.yahoo.com`).

**Figure 5.2** AltaVista (`http://www.altavista.com`).

Jumping from one known Web site to another is easy. You can click on links, type URLs, or select favorite sites from the Favorites menu. But what do you do when you don't know the name of a particular Web site or have no idea where some information can be found?

Unlike highly organized services such as America Online, the Internet is a disorganized array of information distributed across millions of computers. No one group is responsible for organizing the content of the Internet. If you want to learn about butterflies, for example, it's up to you to find the relevant Web sites.

To impart order to this data mishmash, some sites, called *search engines*, are dedicated to the task of searching the Web and are the equivalent of an electronic card catalog system. By entering keywords and phrases, you can find information on almost any topic. **Figures 5.1** and **5.2** show two popular search engines.

IE5 helps you search the Internet in these ways:

◆ Use the Search Assistant to find Web pages, addresses, street maps, etc.

◆ Perform an *autosearch* by typing keywords into IE5's Address bar.

◆ Search your computer or the Internet from the Start > Find menu.

◆ Search for keywords within any Web page displayed in IE5.

# Searching with the Search Assistant

SEARCHING WITH THE SEARCH ASSISTANT

Rather than visit search sites such as AltaVista or Lycos, you can use the Search Assistant to search the Internet for Web pages, addresses, phone numbers, email addresses, company information, maps, encyclopedia articles, and newsgroup messages.

When you click the Search button (**Figure 5.3**), the window splits into two panes (**Figure 5.4**). Click a radio button in the Search Assistant to select the type of information you want to find, enter the search criteria, and click Search.

Most search results are shown as links in the Search Assistant. Followed links are displayed in the right pane. If a link doesn't lead to the information you want, click another one. In some cases, there will be a Next or More button you can click to view additional search results. With the Search Assistant open, you can explore multiple links without having to use the Back button.

## To perform a search with the Search Assistant:

1. Click the Search button, choose View > Explorer Bar > Search, or press Ctrl + E ). The Search Assistant appears (as shown in **Figure 5.5**).

2. Select a search category or click *more* to see additional categories (**Figure 5.6**).

3. Enter your search criteria and click Search.

   Depending on the type of search, the results are displayed as hypertext links in the Search Assistant (Web information, addresses, encyclopedia articles, and newsgroup messages) or as a new Web page (maps and company information).

**Figure 5.3** The Search button.

Search Assistant                          View hits in this pane

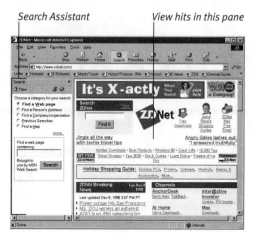

**Figure 5.4** When you click the Search button, the window splits into two panes.

Click to expand the category list

**Figure 5.5** When first summoned, the Search Assistant presents this list of search categories.

**Figure 5.6** Click the More link to see additional search categories.

Links

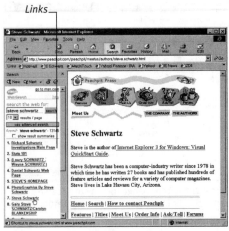

**Figure 5.7** Each link displayed in the Search Assistant represents a potential match for your search criteria.

Next button   Next menu

**Figure 5.8** Click the Next button or open the Next drop-down menu to use a different search engine with the same search criteria.

**Figure 5.9** If you run the cursor over a potential match, summary information often appears.

Logo

**Figure 5.10** Click the search engine's logo to go to its Web site.

**4.** If a list of links is displayed in the Search Assistant, click a link to view its Web page or related information (**Figure 5.7**). Click links until you find what you want.

To move to the previous or next set of search results, click the appropriate text link or button in the Search Assistant (such as Previous and Next).

**5** If additional search engines are available for the type of search you are conducting, click the Next button at the top of the Search Assistant or select an engine from the Next drop-down menu (**Figure 5.8**).

**6.** To perform a new search of the same type, change the criteria and click Search.

*or*

To perform a search of a *different* type, click the New button.

*or*

To close the Search Assistant and display the current Web page full-screen, click the Search button again or click the Search Assistant's close button (the tiny *x*).

## ✔ Tips

- You can repeat a recent search by choosing Previous Searches.

- Need more information about a search result? Move the mouse pointer over a link in the Search Assistant (see **Figure 5.9**).

- To go to the home page for a search engine, click on the site's logo in the Search Assistant (**Figure 5.10**). In many cases, a search engine's home page will provide more advanced search options.

**SEARCHING WITH THE SEARCH ASSISTANT**

# Customizing the Search Assistant

As you determine which types of searches you perform most of the time, you can customize how the Search Assistant displays and works.

## To customize the Search Assistant:

1. Click the Customize button at the top of the Search Assistant.

   The Customize Search Settings page appears (**Figure 5.11**).

2. To remove or add a search category (such as Find a Web Page or Find a Person's Address), click to remove or add the checkmark before the category name.

3. To remove or add search providers within a search category, click to remove or add the checkmark before the provider name.

4. To change the order in which providers are presented within a search category, select a provider in the scrolling list and then click the up or down button to move the provider to a new position (**Figure 5.12**).

5. To change the order in which the search categories appear in the Search Assistant, scroll to the bottom of the Web page, select a search category, and then click the up or down button to move the search category to a new position (**Figure 5.13**).

6. To save your changes, click Update. To ignore the changes you've made, click Cancel. To reset the Search Assistant to its default settings, click Reset.

## ✔ Tip

■ You can replace the Search Assistant with a single search engine of your choice by clicking the link at the bottom of the page (Choose a Default Search Provider).

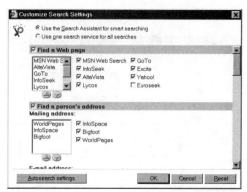

**Figure 5.11** You can change the way the Search Assistant works in the Customize Search Settings page.

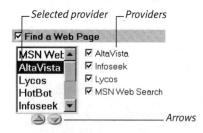

**Figure 5.12** Change the provider order by selecting one in the scrolling list and then clicking the up- or down-arrow button.

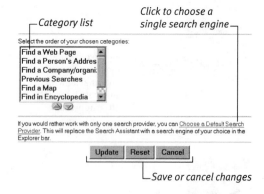

**Figure 5.13** Use the same procedure to change the order in which search categories are listed in the Search Assistant.

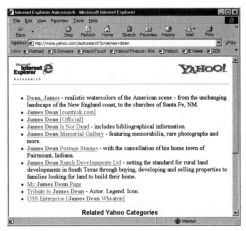

**Figure 5.14** This autosearch for ? James Dean yields these hits in Yahoo!

*Chosen site*

**Figure 5.15** Choose an autosearch site from this dialog box.

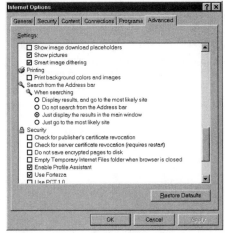

**Figure 5.16** Specify what should be done when performing an autosearch.

# More Search Methods

Other IE5 search options enable you to do the following:

♦ You can quickly perform a Web *auto-search* by typing search terms in the Address box.

♦ You can instruct IE5 to find sites that are similar to the one you are viewing.

♦ You can initiate some searches directly from Window's Start > Find menu.

## To perform an autosearch:

1. In the Address box, type ?, Go, or Find, followed by a space and the search keyword or phrase (such as Find baseball).

2. Press [Enter] or click the Go button to execute the search.

   Possible matches are shown as links in the designated autosearch site (**Figure 5.14**). Click any link to go to that Web page.

To choose an autosearch site, click the Customize button in the Search Assistant followed by the Autosearch Settings button (**Figure 5.15**). You can further customize autosearch in the same dialog box or in the Advanced section of the Internet Options dialog box (**Figure 5.16**).

To find sites that are similar to the page you are viewing, choose Tools > Show Related Sites.

## To search from the Start menu:

1. From the Start menu, choose Find, followed by the command for what you'd like to find (**Figure 5.17**).

   Choose *On the Internet* to launch IE5 and conduct a search using the Search Assistant.

   Choose *People* to find names and addresses in your Windows address book or on the Internet.

   Choose *Files or Folders* to find information on your computer.

   Note that other Find commands may be listed, depending on the particular programs installed on your computer.

2. A dialog box appears (**Figure 5.18–19**), or the Search Assistant opens (if you've chosen On the Internet). Enter search criteria, set options, and execute the search.

## ✔ Tips

- You don't have to precede auotsearch terms with ?, Go, or Find. You can type `Charles Atlas` rather than `Find Charles Atlas`, for example.

- When searching for People from the Start > Find menu (refer to **Figure 5.17**), you can look in your Windows address book (Contacts) or in several Web search sites. Different sites often have different information. If you can't find the person you're seeking, choose another site from the Look In list.

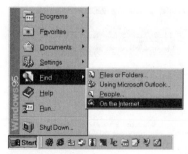

**Figure 5.17** The Find menu.

**Figure 5.18** When searching for files or folders, the Find All Files dialog box appears.

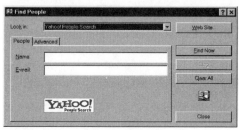

**Figure 5.19** You can use the Find People dialog box to search for contacts in your address book or to search the Internet for information on others.

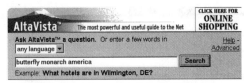

**Figure 5.20** To conduct a search in AltaVista, enter keywords in this box and click Search.

*Search results*    *Search keywords*

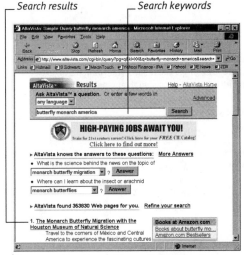

**Figure 5.21** Search results are displayed as links.

# Using a Search Engine

To give you a better idea of how to perform a search with one of the many search engines, I'll show you how it's done in AltaVista.

## To search with AltaVista:

1. Type a list of keywords that you want to find. Separate keywords with spaces.

   Entering butterfly, monarch, and america as keywords (**Figure 5.20**) presents a list of links of possible matches (**Figure 5.21**). The best matches—those that contain as many terms as possible—are listed first. (If you enter keywords in lowercase letters, AltaVista ignores case when searching.)

2. To treat words as a phrase, enclose them in quotes. For example, when searching for a person's name, you'll have *much* better luck using "Bob Smith" than entering the name as separate keywords (i.e., Bob Smith). The former will find only Bob Smith, while the latter will identify all Bobs and all Smiths.

3. Search words can be required or prohibited.

   To require a word, precede it with a plus (+) symbol; to prohibit it, precede it with a minus (–) symbol. For example, +"Steve Schwartz" –music will find links for Steve Schwartz, while omitting those for the composer by that name.

4. Use an asterisk as a wild card to identify variants of a word. For example, enter iron* to find iron, irony, ironed, ironing, ironstone, and ironclad.

## ✔ Tip

- If you usually search with a particular search engine, you can replace the Search Assistant with it. Open the Search Assistant and click Customize. Click the radio button marked *Use one service for all searches*, choose a service, and click OK.

# Tips for Productive Searches

Here are some general strategies for improving the productivity of your searches.

## Try, try again

No search site covers all the information on the Internet. If you can't find what you're looking for at one search site, try another.

## Read the site's instructions

Search procedures can vary dramatically from one site to the next. Words may have to be typed in different boxes, separated by the words OR or AND, or enclosed in quotation marks. By phrasing your search correctly, you'll have a greater likelihood of finding what you want (**Figure 5.22**).

## Be specific, but not too

Most search tools can perform *fuzzy searches* (finding matches that are close to the search terms). Searching for Steve Schwartz may also find Steven, Stephen, and S. Schwartz. Closest matches are usually listed first.

## Use the appropriate search tool

Search sites frequently specialize in different types of information (see **Table 5.1**). Areas of specialization may include Web pages, newsgroups, names, addresses, phone numbers, and e-mail addresses.

## ✔ Tip

- If your Internet service provider doesn't offer newsgroups, you can visit AltaVista (http://www.altavista.com), click the Usenet link, and read newsgroup posts. Deja News (http://www.dejanews.com) is another excellent source of this material.

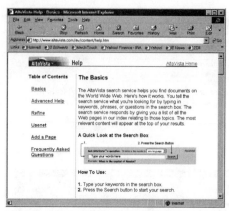

**Figure 5.22** To get the results you want, it's an excellent idea to read each search engine's Help page.

**Table 5.1**

| Web Search Sites | | |
| --- | --- | --- |
| **SITE NAME** | **SPECIALIZATION** | **URL** |
| AltaVista | Web, newsgroups, e-mail addresses, category searches | www.altavista.com |
| AnyWho | Addresses, e-mail addresses, phone numbers | www.anywho.com |
| AOL NetFind | Web, newsgroups, addresses, phone numbers, e-mail addresses, category searches, personal Web pages | www.aol.com/netfind |
| Deja News | Newsgroups | www.dejanews.com |
| HotBot | Web, newsgroups, e-mail addresses, category searches | www.hotbot.com |
| InfoSeek | Web, newsgroups, e-mail addresses, category searches | infoseek.go.com |
| Lycos | Web and category searches | www.lycos.com |
| WebCrawler | Web, addresses, maps, category searches | www.webcrawler.com |
| WhoWhere? | Addresses, phone numbers, e-mail addresses, personal Web pages | www.whowhere .lycos.com |
| Yahoo! | Web, email addresses, phone numbers, category searches | www.yahoo.com |

Search options    Text to find

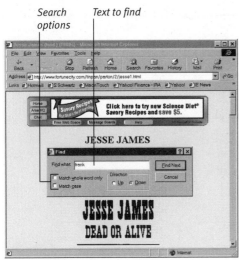

**Figure 5.23** The Find dialog box.

The found text

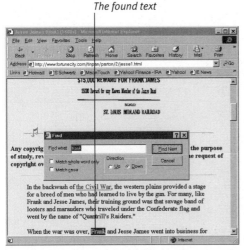

**Figure 5.24** Found text is highlighted by IE5.

# Searching for Text within a Web Page

In addition to giving you quick access to a variety of search sites (via the Search button), IE5 also enables you to search for text in the current Web page—in much the same way as using a word processor's Find command.

## To search within a Web page:

1. Choose Edit > Find (on this page) or press Ctrl+F. The Find dialog box appears (**Figure 5.23**).

2. Enter the search string in the Find what box.

3. *Optional:* To change the direction of the search, click to select Up or Down.

4. *Optional:* To find only exact occurrences of the word, click the Match whole word only check box.

5. *Optional:* Click the Match case check box to restrict matches to those with the same case as that of the search string.

6. Click Find Next to begin the search. If a match is found, IE5 scrolls to select and display it (**Figure 5.24**).

7. Click Find Next to continue searching or click Cancel to dismiss the dialog box.

## ✔ Tip

■ The Find (on this page) command can be very useful immediately after using a search site or the Search Assistant to locate a relevant Web page. Use Find to search for the same text string, enabling you to quickly jump to the first occurrence of the text.

# OFFLINE BROWSING

Using Internet Explorer's offline browsing capabilities, you can read Web pages without being connected to the Internet. If your Internet account charges are based on connect time, you can save money by browsing offline. Even if you have an account with unlimited connect time, there are still instances in which you may want to work offline, such as:

◆ You need to use your Internet phone line for other purposes, such as voice calls or sending and receiving faxes.

◆ You are traveling with a portable computer and have no Internet access (in a car, on an airplane, or at the beach, for example).

◆ You take a portable home from the office to catch up on your Web page reading.

With Internet Explorer 5, you can do any of the following tasks while offline:

◆ Look at favorites that have been downloaded with the Tools > Synchronize command.

◆ View recently visited Web pages that are stored in the History folder.

◆ Open Web pages you have saved on your hard disk.

# Going Offline and Online

If you use the Internet as most people do, the majority of your work will be in online mode; that is, you will have an active Internet connection. Under the circumstances cited at the start of this chapter, however, you can also work offline.

## To switch between online and offline modes:

1. *To switch to offline mode,* choose File > Work Offline. When you are in offline mode, the Work Offline command is preceded by a checkmark (**Figure 6.1**).

2. *To switch back to online mode* (and reconnect to the Internet, if needed), choose File > Work Offline again to deselect it. When you are in online mode, the Work Offline command is unchecked.

## ✔ Tips

■ While browsing in offline mode, if you attempt to display a page that is not stored on your hard disk, a dialog box appears offering the option to reopen your Internet connection and go online (**Figure 6.2**). To go online, click Connect. To continue working in offline mode, click Stay Offline or click the close box.

■ Choosing File > Work Offline in either IE5 or Outlook Express also sets the same command for the other program. If you are currently connected, though, it may have no effect on other Internet programs that are still running. If you really want to work offline, you may have to manually close your connection to the Internet.

**Figure 6.1** Choose the Work Offline command to switch between online and offline modes.

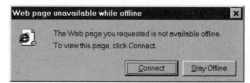

**Figure 6.2** This dialog box appears if you are offline and try to view a page or go to a link that is not stored on your hard disk.

Make the favorite available offline  Set a synchronization schedule for the favorite

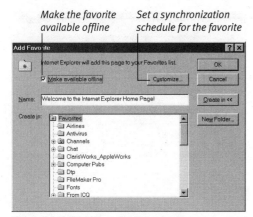

**Figure 6.3** The Add Favorite dialog box.

Click to make the favorite available offline  Select a favorite here

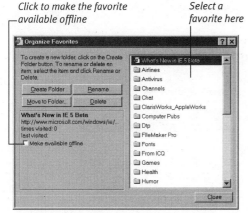

**Figure 6.4** The Organize Favorites dialog box.

# Viewing Favorites Offline

Any Web page saved as a favorite can be made available for offline viewing. (In prior versions of Internet Explorer, this was called *subscribing* to a page; it is now called *synchronizing*.) On a specific schedule (as well as on demand), the content from all subscribed pages is downloaded to your hard disk—making it available for offline viewing.

To include a Web page in the synchronization process, you instruct IE5 to make the page available offline, determine whether you want to follow only that page or all of its links, and then set a synchronization schedule for the page.

A page can be added to the synchronization list at the time it is saved as a favorite or later—at your convenience or as your needs change.

## To mark a page for synchronization:

When creating a new favorite, choose Favorites > Add to Favorites, and click the checkbox labeled *Make available offline* (**Figure 6.3**).

If the page is already a favorite, you can do either of the following:

◆ Choose Favorites > Organize Favorites, select the page name in the Organize Favorites dialog box (**Figure 6.4**), and click the checkbox labeled *Make available offline*. To specify a schedule and other synchronization options for the favorite, click the Properties button that appears in the dialog box.

◆ Open the Favorites bar, right-click the page name, choose Properties, and click the checkbox labeled *Make available offline*.

## Creating synchronization schedules

Because you won't want to set a different synchronization schedule for every favorite (although you *can*), IE5 lets you create basic schedules for daily, weekly, and monthly synchronization. Once created, you can assign favorites to these schedules.

## To establish standard synchronization schedules:

1. Choose Tools > Synchronize.

   The Items to Synchronize dialog box appears (**Figure 6.5**).

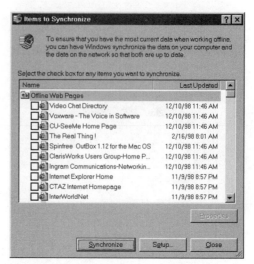

**Figure 6.5** The Items to Synchronize dialog box.

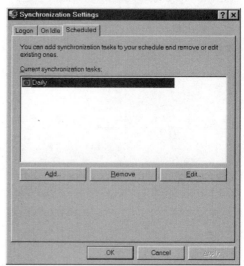

**Figure 6.6** Edit existing schedules or create new ones in this section of the Synchronization Settings dialog box.

**Figure 6.7** Click the Schedule tab to set a starting time and frequency for a schedule.

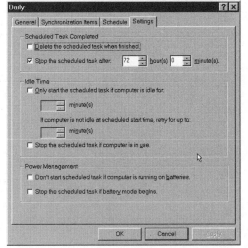

**Figure 6.8** Click the Settings tab to specify the circumstances under which the schedule should and should not be run.

2. Click the Setup button.

   The Synchronization Settings dialog box appears.

3. Click the Scheduled tab.

4. To view or edit an existing schedule (**Figure 6.6**), select it and click Edit. In the dialog box that appears (Daily, for example), click the Schedule and Settings tabs to set a synchronization schedule (**Figures 6.7** and **6.8**).

   *or*

   To create a new schedule (other than the ones already listed), click Add.

5. Close the dialog boxes when you are done.

## Assigning favorites to synchronization schedules

You can associate a Web page with one or more synchronization schedules when you save it as a favorite, or you can simultaneously set a schedule for *many* existing favorites.

### To set a synchronization schedule for a new favorite:

1. Visit the Web page that you want to save as a new favorite.

2. Choose Favorites > Add to Favorites.
   The Add Favorite dialog box appears (refer to **Figure 6.3**).

3. Click the checkbox marked *Make available offline*.

4. If you also want to assign the page to an automatic synchronization schedule, click Customize. Otherwise, skip to Step 7.
   The Offline Favorite Wizard appears.

5. Click Next to begin (**Figure 6.9**).

6. Respond to the Wizard's questions, specifying what is to be downloaded, when it is to be downloaded (manually or on a schedule), and so on. Click Finish when you are done. You return to the Add Favorite dialog box.

7. Select a folder in which to store the favorite, and click OK.

**Figure 6.9** Use the Online Favorite Wizard to help you set a synchronization schedule for a new favorite.

Synchronize favorites at logon    Select favorites from this list    Choose a connection

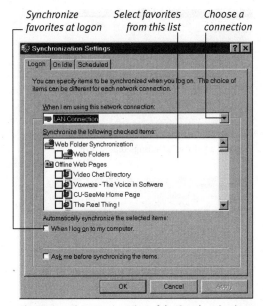

**Figure 6.10** The Logon section of the Synchronization Settings dialog box.

Activate idle time synchronization    Set idle time synchronization options

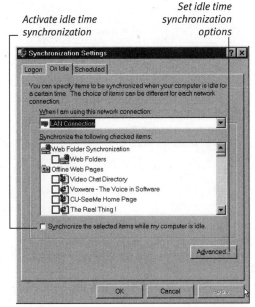

**Figure 6.11** The On Idle section of the Synchronization Settings dialog box.

## To set a schedule for existing favorites:

1. Choose Tools > Synchronize.

   The Items to Synchronize dialog box appears (**Figure 6.5**).

2. Click the Setup button.

   The Synchronization Settings dialog box appears.

3. To specify pages that will automatically be updated at logon or logoff, click the Logon tab (**Figure 6.10**), select a network connection, and choose the desired pages.

   ◆ To synchronize the chosen pages at logon, click the appropriate checkbox.

   ◆ If you want to be prompted before each synchronization (giving you an option to prevent it), click the checkbox labeled *Ask me before synchronizing the items.*

   ◆ If desired, repeat this procedure for any additional network connections.

4. To specify pages that will automatically be updated during idle times on your computer, click the On Idle tab (**Figure 6.11**), select a network connection, and check off the desired pages.

   ◆ Click the checkbox labeled *Synchronize the selected items while my computer is idle.*

   ◆ Click the Advanced button to set an idle time period (such as 15 minutes) and the frequency with which synchronization will be repeated (**Figure 6.12**).

   ◆ If desired, repeat this procedure for any additional network connections.

5. To specify pages that will automatically be updated on a preset schedule, click the Scheduled tab (**Figure 6.13**), select a

VIEWING FAVORITES OFFLINE

schedule (such as Daily), and click Edit.
(If you want to create a new schedule,
click Add.)

◆ Click the Synchronization Items tab
(**Figure 6.14**), select a network connection, and check off the desired
pages.

◆ If you want this schedule to be followed even when your computer isn't
connected to the Internet at the designated time, click the checkbox at
the bottom of the dialog box.

◆ To change the scheduled synchronization time, click the Schedule tab. To
change basic schedule details and procedures, click the Settings tab.

◆ If desired, repeat this procedure for
any additional network connections.

6. To save the new settings, return to the
original dialog box and click Close.

**Figure 6.12** The Idle Settings dialog box.

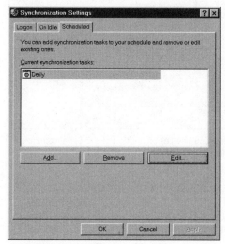

**Figure 6.13** Modify a schedule or create a new one.

*Automatically connect to the Internet,
if needed to synchronize the pages*

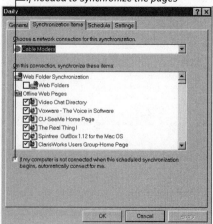

**Figure 6.14** Specify the pages affected by this
synchronization schedule.

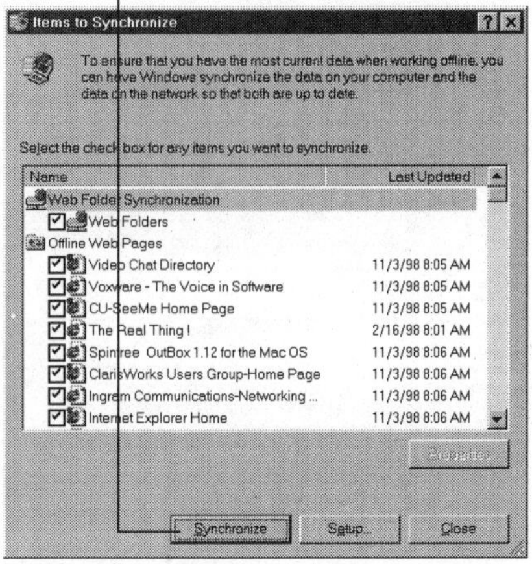

*Click to begin a manual synchronization*

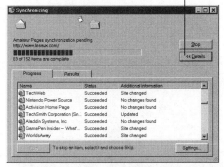

**Figure 6.15** The Items to Synchronize dialog box.

*Click to show or hide the details of the synchronization process*

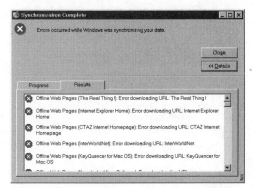

**Figure 6.16** As the synchronization proceeds, its progress is shown in the Synchronizing dialog box.

**Figure 6.17** Click the Results tab to view errors that occurred during the synchronization.

## Manual synchronization

In addition to performing scheduled synchronizations (whether at logon, during idle periods, or at scheduled times), you can instruct IE5 to synchronize immediately.

### To perform a manual synchronization:

1. Choose Tools > Synchronize.

   The Items to Synchronize dialog box appears (**Figure 6.15**).

2. Add or remove checkmarks to select the pages you want to synchronize.

3. Click the Synchronize button.

   The Synchronizing dialog box appears (**Figure 6.16**), showing synchronization progress.

### ✔ Tips

■ In offline mode, you can visit any Web page in the Favorites menu or History folder whose name is listed in black text. Page names that are unavailable while offline are shown in gray text.

■ When you move the cursor over a link on an offline page, it is shown as a pointing hand (if the linked page is available offline) or as a pointing hand accompanied by a circle with a slash through it (if the linked page is *not* available offline).

■ Although there may be a temptation to synchronize several layers of links for pages (rather than the main page alone), be aware that this can result in huge downloads, depending on the number of links on the page and the number of levels followed.

■ Errors during a manual synchronization can be viewed by clicking the Results tab in the Synchronizing dialog box (**Figure 6.17**).

# Viewing Pages in the History Folder

The History folder contains the data necessary to display Web pages that you've recently viewed online. If you want to read the text of a page that's in the History folder, you can readily do so while offline.

## To view a page in the History folder:

1. Launch IE5, if it is not already running.

2. Click the History button on the toolbar. The History bar opens in the left side of the browser window (**Figure 6.18**).

3. Click the View button in the History bar to select a sort order for displaying the pages.

   *or*

   Click the Search button to locate a specific Web page in the History folder.

4. Click the name of a Web page to display it. Note that grayed out page names in the History bar cannot be viewed offline.

5. To dismiss the History bar, click the History button again or the tiny *x* at the top of the History bar.

For more on the History bar, see Chapter 3.

## ✔ Tip

■ Whether a page is currently stored in the History folder depends on the settings you have chosen in the Internet Options dialog box (**Figure 6.19**). To set the number of days pages will be stored in the History folder, choose Tools > Internet Options.

Set a display order for the history list
Search the History folder
Close the History bar

**Figure 6.18** Open the History bar to revisit recently viewed Web pages.

Number of days to store a page in History

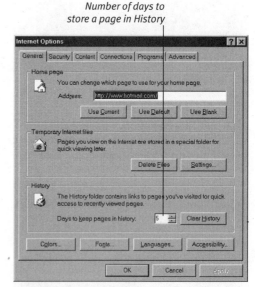

**Figure 6.19** Choose Tools > Internet Options to set options for the History folder.

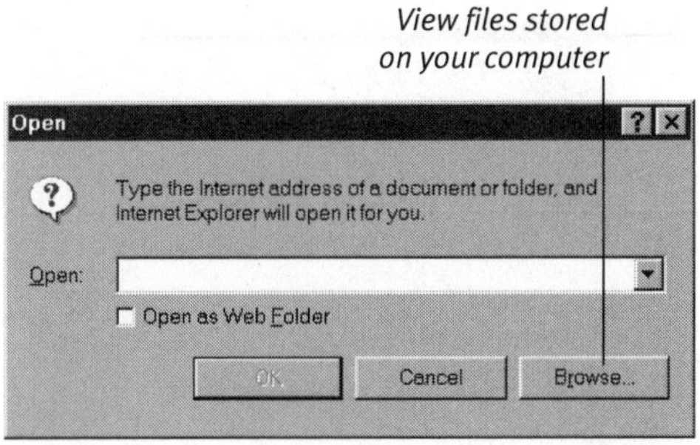

View files stored
on your computer

**Figure 6.20** The Open dialog box.

**Figure 6.21** Select an HTML file to open.

Steve
Schwartz.htm

**Figure 6.22** An HTML
file icon.

# Opening Saved HTML Files

HTML files (Web pages with a .htm or .html extension) that you created yourself or saved from browsing sessions with the File > Save command can be opened and viewed from within IE5.

## To open a stored HTML file:

1. Launch IE5, if it is not already running.

2. Choose File > Open or press Ctrl+O. The Open dialog box appears (**Figure 6.20**).

3. Click the Browse button. A standard file dialog box appears (**Figure 6.21**).

4. Navigate to the drive and folder that contains the HTML file you want to open, select it, and click Open. The Open dialog box reappears with the path of the selected file entered for you.

5. Click Open to display the page in IE5.

See Chapter 7 to learn about opening other types of files in your browser, such as JPG and GIF graphic images, and also for information on saving Web pages to your hard disk.

## ✔ Tip

■ You can also open stored pages by going to the desktop, opening the folder in which the page is stored (if necessary), and then double-clicking the file's icon (**Figure 6.22**). As long as IE5 is your default browser, it launches and displays the selected Web page. If another browser (such as Netscape Navigator) is your default, the page will open in that browser.

OPENING SAVED HTML FILES

# WORKING WITH FILES

7

One of the great things about using Internet Explorer 5 is that you aren't restricted to just browsing the World Wide Web. You can also use IE5 to accomplish these file-related activities:

- ◆ Download files, such as drivers for computer equipment, program updates, templates, documentation, demos, shareware, and freeware.

- ◆ Save the current Web page as a text or HTML file and copy selected text from a Web page.

- ◆ Save any graphic image on a Web page as a file or as Windows wallpaper.

- ◆ Save any background image from a Web page as a graphics file.

- ◆ Save audio and video files found on the Web (see Chapter 8).

- ◆ Use IE5 to open files on your hard disk (such as HTML documents and graphics) and launch programs.

- ◆ Connect to FTP (*File Transfer Protocol*) sites and download or upload files.

# Downloading Files from the Web

Downloading a file from the Web is simple. Web sites usually contain hypertext links or buttons you can click to download files. The only decision you must make is whether to save the file on disk or—in the case of an executable file—to open it at once.

## To download a file:

1. Go to the Web page that contains the file you want to download.

2. Click the hypertext or graphic link for the file (**Figure 7.1**).

    The download begins (**Figure 7.2**), and a dialog box appears (**Figure 7.3**).

3. To save the file, click the *Save this program to disk* radio button. To immediately launch the program (or extract its contents, in the case of an archive), click *Run this program from its current location.*

4. If you are saving the file, a Save As dialog box appears (**Figure 7.4**). Select a location on disk for the new file.

    The download continues (**Figure 7.5**).

5. When the download finishes, the file is saved to disk or opened, depending on the option chosen in Step 3.

## ✔ Tips

■ You can halt a download at any time by clicking the Cancel button in the File Download dialog box (refer to **Figure 7.5**).

■ Not all downloads are automatically saved to disk or launched. Some text files, for example, are displayed by IE5 as Web pages. You can save the current page by choosing File > Save As.

Link

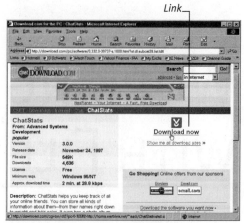

**Figure 7.1** To begin a file download, all you usually have to do is click a graphic or text link.

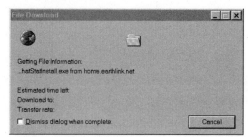

**Figure 7.2** The first thing that happens during a download is that IE5 obtains information about the file, such as its size.

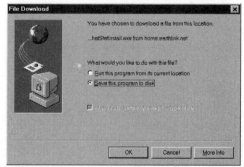

**Figure 7.3** Decide whether you want to open the file the moment it is received or save it to disk.

**Figure 7.4** When using the *Save this program to disk* option, you must choose a location on disk in which to save the downloaded file.

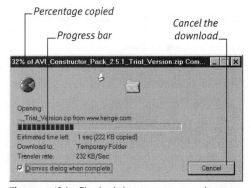

**Figure 7.5** If the file size is known, a progress bar shows how the download is faring.

**Figure 7.6** You can also download a file by right-clicking its link and choosing Save Target As.

- You can download any file directly to disk by right-clicking its link and choosing Save Target As from the pop-up menu that appears (**Figure 7.6**). See "Saving Multimedia Files" in Chapter 8 for instructions.

- You can also download a file from an FTP site by typing the file's URL in the Address box, such as:

  `ftp://ftp.aznet.com/pub/test.exe`

  For additional information about downloading files from FTP sites, see "Using FTP Sites," later in this chapter.

- When downloading an installation program, it is often smarter to save it than to open it immediately. Then if you ever need to reinstall the application, you can do so without having to download it again.

- Depending on how you have programs on your computer configured, when downloading some file types, you may not be given an option to save or open the file. ZIP archives may automatically be downloaded and then opened by WinZip, for example.

- The amount of time that a download takes is directly affected by the amount of network traffic. If it seems to be taking too long, try again at a different time of day. You may also find that the same file downloads faster from a different site. In general, when you are offered a choice of download sites, choose the one closest to you.

- Some download attempts will be met with an error message of one sort or another. Don't give up too quickly. Not all errors are meaningful. It's often worth a second—or third—try.

# Saving Files from the Web

By following the procedures in this section, you can save entire Web pages, graphics found on Web pages, and page backgrounds.

## Saving a Web page

If you want to be able to view a Web page while off-line or work with its HTML code, you can save the current Web page in a variety of formats.

To save a complete Web page (including all graphic images needed to create the page), save it as *Web Page, complete* or *Web Archive*. The former method saves the HTML code and then stores the graphics in a separate folder. The latter method stores all elements in a single archive file.

To save only the HTML code needed to create the page (without saving the graphics), save the page in *Web Page, HTML only* format. You will still be able to view the page in your browser (whether you are on- or off-line), but all graphics will be missing.

If you're only interested in the page's text (to paste it into a word processing document, for example), choose the Text File save option.

## To save a Web page:

1. Display the page that you want to save.

2. Choose File > Save As.

   The Save As dialog box appears (**Figure 7.7**).

3. Enter a name for the file in the File name box or accept the name that is proposed.

4. Select a type for the file from the Save as type pop-up menu.

5. Click Save.

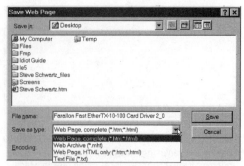

**Figure 7.7** When saving a Web page, choose a save format by clicking this down arrow.

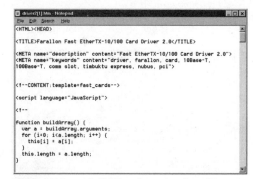

**Figure 7.8** A page's HTML code can be viewed in Notepad. You can make it easier to read by choosing Edit > Word Wrap.

*Selected text*

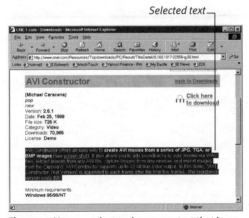

**Figure 7.9** You can select and copy any text that is on a Web page. Remember that text that is part of an image is a graphic, not real text.

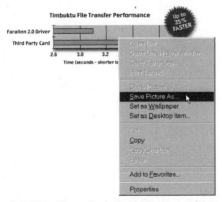

**Figure 7.10** Choose Save Picture As to save the selected element as a file.

*Filename* — *File type menu*

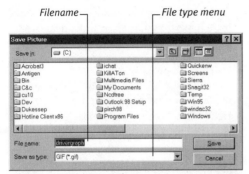

**Figure 7.11** Name and select a file type for the item. (Or you can accept the original filename and type.)

## ✔ Tips

■ Another way to examine a page's HTML code is to choose View > Source. The code is displayed in Notepad (**Figure 7.8**), where it can be examined, edited, and saved.

■ To save only selected text from a page (**Figure 7.9**), highlight the text, choose Edit > Copy (or press Ctrl+C), and then paste it into a Notepad or WordPad document. Any graphic element (a picture, icon, or advertisement, for example) can be saved on disk as a separate file.

## To save a page element:

1. Right-click the page element that you want to save.

   A pop-up menu appears (**Figure 7.10**).

2. Choose Save Picture As from the pop-up menu.

   The Save Picture dialog box appears (**Figure 7.11**).

3. Navigate to the drive and folder where you wish to save the file.

   *Optional:* The name proposed for the file is the name that the Web page creator assigned to it. You can rename the file, if you wish.

   *Optional:* The file format is automatically shown in the Save as type box. You can select a different file type, if you wish.

4. Click Save.

**SAVING FILES FROM THE WEB**

## ✔ Tips

- You can copy a selected page element to the clipboard by right-clicking it and choosing Copy from the pop-up menu. The item is then available for pasting into other documents (WordPad, for example).

- If you right-click a hypertext or graphic link to another Web page, a new choice appears on the pop-up menu: Save Target As. Choose this command to save a link as an HTML file (without graphics).

- You can also save most types of page elements (links and graphics, for example) by simply dragging them onto the desktop.

## Saving a graphic as wallpaper

There are many eye-catching images on the Web. If you find one that really appeals to you, it's easy to capture and use it as your desktop wallpaper.

## To save an element as wallpaper:

1. Right-click the page element that you want to use as wallpaper.

    The pop-up menu shown previously in **Figure 7.10** appears.

2. Choose *Set as Wallpaper* from the menu.

    The image is saved as the Internet Explorer Wallpaper and becomes the new wallpaper (**Figures 7.12**).

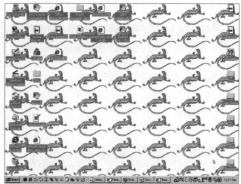

**Figure 7.12** You can use many of the images on the Web as interesting wallpaper.

### Using a Web Page as Wallpaper

If you have Active Desktop installed (see Chapter 1), you may find it useful to use a favorite Web page as your wallpaper. Clicking a hypertext or graphic link on the wallpaper will launch your browser to display the linked information.

Start by saving an HTML file to disk, as explained earlier in this chapter. Next, right-click the desktop, choose Properties, click the Background tab in the Display Properties dialog box, and click the Browse button. Select the HTML file from its location on your hard disk.

— *Original IE5 wallpaper file*

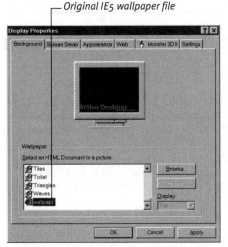

**Figure 7.13** Choose the wallpapr HTML document to revert to IE5's original wallpaper.

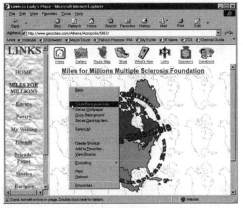

**Figure 7.14** To save a page background, such as this North American map, right-click it to make the pop-up menu appear.

**Figure 7.15** Specify a location on disk, filename, and file type for the background.

## ✔ Tips

- You don't have to be viewing a Web page when saving an image as wallpaper. You can use IE5's Open command to view JPEG or GIF files from your hard disk and then save them as wallpaper.

- Even if you didn't save a particular image when you were on-line, there is a good chance that you can find it in the Temporary Internet Files folder. To use such an image file as wallpaper, copy it to another directory, open it in IE5 and then follow the procedure to save it as wallpaper.

- To restore the original IE5 wallpaper, open the Display control panel (**Figure 7.13**), click the Background tab, and choose wallpapr.

    Many Web pages have decorative backgrounds. If you'd like to examine a background more closely or use it in your own pages, you can save it as a graphic file.

## To save a background graphic:

1. Right-click the background and choose *Save Background As* from the pop-up menu that appears (**Figure 7.14**).

    The Save Picture dialog box appears (**Figure 7.15**).

2. Specify a name, location, and file type.

3. Click Save.

## ✔ Tip

- If you prefer, you can simply copy a background to the clipboard by choosing Copy Background from the pop-up menu. After it has been copied, the background can be pasted into other documents by choosing Edit > Paste or pressing Ctrl+V.

# Opening Files on Your Hard Disk

You can open *any* file on your hard disk from within IE5, and you can use it to launch programs as well. Depending on the type of file opened, the IE5 add-ons you have installed, and the Windows file associations you have set, the file will either open in IE5 (text, HTML, JPEG, and GIF files, for example) or in a different program.

## To open a file from disk:

1. Choose File > Open (or press Ctrl+O). The Open dialog box appears (**Figure 7.16**).

2. In the Open box, type the path of the file or folder to open (C:\Screens\Ball.jpg, for example) or the program to launch.

   Alternately, you can click Browse. A standard file dialog box appears. Navigate to the appropriate drive and directory. If the file is not listed, choose its type from the Files of type list or choose *All Files*. Select a file or program, and click Open.

3. Click OK.

4. For some file types, the File Download dialog box appears (**Figure 7.17**). Choose *Open this file from its current location* and click OK.

   If a document file was selected, the file is either displayed in the browser (**Figure 7.18**) or opened in another program. If a program was selected, it launches.

## ✔ Tips

- You can also open files and run programs by typing the path into the Address box.

- Choose View > Toolbars > Folders to make IE5 work like Windows Explorer.

Path for the file, folder, or program

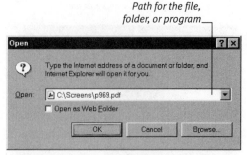

**Figure 7.16** You can open a file, folder, or program by typing its path in the Open dialog box. If you don't know the path, click Browse to look for the item.

Open file

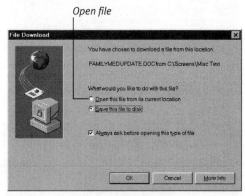

**Figure 7.17** The File Download dialog box sometimes appears when opening items on your hard disk. Since you normally do not want to resave the document, click *Open it from its current location*.

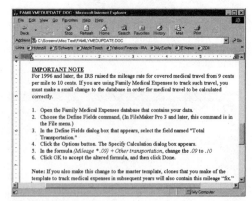

**Figure 7.18** With Word Viewer 97 installed, Word documents can be viewed within IE5.

# Using FTP Sites

FTP (*File Transfer Protocol*) sites abound on the Internet. These sites are file repositories; files are transferred in and out using FTP. The prefix for an FTP site is `ftp://` rather than `http://`.

If you have your own Web page, chances are good that your HTML and graphic files are stored on your Internet service provider's FTP site. Many computer software and hardware vendors maintain public areas on their FTP sites where customers can download the latest device drivers, patches, updates, and demos.

## Connecting to an FTP site

There are two ways to connect to an FTP site: as an *anonymous user* (the default method) and as a *named user* (requires an assigned user name and password). The system administrator for each FTP site determines the privileges afforded each type of user. It is not unusual for anonymous users to have downloading privileges from public directories, but they may not be allowed to upload files to the site (or may only do so to specific directories).

## To log onto an FTP site as an anonymous user:

To connect to an FTP site as an anonymous user, simply type the site's URL in the Address box (`ftp://ftp.microsoft.com`, for example) or choose it from the Favorites menu.

---

### Setting File Associations

Windows uses file associations to determine which program launches when you double-click a particular type of document. For example, you can associate various types of Microsoft Word documents with Microsoft Word, Word Viewer 97, or WordPad. When you install IE5, it automatically assigns the file associations for GIF and JPEG graphics to itself.

To see a list of the current file associations, open any folder, choose View > Folder Options, and click the File Types tab at the top of the Folder Options dialog box. If you'd like to associate a particular file type with a program other than IE5 (linking JPEG files with a graphics viewer, for example), refer to "File types, associating with programs" in Windows Help.

## To log onto an FTP site as a named user:

1. Begin by connecting as an anonymous user.

2. Choose File > Login As.

   The FTP Login dialog box appears (**Figure 7.19**).

3. Enter your user name and password.

4. Click Login.

## Downloading and uploading files

Depending on the privileges you have at a given FTP site, you may be allowed to view files, download files, upload files, or perform any combination of these activities. (Note that downloading and uploading privileges may be directory-specific; that is, you may be able to download files from some directories but not others.)

## To download files from an FTP site:

1. Use IE5 to connect to the FTP site, as explained previously.

2. Right-click the file or folder you want to download and choose Copy to Folder (**Figure 7.20**).

   The Browse for Folder dialog box appears (**Figure 7.21**).

3. Select the folder to which the downloaded file(s) will be copied.

4. Click OK.

   The file(s) are copied from the FTP site to the designated folder (**Figure 7.22**).

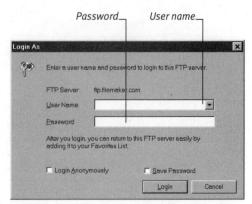

Figure 7.19 To log onto an FTP site as an authorized user, enter your user name and password in the FTP Login dialog box.

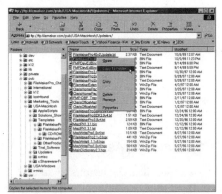

Figure 7.20 To download a file from an FTP site, right-click it and choose Copy to Folder.

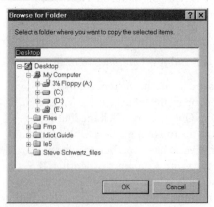

Figure 7.21 Navigate to the drive and folder in which the downloaded item(s) will be saved.

_Progress bar_

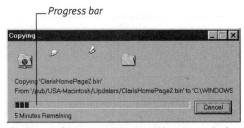

**Figure 7.22** If you are copying many items or a single large file, a progress dialog box appears.

_Site information_

**Figure 7.23** When viewed as a Web page, site information may be provided in the left side of the window.

_Site folders_

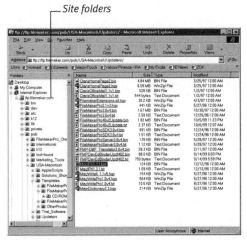

**Figure 7.24** When the Folders Explorer bar is enabled, you can quickly change directories by choosing a folder.

## To upload files to an FTP site:

1. Use IE5 to connect to the FTP site, as explained previously.

2. Use IE5, Windows Explorer, or a standard folder to display the file(s) or folder(s) you want to send to the FTP site.

3. Drag the files(s) or folder(s) into the desired folder on the FTP site.

   The file(s) or folder(s) are transmitted and stored in the chosen folder at the FTP site.

## ✔ Tips

- You can alter the display of an FTP site in several useful ways. Choosing View > as Web Page may provide useful information about the site (**Figure 7.23**). Choosing View > Explorer Bar > Folders makes it simple to navigate through the site (**Figure 7.24**).

- Some FTP sites can be configured to work exactly like Windows Explorer (although few sites currently support this feature). To determine if a site can be made to work this way, choose File > Open, paste or type the FTP site's URL into the Open text box, and click the option to _Open as Web Folder_.

**USING FTP SITES**

# WORKING
# WITH MULTIMEDIA

Not all Web pages consist merely of static text and pictures. Some feature multimedia elements, such as streaming video or audio. Other pages may include movie and audio clips that you can download and play at your leisure.

In previous versions of Internet Explorer, audio and video were played by *ActiveMovie controls* (ActiveX multimedia handlers designed to run from within Internet Explorer). Although this worked fairly well, it wasn't uncommon to discover that you didn't have the player needed for a particular audio or video format. So your multimedia experience was put on hold until you downloaded the necessary player.

IE5, on the other hand, relies on the revamped Windows Media Player (version 6). Without modification, it can play most of the popular multimedia audio and video formats. Not only can it be invoked from Web pages, but it can also run as a standalone application, playing multimedia files that you have stored on your hard disk—such as WAV files and video clips.

## ✔ Tip

■ Windows Media Player is a component of Windows 98 and is installed as part of IE5.

# Playing Multimedia Files

Windows Media Player can play all the following file types: ASF, RealVideo and RealAudio 4.0, MPEG 1, MPEG 2, WAV, AVI, MIDI, MOV, VOD, AU, QuickTime, and MP3. If a new file format is encountered for which a *codec* (an interpreter) can be found, the codec is automatically downloaded.

## To play a file on a Web page:

Click the graphic or text link for the file.

The file downloads to your computer and plays as part of the Web page (**Figure 8.1**) or within Windows Media Player (**Figure 8.2**). Whether the audio or video plays in an embedded multimedia controller or in a separate Windows Media Player window depends on how the designer created the Web page.

*Windows Media Player*

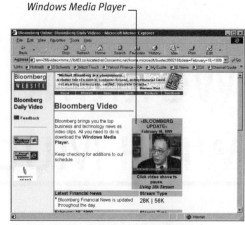

**Figure 8.2** Some designers embed the Windows Media Player in the Web page.

*Playback controls*       *Volume control*

**Figure 8.2** The Windows Media Player controls work similarly to those of a tape deck or VCR: play, pause, stop, beginning, end, and step.

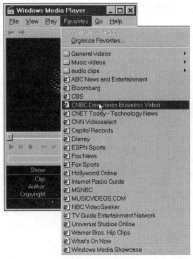

**Figure 8.3** The Favorites menu comes with a built-in list of popular audio and video sites. You can add your own sites and files to the menu, as well as create new folders to better organize the material.

*Choose a file from your hard disk*

*Click to choose a recently played file*

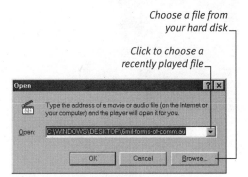

**Figure 8.4** The Open dialog box.

## To open a file with Windows Media Player:

1. Launch Windows Media Player by clicking Start > Accessories > Multimedia > Windows Media Player, or Start > Internet Explorer > Windows Media Player.

2. Choose a Web site or audio/video file from the Favorites menu (**Figure 8.3**).

   If you choose a specific file, it loads in Windows Media Player and then plays. If you choose a Web site, IE5 launches and opens the site.

3. To open a different file on the Web or one on your hard disk, choose File > Open (or press Ctrl+O). An Open dialog box appears (**Figure 8.4**).

4. Do one of the following:
   - ◆ Choose a recently opened file from the drop-down list and click OK.
   - ◆ In the Open text box, type or paste the file's Internet address or its location on your hard drive and click OK.
   - ◆ Click the Browse button to select a file from your hard disk. Click Open and then click OK.

**PLAYING MULTIMEDIA FILES**

## Playing RealAudio/Video files

RealAudio and RealVideo are popular formats for *streaming audio and video* (audio and video that plays as it downloads). Although Windows Media Player can currently handle RealAudio/RealVideo 4.0 feeds, it cannot play those from version 5.0. To play 5.0 feeds, you have to download RealPlayer G2 (free version) or RealPlayer Plus G2 (commercial version) from http://www.real.com. Then, when IE5 encounters a RealAudio or RealVideo 5 feed, RealPlayer Plus launches (**Figure 8.5**).

To change the size of the Windows Media Player playback window, you can:

◆ Click and drag a corner of the window.

◆ Choose View > Zoom or right-click the player and choose Zoom (**Figure 8.6**).

◆ Choose View > Full Screen (or press Alt + Enter).

## ✔ Tips

■ If you encounter a video or audio file that Windows Media Player cannot play, look to see if the Web site directs you to a page where you can download the necessary ActiveMovie control or a standalone player (**Figure 8.7**).

■ To specify default settings for Windows Media Player, choose View > Options.

*Playback controls*    *Volume control*

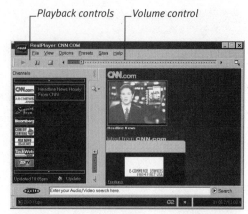

**Figure 8.5** RealPlayer G2 works much like Windows Media Player, but is restricted to playing RealAudio and RealVideo files.

**Figure 8.6** You can access the Zoom menu and other main commands by right-clicking the player window.

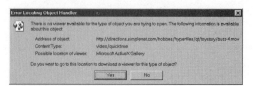

**Figure 8.7** Click Yes to open IE5 to a Web site that may contain the appropriate ActiveX control for this type of file.

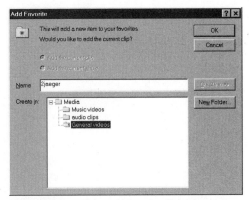

**Figure 8.8** Expand the Add Favorite dialog box to select a different folder or subfolder in which to store a new favorite.

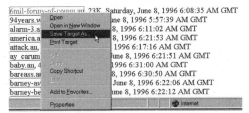

**Figure 8.9** To download an audio or video file to disk, right-click the file's link.

**Figure 8.10** Choose a location on disk where you wish to save the downloaded file.

# Saving Multimedia Files

You can save multimedia files as favorites (storing their location on the Internet rather than the actual file), save them directly to disk as playable files, or save them after viewing or listening to them on the Web.

## To store a multimedia item as a favorite:

1. After playing a multimedia file from the Web that you want to save, choose Favorites > Add to Favorites.

   The Add Favorite dialog box appears.

2. Click the Create in button to expand the window (**Figure 8.8**).

3. Select a location within the Media folder (creating a new folder, if necessary) and click OK.

## To download a multimedia item directly to disk:

1. Right-click the hypertext or graphic link for the item.

   A pop-up menu appears (**Figure 8.9**).

2. Choose Save Target As.

   The Save As dialog box appears (**Figure 8.10**).

3. Choose a location for the file.

4. Click Save.

   When the download completes, the file is saved as directed.

Although downloading an item to disk is the easiest way to save multimedia files, most users don't decide to save an item until after they have listened to or viewed it. The more common procedure is to open the item by clicking the link, listen to or view it, and then save it.

## To save a previously opened multimedia item:

**1.** Open the `C:\Windows\Temporary Internet Files` folder. (If Windows was installed on a drive other than C:, substitute its drive letter for C:.)

Audio and video files downloaded by IE5 are automatically stored in this folder.

**2.** Locate the multimedia file.

**3.** Copy the file to another disk or folder.

### ✔ Tips

■ If you want to make your favorite multimedia files easier to find, create additional folders to help organize them—just as you do with IE5 favorites.

■ Not all multimedia files can be saved to disk. When you attempt this with some file types (for example, RealAudio/RealVideo files), you'll find that all you can save is the setup and location data for the file rather than the actual audio or video.

**Figure 8.11** The radio bar.

---

### The Radio Bar

The radio bar (**Figure 8.11**) is a new IE5 feature that you can use to listen to radio stations as you Web surf. Because radio transmits continuously, it is best used with high speed connections (56K or faster).

To display the radio bar, choose View > Toolbars > Radio. To select a station, click the Radio Stations drop-down menu. Choose *Radio Station Guide* to see a list of available stations. Click Stop to end or pause a transmission; click Play to continue. If you enjoy the current station, you can add it to the Radio Stations menu by choosing Radio Stations > Add Station to Favorites.

To permanently enable the radio bar, choose Tools > Internet Options, click the Advanced tab, scroll to the Multimedia section, and click *Always show Internet Explorer Radio bar.*

# PRINTING

In this chapter, you'll learn how to install a printer (if you haven't set up your new or current printer to work with Windows), specify print settings (such as orientation and headers/footers), and generate all of the different types of printouts that IE5 offers.

Print options have been expanded dramatically in IE5. You can now print:

◆ A single Web page—with or without background graphics and colors.

◆ The current page and all linked pages.

◆ A single frame from a page (or create a separate printout for each frame).

◆ Selected text on a page.

◆ A list of URLs for all links cited on a page.

# Installing a Printer

When printing Web pages, IE5 uses the printer drivers you have installed for Windows. If you have not installed a driver for your printer, you can do so by following these steps. (These instructions are for Windows 95. If you use a different version of Windows, the instructions may be slightly different.)

## To install a printer driver:

1. Open the Printers control panel and double-click Add a Printer.

   The Add Printer Wizard appears.

2. Click the Next button.

   The dialog box lists the supported printer manufacturers and models (**Figure 9.1**).

3. Select the manufacturer and model of your printer.

4. *Optional:* If your printer came with its own driver, click Have Disk and then indicate where to find the driver (**Figure 9.2**).

5. Click Next to view the list of communications ports on your computer (**Figure 9.3**).

6. Select the port to which your printer is connected.

   For a parallel printer, the correct choice is usually *LPT1*. Serial printers are connected to *COM* ports.

7. *Optional:* Click Configure Port to see how the port is configured or to change its settings.

8. Click Next. The dialog box shown in **Figure 9.4** appears.

9. Accept the proposed printer name or enter a different name.

Choose a manufacturer    Choose a printer model    Click if the driver is on disk

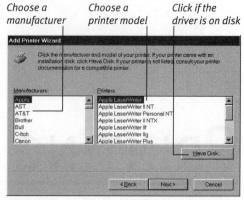

**Figure 9.1** After selecting a manufacturer from the left side of this dialog box, a list of all its supported printer models appears in the right side of the window.

Click to select the drive or directory

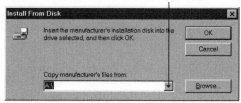

**Figure 9.2** Select the disk or directory that contains the printer driver.

Click to view or change the selected port's settings

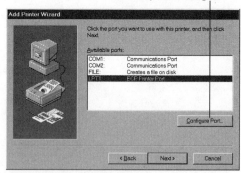

**Figure 9.3** This dialog box lists all of your computer's communications ports.

*Click to make this the default printer*     *Enter or edit the printer's name*

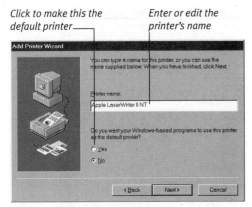

**Figure 9.4** Specify the printer's name and whether Windows should use it as the default printer.

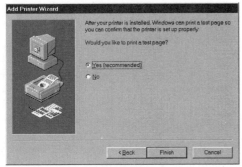

**Figure 9.5** To print a test page, turn the printer on, click Yes, and click Finish.

**10.** If this is your only printer or the one that you will generally use, click Yes to make it the default.

**11.** Click Next. The dialog box shown in **Figure 9.5** appears.

**12.** Click Yes to print a test page or click No to continue without printing a test page.

**13.** Click Finish.

If asked, insert the requested Windows disk or CD-ROM to complete the installation. After the driver has been copied to your hard disk, the print test commences.

## ✔ Tips

- Any installed printer can be used for any print job. It doesn't matter which printer you've set as your default in step 10.

- Some printers come with special programs for configuring the printer, cleaning its jets (if it's an ink jet printer), and so on. See your printer manual for instructions on installing and using such software.

- If you intend to print documents on a printer that is not at this location (it may be in your home, for example), choose File in step 6. Then when you issue the Print command from a Windows program, a print file is created on disk rather than printing. Bring the print file to the printer's location and then either download it to the printer with an appropriate utility or use the DOS COPY command to copy it to the printer port, as follows:

  ```
  C:> COPY a:file1.prn lpt1:
  ```

  Substitute the appropriate drive letter, filename, and communications port when using this procedure.

# Print Settings

Settings for print and paper options—such as size, orientation, source of paper, graphics resolution—can be set globally for all print jobs (to be used as defaults when a given printer is chosen) or individually set for each print job.

◆ *Default print settings* are established by selecting your printer's icon in the Printers control panel and choosing File > Properties or right-clicking the icon and choosing Properties (**Figure 9.6**). Default print settings are automatically used for each document printed with the printer—except when overridden by document-specific settings.

◆ *Document-specific print settings* are set by choosing File > Page Setup (or Print Setup) from within any Windows program (**Figure 9.7**), such as Internet Explorer 5. These settings apply only to the current document and—if the document is saved—are stored as part of the document.

## ✔ Tips

■ Most of the Properties and Page Setup options are self-explanatory. Generally, the best way to handle these options is to check them once, make any necessary changes (to reflect the way you usually print), and then forget about them.

■ To set header and footer text (to print at the top and bottom of each page, respectively), click Headers/Footers in the Page Setup dialog box and enter the option codes listed in **Table 9.1**. Codes are frequently used in combination, as you can see if you examine the Page Setup dialog box. To print a Web page's URL and the current date (long format), for example, you would enter:

&u&b&D

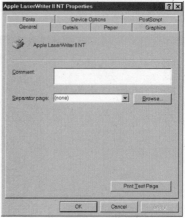

**Figure 9.6** Click the tabs at the top of this Properties dialog box to view or alter the default settings for the selected printer.

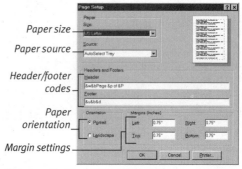

Paper size — 
Paper source — 
Header/footer codes — 
Paper orientation — 
Margin settings — 

**Figure 9.7** The Page Setup dialog box.

**Table 9.1**

## Header and Footer Codes

| Description | Code |
| --- | --- |
| Window title | &w |
| Page URL | &u |
| Date (short format) | &d |
| Date (long format) | &D |
| Time | &t |
| Time (24-hour format) | &T |
| Current page number | &p |
| Total pages | &P |
| Centered text | &b |
| Right-aligned text | &b&b |

Print range  Select a printer  Change printer properties

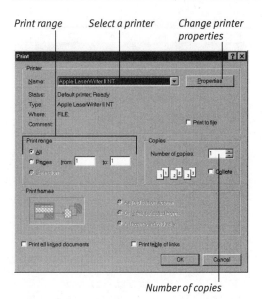

Number of copies

**Figure 9.8** The Print dialog box.

Selected text

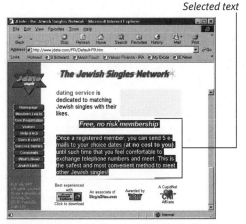

**Figure 9.9** IE5 enables you to print selected text from a Web page.

# Printing a Web Page

Here is how to print the current Web page–and a description of the options you can set.

## To print a single Web page:

1. Display the page you want to print.

2. Choose File > Print, click the Print button, or press ⌈Ctrl⌉+⌈P⌉.
   The Print dialog box appears (**Figure 9.8**).

3. Select a printer to use from the list of currently installed printers.

4. *Optional:* To specify properties for this print job, such as the type and size of paper, graphics quality, and so on, click the Properties button.

5. Set a print range by clicking the All button or by entering numbers in From and To.
   Note that the From/To range refers to the number of pieces of paper to print rather than to the number of Web pages. *All* prints the entire Web page, regardless of the number of sheets of paper needed.

6. Specify the number of copies to be printed.

7. *Optional:* If you're printing several copies, you can print them in collated order by clicking the Collate check box.

8. Click OK to begin printing.

## ✔ Tips

- To print more pages from the same Web site, display each page and issue the Print command for each one.

- To print specific text (**Figure 9.9**), highlight the text, choose File > Print, and click Selection in the Print Range section of the Print dialog box.

## Printing a page's background color or image

By default, Web page printouts do *not* contain the page designer's background graphic or color (if one was used). Thus, your printout may not be an exact match to what you see onscreen. In many cases, however, excluding the background color or graphic will result in a more readable printout.

If you want to include the page's background color or graphic image in the printout, choose Tools > Internet Options, click the Advanced tab in the Internet Options dialog box, scroll down to the Printing section, and check the box marked *Print background colors and images* (**Figure 9.10**).

Note that this option will affect *all* your future Web page printouts. You can use this feature selectively by turning the option off and on as needed.

*Print background colors and images*

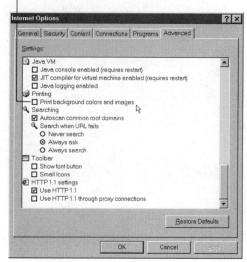

**Figure 9.10** Whether or not background images and colors are printed is determined by an Internet Options setting.

*Frames*

**Figure 9.11** This Web page is divided into three frames; one for the menu, one for the page title, and one for the body text.

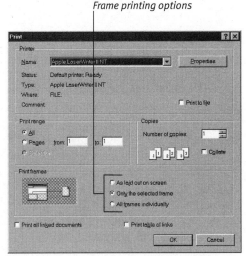

*Frame printing options*

**Figure 9.12** When printing a page that contains frames, the Print frames section of the Print dialog box appears.

# Printing a Page with Frames

When you print a page that is divided into *frames* (**Figure 9.11**), a new section of the Print dialog box appears, enabling you to print the page normally, print the currently selected frame, or create a separate printout from each frame area.

## To print a page with frames:

1. Display the Web page that you want to print.

2. Choose File > Print, click the Print button, or press Ctrl+P.

    The Print dialog box appears (**Figure 9.12**).

3. Set print settings as specified in *To print a Web page* earlier in this chapter.

4. In the Print Frames area of the dialog box, choose the desired frame-printing option.

    Note that "Only the selected frame" can be chosen if you initiated the print job by right-clicking in the frame and choosing Print from the pop-up menu.

    *As laid out on screen* generates a normal printout, as though the page does not contain separate frames. *Only the selected frame* creates a single printout from the chosen frame. *All frames individually* generates a separate print job for each frame on the Web page.

5. Click OK to begin printing.

# Print Options for Pages with Links

Many Web pages contain links to other Web pages, files on FTP sites, and email address links. IE5 provides two Print options that are useful for listing and viewing links: Print all linked documents and Print table of links.

## To print all linked documents:

1. Issue the Print command by choosing File > Print, clicking the Print button, pressing Ctrl+P, or right-clicking the page and choosing Print.

   The Print dialog box appears.

2. Follow the normal steps for printing a single Web page (with or without frames).

3. Check the box labeled Print all linked documents (**Figure 9.13**).

4. Click OK to begin the print job.

IE5 will print the current page and then create a separate print job for each link on the page.

## To print a table of links:

1. Issue the Print command by choosing File > Print, pressing Ctrl+P, or clicking the Print button, clicking the page and choosing Print.

   The Print dialog box appears.

2. Follow the normal steps for printing a single Web page (with or without frames).

3. Check the box labeled Print table of links (refer to **Figure 9.13**).

4. Click OK to begin the print job.

The current Web page will print as directed and conclude with a table listing the linking text and address for each link found on the page.

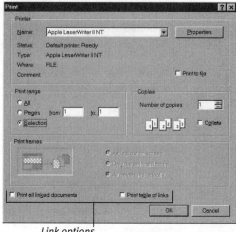

Link options

**Figure 9.13** These print options enable you to print all linked documents or a list of link addresses (in addition to printing the current Web page).

### Printing All Linked Documents

You should be aware that the result of checking "Print all linked documents" is often not the same as individually printing each page in a Web site—although this may well be what you intended to do. Instead, this command prints all linked documents, whether they are pages in the current site or different sites, such as those linked by banner ads.

In addition to the possibility of printing pages in which you may have no interest, this command has the potential to generate *huge* printouts. Use it with caution.

If what you really want is a record of the contents of a single Web site, it is better to visit each desired page and issue a separate Print command.

# WORKING WITH CHANNELS

Major information providers—such as CNET, MTV, and ESPN—offer timely news, feature articles, and downloads over the Internet. These information feeds are a special type of favorite called *Active Channels*. Channel content is automatically updated on a schedule set by the provider, enabling you to view the most current information whether you are on or offline.

# Adding Channels with Active Desktop

If your computer has Active Desktop enabled (see Chapter 1), channels can be added as desktop components (**Figure 10.1**). With or without Active Desktop, you can view channels in your browser by selecting them from the Favorites > Channels folder (**Figure 10.2**) or from the channel bar (**Figure 10.3**).

## To add the channel bar to the desktop (with Active Desktop):

1. Right-click the desktop and choose Active Desktop > Customize my Desktop. The Web section of the Display Properties dialog box appears (**Figure 10.4**).

2. Enter checkmarks for *View my Active Desktop as a Web page* and *Internet Explorer Channel Bar* and click OK.

To use the channel bar if you do not have Active Desktop installed, choose Start > Programs > Internet Explorer > Channel Bar.

**Figure 10.1** Some channels can be added as Active Desktop items, allowing you to view and work with them without opening the browser.

_Channels folder

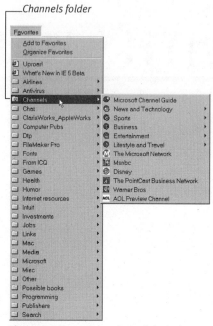

**Figure 10.2** You can view channels in the browser by selecting them from the Favorites > Channels folder.

**Figure 10.3** The channel bar.

_Check to enable the channel bar

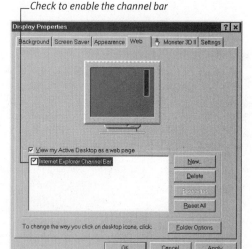

**Figure 10.4** If you have Active Desktop installed and enabled, you can add the channel bar to the desktop.

**Figure 10.5** The Add Active Channel button.

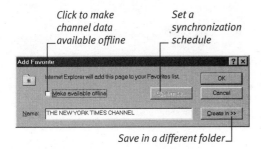

*Click to make channel data available offline*

*Set a synchronization schedule*

*Save in a different folder*

**Figure 10.6** The Add Favorite dialog box.

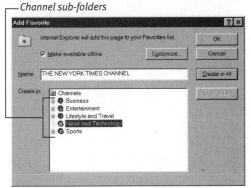

*Channel sub-folders*

**Figure 10.7** When expanded, the Add Favorite dialog box shows the folders and sub-folders in which the current channel can be stored.

# Adding Channels as Favorites

If you don't want a channel added as an Active Desktop item (or if you don't *have* Active Desktop), you can store any channel as a favorite and set a synchronization schedule in a manner similar to storing an ordinary Web page as a favorite (discussed in Chapter 4).

## To add a channel as a favorite:

1. Choose Start > Favorites > Channels, followed by the channel you want to add; in IE5, choose Favorites > Channels, followed by the channel you want to add; or click the channel or category on the channel bar.

   Your browser opens to the channel's Web page.

2. Click the Add Active Channel button (**Figure 10.5**). Note that the button or link may have a slightly different label, such as Add Channel.

   The Add Favorite dialog box appears (**Figure 10.6**).

3. Click the checkbox to *Make available offline*.

   The Customize button appears.

4. To accept the default location in the Favorites folder and the download schedule specified by the channel provider, click OK. Otherwise, go to Step 5.

   The channel is stored as a favorite and added to the bottom of the channel bar, if displayed on the desktop.

5. *Optional*: To specify a different location in which to store the channel, click Create in.

   The dialog box expands (**Figure 10.7**). Select a folder in which to store the channel.

**6.** To set a synchronization schedule for the channel, click Customize.

The Offline Favorite Wizard appears (**Figure 10.8**). Click Next.

**7.** Click No to limit downloads to the main page and site index; or click Yes to download information from linked pages (**Figure 10.9**). Click Next.

**8.** To accept the provider's synchronization schedule for downloads, click Finish (**Figure 10.10**). Otherwise, set another schedule, and then click Finish.

The channel is stored as a favorite and added to the bottom of the channel bar, if displayed.

## ✔ Tips

■ The procedure for adding an Active Channel varies substantially from one site to the next. Some begin with the Add Favorite dialog box, while others start with the Offline Favorite Wizard, for example.

■ You may need to increase the height of the channel bar in order to view the new channels you've added. Click and drag a corner of the bar. Alternately, if there are more channels than there is room to display, click the down arrow at the bottom of the channel bar.

■ To remove a channel from the channel bar, right-click the channel's logo and choose Delete from the pop-up menu that appears.

■ To learn more about setting synchronization schedules for favorites and changing other options for favorites, see Chapters 4 and 6.

**Figure 10.8** Use the Offline Favorite Wizard to set a synchronization schedule to use for channel updates.

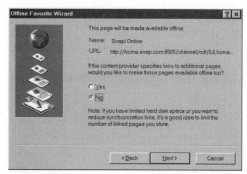

**Figure 10.9** Decide whether you want to limit content downloads to the channel's index page or to additional links as well.

**Figure 10.10** Specify a synchronization schedule, or accept the default schedule suggested by the channel provider.

_Add Active Channel_     _Add to Active Desktop_

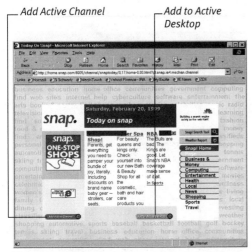

**Figure 10.11** Channel providers usually make it simple to add new channels by including buttons on their Web pages.

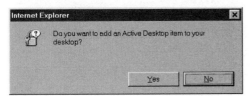

**Figure 10.12** The Internet Explorer dialog box.

_Add using custom settings_

_Add using default settings_

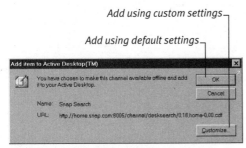

**Figure 10.13** The Add items to Active Desktop dialog box.

# Viewing Channels

If you have Active Desktop installed (see Chapter 1), you can view channels as desktop components or in an IE5 browser window. (This option is available for every channel you add as a favorite, rather than as an all-or-nothing choice.) Without Active Desktop installed and enabled, channels can _only_ be viewed in the browser.

## To add a channel as a desktop item:

1. From the desktop, choose Start > Favorites > Channels, followed by the channel you want to install. Alternately, from any IE5 browser window, choose Favorites > Channels, followed by the channel you want to install.

2. If the channel can be added to your desktop, an Add to Active Desktop button will be shown (or one with a similar label). Click the button (**Figure 10.11**).

   The Internet Explorer dialog box appears (**Figure 10.12**).

3. Click Yes.

   The Add item to Active Desktop dialog box appears (**Figure 10.13**).

4. To accept the default settings (such as the synchronization schedule) for the item, click OK. The item is added to the desktop.

   Otherwise, to examine or change the settings for the item, click Customize. The Offline Favorite Wizard appears (refer to **Figure 10.8**). Click Next.

**5.** Click No to limit downloads to the main page and site index; or click Yes to download information from linked pages (refer to **Figure 10.9**). Click Next.

**6.** To accept the provider's synchronization schedule for downloads, click Finish (refer to **Figure 10.10**). Otherwise, set another schedule and then click Finish.

The channel is added to your desktop. You can move it to a new position by dragging in the gray area at the top of the desktop item.

## To view channels in the browser:

**1.** Add the channel, as explained in "To add a channel as a favorite," earlier in this chapter.

**2.** Choose a channel to display from the channel bar, the Channels folder in the Favorites menu, or the Channels folder in the IE5 Favorites bar.

The selected channel is displayed in an IE5 browser window (**Figure 10.14**).

## ✔ Tips

- You interact with desktop channels in the same manner as you do with any other desktop item. You can click links to view related Web pages, enter information into boxes, and so on.

- You can manually synchronize an Active Desktop channel at any time by clicking the down arrow at the top of the item and choosing Synchronize (**Figure 10.15**).

*Favorites bar*

**Figure 10.14** You can view channels in your browser by selecting them from the Favorites bar or the Favorites menu.

**Figure 10.15** If you want to be sure you are viewing the latest information in a desktop channel, you can force an update by choosing the Synchronize command.

Checked items
are enabled

Delete the
selected item

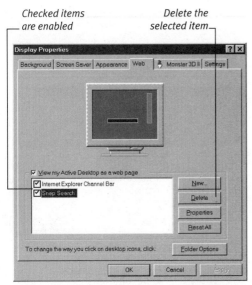

**Figure 10.16** To temporarily disable a desktop item, remove its checkmark.

- To remove an Active Desktop item from the desktop, click its close box.

- You can also remove an Active Desktop item from the desktop without deleting it by right-clicking the desktop, choosing Active Desktop > Customize my Desktop, and clearing the item's checkmark in the Web section of the Display Properties dialog box (**Figure 10.16**).

- If you want to permanently delete an Active Desktop item, right-click the desktop, choose Active Desktop > Customize my Desktop, highlight the item in the Web section of the Display Properties dialog box, and click Delete (refer to **Figure 10.16**).

# Using Channels as Screen Savers

Many channels contain content that can be displayed as a Windows *screen saver*. A screen saver is an image that is displayed on your monitor during periods of system inactivity.

## To use channels as a screen saver:

1. Open the Display Properties control panel by doing one of the following:

   ◆ Choose Start > Settings > Control Panel and double-click Display.

   ◆ Right-click the desktop and choose Properties.

   ◆ Right-click the desktop and choose Active Desktop > Customize my Desktop.

2. Click the Screen Saver tab (**Figure 10.17**) at the top of the Display Properties dialog box.

3. From the Screen Saver list, choose Channel Screen Saver.

4. Click the Settings button. The Screen Saver Properties dialog box appears (**Figure 10.18**).

5. Check the channels you want to include as screen savers. (Each time the screen saver runs, it cycles through the checked channels.)

6. Set a display time for each checked channel. Default is 30 seconds.

7. If you want to hear channel background sounds, add a checkmark for Play background sounds.

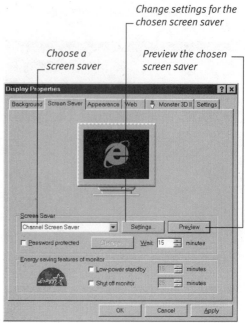

*Change settings for the chosen screen saver*

*Choose a screen saver*

*Preview the chosen screen saver*

**Figure 10.17** Select a screen saver and specify how it will work in the Screen Saver section of the Display Properties dialog box.

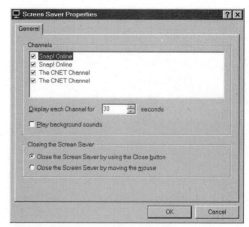

**Figure 10.18** Set options for the screen saver in the Screen Saver Properties dialog box.

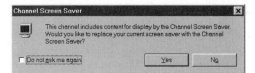

**Figure 10.19** The Channel Screen Saver dialog box.

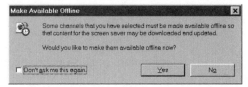

**Figure 10.20** The Make Available Offline dialog box.

**8.** Specify the method you want to use to quit the screen saver. If you want to be able to interact with the channel data (clicking links, for example), choose *Close the Screen Saver by using the Close button.* (A close button automatically appears in the upper-right corner of the screen whenever you move the mouse pointer.)

To dismiss the screen saver whenever you move the mouse, choose the second option.

**9.** Click OK to return to the Screen Savers section of the Display Properties dialog box.

**10.** *Optional:* Click Preview to see an example of the Channel Screen Saver.

**11.** Click OK to dismiss the dialog box and save the new settings.

## ✔ Tips

■ If you have a non-channel screen saver in effect when you add a channel that contains a screen saver component, you'll see the Channel Screen Saver dialog box (**Figure 10.19**). If you wish, you can click Yes to switch to the Channel Screen Saver without having to open the Display Properties dialog box.

■ If you include a channel in the screen saver list that is not currently set for offline viewing, you will be asked to make it available offline (**Figure 10.20**). Click the Yes button.

USING CHANNELS AS SCREEN SAVERS

# INTERNET EXPLORER OPTIONS

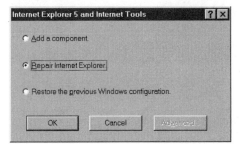

**Figure 11.1** Choose *Repair Internet Explorer* to check IE5 for damage.

You can customize Internet Explorer to work the way you prefer. You set preferences (called *options*) in the Internet Options dialog box. After setting options, IE5 uses them from that moment on. Of course, you can modify the options if your needs change.

Options are divided into the following categories, each represented by a tab at the top of the Internet Options dialog box:

◆ *General*. Set a start page, manage the History and Temporary Internet Files folders, and set default Web page appearance settings.

◆ *Security*. Set a standard method for handling ActiveX controls and Java applets, file downloads, site log-ons, and so on.

◆ *Content*. Enable site ratings (parental controls), protect yourself against sites with invalid certificates, set AutoComplete procedures, and store personal information.

◆ *Connections*. Set Internet connection options.

◆ *Programs*. Specify default email, newsgroup, videoconferencing, calendar, contact list, and HTML editing programs.

◆ *Advanced*. Set miscellaneous options.

To set options for any of these categories, follow this procedure.

## IE5: The Self-Healing Program

If you find that you're having an unusual number of Internet-related crashes (where your computer locks up or exhibits other inexplicable behaviors), it may be that IE5 has become damaged. To repair the program, open the Add/Remove Programs control panel, choose *Microsoft Internet Explorer 5 and Internet Tools*, and click Add/Remove. In the dialog box that appears (**Figure 11.1**), choose *Repair Internet Explorer* and click OK.

## To set IE5 options:

1. Choose Tools > Internet Options. (Or right-click the IE5 icon on your desktop and choose Properties.)

   The Internet Options dialog box appears, open to the General tab (**Figure 11.2**).

2. Choose an options category by clicking its tab at the top of the dialog box.

3. Make the desired changes.

4. To put the changes into effect without closing the dialog box (so you can set other preferences), click Apply. To put the changes into effect and dismiss the dialog box, click OK.

## ✔ Tip

- If you're not sure how a particular option should be set, it may be safer to leave it alone. The default settings for Internet Options are appropriate for most users. You can obtain a brief explanation of many options and settings by clicking the question mark symbol in the upper-right corner of the dialog box and then clicking the option you need help with (**Figure 11.3**).

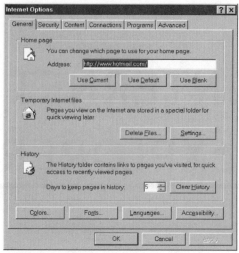

**Figure 11.2** General options.

*Help information* —      *Click to request help* —

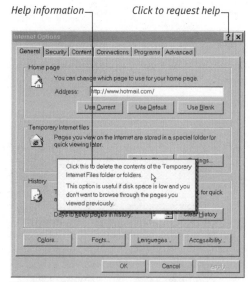

**Figure 11.3** To get help with an item in any of the Internet Options dialog boxes, click the question mark icon and then click the item.

# General Options

In the General section, you can set your start page, manage the History and Temporary Internet Files folders, and specify default Web page appearance settings.

## Setting a home page

A *home page* is the Web page that IE5 automatically opens at the start of each browsing section. After choosing a home page, you can visit it at any time by clicking the Home button, choosing View > Go To > Home Page, or pressing [Alt]+[Home].

You can set or change your home page by doing any of the following (refer to **Figure 11.2**):

◆ Type or paste the page's URL into the Address box.

◆ Visit the prospective home page in IE5, and then click Use Current. The page's URL is automatically recorded in the Address box.

◆ Click Use Default to set Microsoft's Web site as your home page. (If you downloaded IE5 from a different Web site, the default home page may be linked to that site.)

◆ If you want to open to a blank page (rather than visiting a particular Web page), click Use Blank.

## Temporary Internet Files

IE5's *cache* is stored in the Temporary Internet Files folder. The cache contains the Web pages you have recently visited, as well as any graphic and multimedia files you have seen and heard. To empty the cache, click Delete Files.

To manage the cache, change its settings, or view its current contents, click the Settings button.

## To view or open files in the cache:

1. Click the Settings button.

   The Settings dialog box appears (**Figure 11.4**).

2. Click View Files.

   The C:\WINDOWS\Temporary Internet Files folder opens (**Figure 11.5**), showing all Web pages, graphics, and text files you have viewed in recent browsing sessions.

3. If you want to examine one of these items, drag it to the desktop to create a copy of the file.

   Opening these items while they are still in the cache can cause serious problems (**Figure 11.6**). However, it is safe to open the desktop copy of such an item.

4. Click the window's close box when you are done.

## To view installed ActiveX controls and Java applets:

1. Click View Objects.

   The C:\WINDOWS\Downloaded Program Files folder opens (**Figure 11.7**).

2. Click (or double-click) any item to learn more about it.

3. Click the window's close box when you are done.

## To manage the cache:

1. Click the Settings button.

   The Settings dialog box appears (refer to **Figure 11.4**).

2. The setting for *Check for newer versions of stored pages* determines how often IE5 checks to see if the current Web page has changed; that is, whether it is different from the copy in the cache.

   ◆ *Every visit to the page* is the safest— but slowest—choice. If you visit the

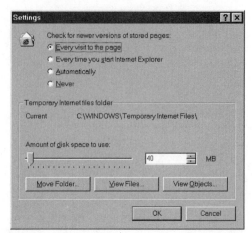

**Figure 11.4** Use the Settings dialog box to manage the cache.

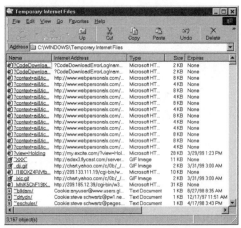

**Figure 11.5** To speed up subsequent visits to pages, IE5 stores copies of pages and other items (such as graphics) in the Temporary Internet Files folder. When IE5 needs them, it draws these elements from your hard disk rather than downloading them again.

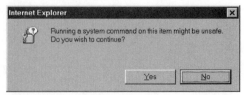

**Figure 11.6** As this warning illustrates, you should not open items that are in the cache. Instead, copy them to the desktop or another folder and open the copy.

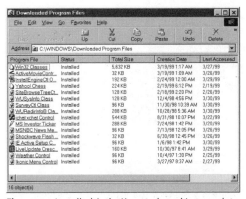

**Figure 11.7** Installed ActiveX controls and Java applets can be found in the Downloaded Program Files folder.

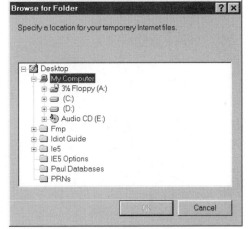

**Figure 11.8** Select a drive and/or folder in which to locate the new cache.

same page five times in a session, it is checked for changes every time.

♦ *Every time you start Internet Explorer* causes IE5 to check for a changed page once per session. This is a compromise. If you visit a page more than once in a session, you run a risk—in most cases, a small one—that the page will have changed.

♦ *Automatically* has a similar effect to *Every time you start Internet Explorer;* that is, it checks for page changes only when you visit a page that you have viewed in previous sessions. (If you visit a page more than once in a session, IE5 will not check it for changes.) If you seldom visit some pages, IE5 learns to check those pages less frequently.

♦ *Never* is the fastest option. If the page you're visiting is in the cache, the cached version is automatically displayed. If the page isn't in the cache, a fresh copy is downloaded from the Web. Your risk is that you will be viewing an outdated page—in the event that the page has changed, but an older copy of it is still in the cache.

**3.** Move the slider to allocate a percentage of your hard drive to be used for the cache. As the cache fills, the oldest items are automatically deleted to make room for new ones. You can also set this option by typing or choosing a number of MB in the text box to the right of the slider.

**4.** To change the drive or folder where the cache is stored, click Move Folder and choose a location from the Browse for Folder dialog box (**Figure 11.8**).

**5.** Click OK to save the new cache settings and return to the Internet Options dialog box.

## History settings

You use the History section to manage the History folder, a repository for Web pages you've recently visited. You can view History pages while online or offline by clicking the History button and then opening the desired page. Refer to Chapter 3 for more information.

To set the number of days that Web pages are stored in the History folder, type a number in the *Days to keep pages in history* box or click the tiny up- and down-arrows (refer to **Figure 11.2**). To delete all items in the History folder, click Clear History.

## ✔ Tips

- Regardless of how often Internet Explorer has been set to check for page changes, you can force it to display the most current version of a page by clicking the Refresh button.

- Generally, the only reason you would want to change the location of IE5's cache is because you have more free space on a different hard disk.

- IE5 automatically deletes expired items in the History folder. You never have to manually clear the History.

- You can go to the most recent pages viewed in the current session by choosing them from the View > Go To menu (**Figure 11.9**).

## Setting default colors and fonts

In more advanced Web pages, designers may specify the background color, links color, fonts, and text colors that will display. Click the Colors and Fonts buttons to select the colors and fonts you want to use when a designer has *not* specified them.

If you like, you can go a step further. Click the Accessibility button to cause your font and color choices to *always* be used—overriding page designers' settings.

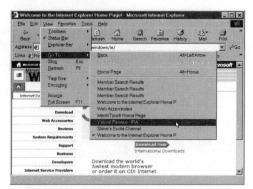

**Figure 11.9** The View > Go To menu lists the most recent pages you've visited during the current browsing session.

**Figure 11.10** Use the Colors dialog box to set default colors for text, page backgrounds, and visited and unvisited links.

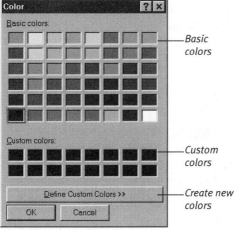

**Figure 11.11** Choose a color by clicking it. To create a new color, click Define Custom Colors.

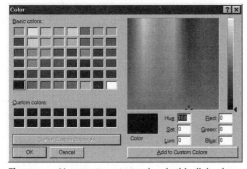

**Figure 11.12** You create custom colors in this dialog box.

## To set default text, background, or link colors:

1. In the General section of the Options dialog box, click the Colors button.

   The Colors dialog box appears (**Figure 11.10**).

2. Click *Use Windows colors* if you want to use the text and background colors you've chosen for Windows. Go to Step 7.

3. If you'd like to choose different colors, remove the check mark from the *Use Windows colors* option.

4. Click the box for the color you want to change (Text or Background).

   The Color dialog box appears (**Figure 11.11**).

5. Click a basic or custom color box to select that color.

   *or*

   Define a custom color by clicking the color box that you want to replace, and then clicking *Define Custom Colors*. The Color dialog box expands (**Figure 11.12**). Create a new color by moving the slider, typing numbers into the boxes, or clicking in the color panel. When you are satisfied with the new color, click *Add to Custom Colors*.

6. Click OK to select the current color, choose another color and click OK, or click Cancel.

7. Set colors for Visited and Unvisited links in the same manner that you chose Text and Background colors.

8. If you like, you can also choose a *hover color* (the color that a link turns when the cursor passes over it). Click *Use hover color*, and click the box to select a color.

**GENERAL OPTIONS**

**125**

## To set default display fonts:

1. In the General section of the Options dialog box, click the Fonts button.

   The Fonts dialog box appears (**Figure 11.13**).

2. Choose a proportional (Web page font) and a fixed-width (Plain text) font from the lists.

   Samples of the selected fonts are shown beneath the font lists.

3. Click OK to accept the new font choices, or Cancel to use the prior font choices.

## Accessibility options

Set accessibility options to override page designers' choices of background color, font style, font size, and text formatting. Settings in the Fonts and Colors dialog boxes will always be used rather than the designers' choices.

## To override specified fonts and colors:

1. Click the Accessibility button.

   The Accessibility dialog box appears (**Figure 11.14**).

2. Enter checkmarks for the design options you want to override.

3. If you have designed or been given a style sheet that you want to use to format all Web pages (specifying fonts, colors, and so on), click *Format documents using my style sheet*. Then type the path to the file or click Browse to select the style sheet file from a dialog box.

4. Click OK.

## Language options

If you're multilingual and you visit Web sites that are available in multiple languages, you can create a prioritized list of languages that determines which one will be used.

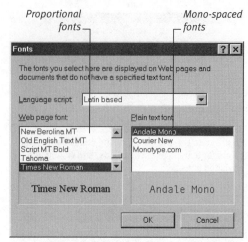

**Figure 11.13** Select default fonts for proportional and mono-spaced text.

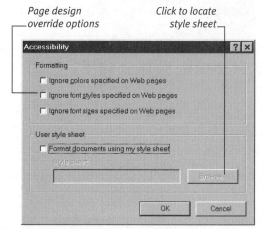

**Figure 11.14** The Accessibility dialog box.

Preferred language list ⎯ Add a language ⎯

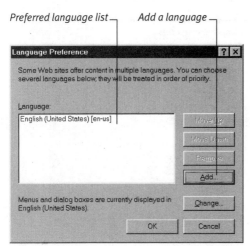

**Figure 11.15** The Language Preference dialog box lists your preferred languages for displaying Web pages. The higher in the list a language appears, the greater your preference for it.

**Figure 11.16** Select a language or variant, and click OK.

## To create a language priority list:

1. Click the Languages button.
   The Language Preference dialog box appears (**Figure 11.15**).

2. Click Add to add a language to the list.
   The Add Language dialog box appears (**Figure 11.16**).

3. Choose a language to add, and click OK.

4. Repeat Steps 2–3 to add other languages.

5. Organize the list in the Language Preference dialog box by selecting a language and clicking Move Up or Move Down.

6. Click OK to dismiss the dialog box.

## ✔ Tips

- The custom colors you can create depend on the color palette setting in the Display control panel. When set for 256 or fewer colors, your choices are limited.

- Enabling a hover color makes it easy to distinguish links from normal text or graphics.

- Before changing fonts or selecting different colors for links and text, make a note of the settings. There is no Use Default button that you can click to restore the original settings.

- As with the other General options, the easiest way to see how new font choices affect the display is to try them out. Select fonts, and then visit several Web sites. Remember that these fonts will only be used when a designer has not specified fonts for a page.

- Web pages generally contain instructions that tell browsers which language and character set should be used to display text. If these instructions are not present, IE5 can often make its own determination if you have View > Encoding > Auto-Select checked.

**GENERAL OPTIONS**

# Security Options

Security settings (**Figure 11.17**) determine the types of page-enhancement controls that Web sites can automatically download to your computer, as well as the prompts you will see before downloading potentially unsafe content. Using the four security zone icons at the top of the dialog box, you can create four security specifications rather than just one global one.

◆ The *Internet* zone settings are applied to all Web sites that are not specifically included in any of the other three zones.

◆ The *Local Intranet* zone covers all pages on your company Intranet (if you have one).

◆ The *Trusted sites* zone is a user-provided list of Web sites that you trust.

◆ The *Restricted sites* zone is a user-provided list of sites that you do *not* trust.

You can set a different security level for each zone by selecting its icon and moving the slider at the bottom of the dialog box. As you move the slider, a text description of the zone settings appears. To change some of the security component settings, click the Custom Level button (**Figure 11.18**).

To specify sites for the *Trusted sites* or *Restricted sites* zone, select its icon and click the Sites button. A new dialog box appears (**Figure 11.19**). Type or paste a URL into the text box and click Add. (Note that you can limit Trusted sites to secure Web sites; i.e., those that begin with `https:` rather than `http:`). Secure sites are generally used for online commerce.

## ✔ Tips

■ You can always tell if you're in a secure Web site. Check the status bar for a lock icon.

■ To restore the original, recommended settings for a zone, select the zone icon and click the Default Level button.

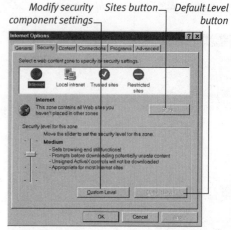

Modify security component settings · Sites button · Default Level button

**Figure 11.17** To set Security options, select a zone icon and adjust the security level slider.

**Figure 11.18** Use the Security Settings dialog box to gain greater control over a zone's settings.

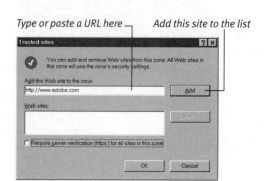

Type or paste a URL here · Add this site to the list

**Figure 11.19** To add a site to the Trusted sites or Restricted sites list, type its URL and click Add.

**SECURITY OPTIONS**

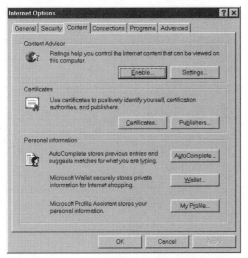

**Figure 11.20** Content options.

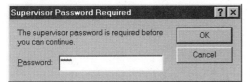

**Figure 11.21** You are prompted to enter the supervisor password each time you try to view or change the rating settings.

*Choose an acceptable level*     *Rating categories*

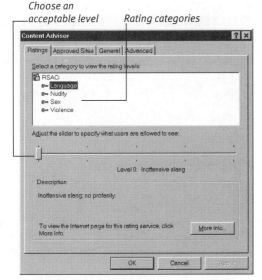

**Figure 11.22** Select a rating category and move the slider to reflect the type of content you will allow.

# Content Options

By setting Content options (**Figure 11.20**), you can control the types of Web pages that you and your children can view; specify certificates that are used to positively identify yourself, Web sites, and software publishers; avoid repetitive typing; and store personal and online shopping-related information.

## Content Advisor

By clicking Enable Ratings, you can specify the types and amounts of sex, nudity, offensive language, and violence that you want to allow. IE5 includes a ratings file from the Recreational Software Advisory Council (RSAC) covering these content areas. If any user attempts to view a site whose ratings exceed the levels you've set, admission is denied.

When you enable ratings, you must create a supervisor password. This password is requested each time you view or change settings (**Figure 11.21**). Next, click Settings to set content restrictions. The Content Advisor dialog box appears (**Figure 11.22**) and is divided into four sections: Ratings, Approved Sites, General, and Advanced.

## Ratings tab

Set ratings by selecting a category and then dragging the slider to the desired position. When you're done, click Apply or OK.

To go to RSAC's Web site and learn more about the rating system, click More Info.

## Approved Sites tab

If you like, you can create a list of approved and restricted Web sites. Type or paste the URL into the text box, and click Always (for trusted sites) or Never (for suspect sites).

## General tab

You can set user options, change the supervisor password, and add other site rating systems in this section of the dialog box.

User options (**Figure 11.23**) include:

◆ *Users can see sites that have no rating.* Check this option to allow access to unrated sites. When unchecked, users can visit only rated sites; access is denied to all others.

◆ *Supervisor can type a password to allow users to view restricted content.* Checking this option allows persons with the supervisor password to view (or grant permission to view) any site.

To change the supervisor password, click Change Password. The Change Supervisor Password dialog box appears (**Figure 11.24**). Enter the old and new passwords in the appropriate boxes, and then click OK.

Depending on the combination of options chosen, if you try to visit an unrated site, one that is rated by a system you don't have installed, or one that exceeds your rating settings, you will be refused entrance or prompted for the supervisor password.

You can also add or remove rating systems. To view or modify your installed rating systems, click Rating Systems. If you have obtained a rating (.rat) file from another rating system, click Add and locate the file on your hard disk. To remove a rating system, select it and click Remove.

## Advanced tab

If you subscribe to or have access to a ratings bureau, type its name in the Ratings bureau text box (**Figure 11.25**). If you have a PICS-Rules (.prf) file, click the Import button to add its rating criteria to the ones already in effect.

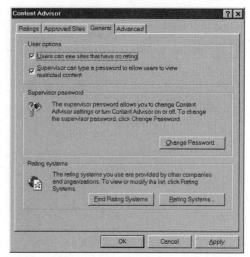

**Figure 11.23** The General subsection of the Content options.

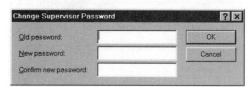

**Figure 11.24** You must provide the old password before you will be allowed to set a new password.

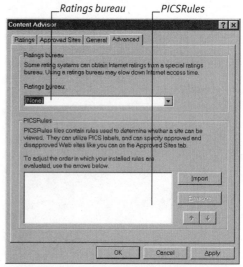

**Figure 11.25** Use the Advanced section of the dialog box to specify a ratings bureau (if you have one) and a PICSRules file containing rating rules.

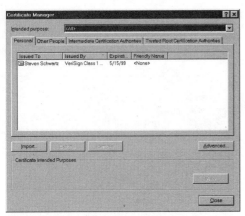

**Figure 11.26** You can see the list of personal certificates that IE5 has acknowledged.

*Click to add the publisher to the trusted list*

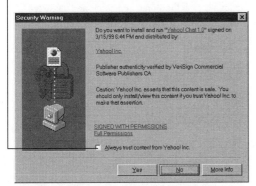

**Figure 11.27** Before a publisher downloads and installs an ActiveX control or Java applet on your computer, this warning appears.

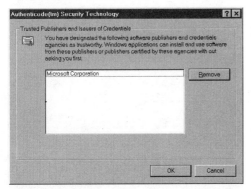

**Figure 11.28** Your personal list of trusted publishers can be viewed in this dialog box.

## ✔ Tips

■ Ratings are not done "on the fly." IE5 doesn't examine the content of pages before displaying them. Either a given page or site is already rated—and is included in one of the installed rating databases—or it isn't.

■ Only a tiny fraction of all sites are rated by RSAC. If you restrict viewing to only rated sites, you will find yourself blocked from viewing many pages—even those of innocuous sites. On the other hand, if you allow access to unrated sites, you relinquish all content control.

One compromise is to check *Supervisor can type a password...* With ratings enabled, your children will have to ask permission to enter unrated sites. During your own sessions, you can disable ratings and enable them again when you quit. Otherwise, you will spend an inordinate amount of time typing the password to enter unrated sites.

■ Rating system (.rat) files are stored in the C:\Windows\System directory of your hard disk. You can learn about other rating systems, rating bureaus, and available rating files at http://www.w3.org/PICS/.

## Certificates

Exploring the Internet is like using a telephone on an open party line. You never know who may be "listening in," so to speak. Certificates provide security for your on-line transactions. Click Certificates to see the certificates that are installed. The Certificate Manager dialog box appears (**Figure 11.26**).

When displayed by a software publisher, a certificate (**Figure 11.27**) helps insure that the file you are about to download actually comes from that vendor and that it hasn't been altered. If you click the checkbox for *Always trust content from...*, the publisher's name is added to the trusted publishers list. To view this list (**Figure 11.28**), click the Publishers button.

## ✔ Tip

■ You can obtain a free trial personal certificate from VeriSign. For details, launch Outlook Express, choose Tools > Options, click the Security tab, and click the Get Digital ID button.

## AutoComplete

IE5's new AutoComplete feature can save you a tremendous amount of time when typing URLs, filling in forms, and entering user names and passwords. Click the Auto-Complete button to view or change your settings (**Figure 11.29**).

◆ *Web addresses.* Check this option to instruct IE5 to remember URLs that you have typed or pasted into the Address bar. The next time you type the URL, IE5 will attempt to complete it for you and present a drop-down list of potential matches.

◆ *Forms.* If you often fill in forms on Web pages (to send your name and address information, for instance), you can use AutoComplete to speed the process. The next time you return to the same form (or another form that uses the same field names, such as City or Email address), AutoComplete will display the text needed to complete the field.

◆ *User names and passwords on forms.* Many Web sites require you to obtain a user name and password and enter that information each time you visit. Check this option to cause IE5 to remember your user names and associated passwords (**Figure 11.30**). If you also check the option to *Prompt me to save passwords*, you can tell IE5 to remember some user names and passwords but not others (**Figure 11.31**).

To clear your AutoComplete history, click the appropriate Clear button (Forms or

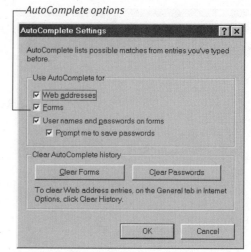
AutoComplete options

**Figure 11.29** Use the AutoComplete Settings dialog box to specify the page features it should affect and to optionally clear the stored form terms and passwords.

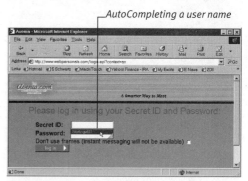
AutoCompleting a user name

**Figure 11.30** To complete a user name or field in a form, double-click the field to open the AutoComplete list or simply start typing to see only terms that match.

**Figure 11.31** If you've set the option for *Prompt me to save passwords*, this dialog box appears the first time you enter a user name and password on a given Web page. Click Yes if you want the password to be stored, or No if you want to type it each time.

Choose a credit card ⎯

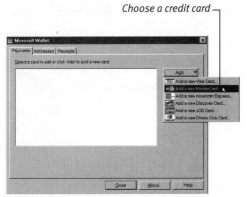

**Figure 11.32** Microsoft Wallet can store your credit card data, personal address information, and online purchasing records.

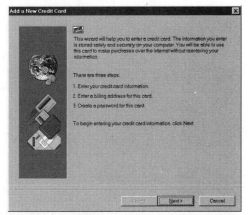

**Figure 11.33** The Add a New Credit Card wizard walks you through the process of entering information about the credit card.

Passwords). To clear the Web history, click the General tab above the Options dialog box and click Clear History.

## ✔ Tips

- If your computer is accessible by others, you may want to be selective with the user names and passwords stored by AutoComplete.

- When an AutoComplete drop-down list appears, you can select an entry by clicking it or by pressing the down- and up-arrow keys. To restrict the entries that are displayed, type the first letter or two.

- If you're not sure whether a field has an associated AutoComplete list, double-click in the field box.

## Microsoft Wallet

If you like, you can use Microsoft Wallet to store your credit card numbers, making it easy to do online shopping. Wallet can also store your personal and business address information (and provide it to sites who request it), and keep track of your online purchases. Your credit card and address information is only released when you authorize it. And your purchase record can only be viewed after supplying the required password.

## To add a credit card:

1. Click the Wallet button.

   The Microsoft Wallet dialog box appears (**Figure 11.32**), open to the Payments tab.

2. To record the information for a credit card, click Add and select the card from the menu that appears.

   The Add a New Credit Card wizard appears (**Figure 11.33**).

3. Enter the information requested (credit card number, billing address, and a password).

## To record your personal and business address information:

1. Click the Wallet button.

   The Microsoft Wallet dialog box appears.

2. Click the Addresses tab (**Figure 11.34**).

3. If the Add a New Address dialog box doesn't appear automatically, click Add.

   The Add a New Address dialog box appears (**Figure 11.35**).

4. If you've created a contact record for yourself in Address Book, click the Address Book button and select the record.

*or*

   Create the record on the provided form. Be sure to indicate whether it is a Home or Business address.

## ✔ Tip

■ Be sure that the option to *Warn before sending addresses over the Internet* is checked. That way, you can choose who does or does not receive your address information.

## Microsoft Profile Assistant

When a Web site requests personal information about you, it can obtain it—with your permission—from the Microsoft Profile Assistant. Click My Profile to enter or view detailed address and related information about yourself. When a Web site requests information on you that is stored in the Profile Assistant, you will receive an onscreen notification. (Like the address data stored in Wallet, Profile Assistant can extract your information from an Address Book contact card.)

*Warn before sending* ⎯⎯⎯⎯⎯ *Stored addresses*

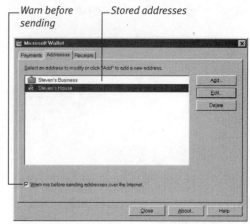

**Figure 11.34** The Addresses section of Microsoft Wallet can store your personal and business address information.

*Select your contact card from Address Book*

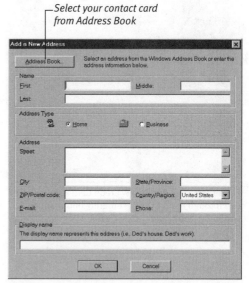

**Figure 11.35** If you've created a contact record for yourself in Address Book, you can also use its data with Microsoft Wallet.

Defined — Create additional — Create a new
connections — connections — connection

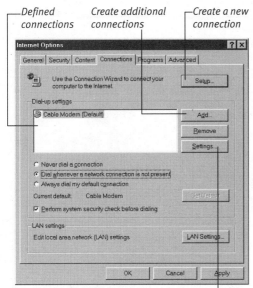

*View or edit connection settings*

**Figure 11.36** Connections options.

**Figure 11.37** The Internet Connection Wizard makes it simple to set up a new Internet connection.

# Connections Options

Settings in Connections options (**Figure 11.36**) specify when and how you connect to the Internet. The options are explained below.

## The Internet Connection Wizard

If you haven't already created a Dial-up Networking connection for this computer, click the Setup button. The Internet Connection Wizard appears (**Figure 11.37**). Pick the option that best describes your situation, and then enter the requested information.

## ✔ Note

■ If you have an Internet account that you've previously used to connect this computer to the Internet, you already have a Dial-up Networking connection. If the connection is listed in the Dial-up settings box, you only need to run the Internet Connection Wizard if you have other connections you also use.

## Dial-up settings

For each defined connection method (you can have multiple connections if you have more than one ISP, for example), you can specify how a connection is made. IE5 will only initiate a connection when you launch it without first connecting to the Internet.

Select a connection, and then choose one of the following options:

◆ *Never dial a connection.* Choose this option if you prefer to manually connect to the Internet or if you use software other than Dial-up Networking.

◆ *Dial whenever a networking connection is not present.* Choose this option to instruct your computer to automatically connect as needed to perform Internet-related activities. For example, launching IE5 and going to a page that isn't in the cache will cause a connection to be made.

◆ *Always dial my default connection.* Choose this option to force your default connection to be dialed.

To examine the settings for any connection, select the connection and click Settings. A Settings dialog box appears (**Figure 11.38**). If you connect via a personal modem, all the necessary information is contained in the Dial-up settings section of the dialog box. It's unlikely you'll have to make changes.

However, be sure to click the Advanced button (**Figure 11.39**). Unless you remove the checkmarks from the two Disconnect options, you'll find that your computer tries to disconnect from the Internet if left unattended or if you quit IE5.

Other options in the Settings dialog box pertain primarily to users connected to a company LAN. See your LAN administrator for proxy server and automatic settings information.

## ✔ Tip

■ One instance in which you might choose *Always dial my default connection* is if you subscribe to an information service but there is no local access number. In this case, you could set a local ISP as your default connection. After connecting to the Internet through the ISP, you can then run your information service's software—and avoid long-distance charges.

## Adding other connections

All connections are stored as icons in the Dial-Up Networking folder. To create a new Dial-up Networking connection, click the Add button. A wizard—similar to the Internet Connection Wizard—will help you enter the necessary information. To edit an existing connection, select it and click Settings.

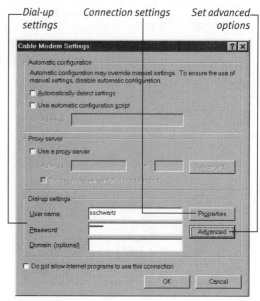

*Dial-up settings*     *Connection settings*     *Set advanced options*

**Figure 11.38** The Settings dialog box for a defined connection.

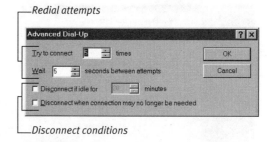

*Redial attempts*

*Disconnect conditions*

**Figure 11.39** Use the Advanced Dial-Up dialog box to set the number of redial attempts for the current connection, and the conditions under which it will automatically disconnect.

*Disconnect from the Internet*

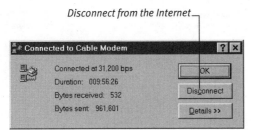

**Figure 11.40** Click Disconnect to end an Internet session.

## ✔ Tips

- You can also create a connection by double-clicking the Make New Connection icon in the Dial-Up Networking folder on your hard disk. To edit an existing connection, right-click its icon and choose Properties.

- If you pay for Internet use by the minute or hour, you'll probably want to pick a low number for the Advanced Dial-up setting of *Disconnect if idle*. If you ever forget you're online IE5 will automatically disconnect.

- If you want to remain constantly connected (so you can instantly receive new email, for example), remove the check mark from the *Disconnect if idle* option. You will have to manually end each session by clicking the Disconnect button in the Connected To dialog box (**Figure 11.40**).

- You can also avoid disconnects caused by time outs by leaving Outlook Express running with instructions to check for new mail every 10 minutes. This ensures that there will be periodic line activity. Then set *Disconnect if idle* for a longer period, such as 15 minutes.

## Perform system security check before dialing

When this option is checked (refer to **Figure 11.36**), IE5 will perform a security check before allowing a connection to be made. If your computer is shared by others or is in an open area, this will help prevent unauthorized use of your Internet account.

## LAN settings

If you connect to the Internet through a local area network, click the LAN Settings button (refer to **Figure 11.36**). Ask your LAN administrator for the proxy server and automatic settings information.

**CONNECTIONS OPTIONS**

# Programs Options

The Programs section (**Figure 11.41**) is used to set the default Internet programs for your computer. For example, when you issue an email command in IE5 (such as Tools > Mail and News > New Message) or in any other program, your default email program automatically opens to create the message.

The program choices for each of the six categories are restricted to programs that are installed on your computer. In addition, listed programs must be registered with IE5 and known to be the correct type. (For example, although there are many HTML editors, it is likely that IE5 only lists *Notepad* and *FrontPage* as choices. This will change as existing programs are updated and new ones are released.) Choose a default program for each category.

If you ever want to return to the original settings for home and search pages, click the Reset Web Settings button.

Finally, you can have only one default browser—although you may have several browsers installed. The default browser is the one that runs when you double-click a Web page shortcut. If you check *Internet Explorer should check to see whether it is the default browser*, it will remain your default browser even if another is later installed. When you next run IE5, it will automatically reset itself as the default browser.

*Restore the default home and search pages*   *Default Internet programs*

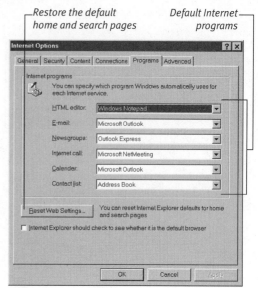

**Figure 11.41** Programs options.

Revert to original settings

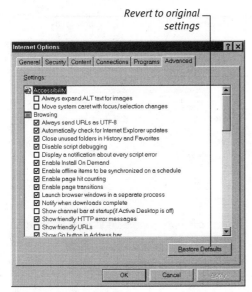

**Figure 11.42** Advanced options.

# Advanced Options

Although the default settings in the Advanced section of the Options dialog box (**Figure 11.42**) will meet the needs of most users, you may want to examine and/or change some of them. Several of the most important options are described in the following paragraphs.

## Browsing settings

*Enable Install On Demand.* When enabled, this option permits IE5 to automatically download and install new components that are needed to display the current Web page.

*Enable page hit counting.* If you are concerned about privacy, you may want to disable this option. It permits Web sites to track your browsing sessions—even when you are offline—by creating a log file on your computer and transmitting it to the site when requested.

*Launch browser windows in a separate process.* If IE5 is already running, and you perform an action such as clicking a URL shortcut on the desktop, IE5 displays the URL in a new window—rather than replacing the contents of the window that is already open.

*Show friendly URLs.* If you want complete URLs to be displayed in the status bar, this option should be unchecked.

*Show Go button in Address bar.* New IE5 users sometimes don't realize that they must press Enter to complete a URL that they've typed or pasted into the Address bar. To alleviate this confusion, Microsoft added a Go button at the end of the Address bar that—when clicked—also completes a URL. If you feel that the Go button is superfluous, you can eliminate it by clearing this checkbox.

ADVANCED OPTIONS

*Show Internet Explorer on the desktop.* Clear this checkbox if you do not want an IE5 shortcut on your desktop.

*Use inline AutoComplete for Web addresses.* When checked and you begin to type a URL in the Address bar, IE5 checks to see if it is an address it already knows. If so, it attempts to complete the address for you. If the URL entered is incorrect, you can continue typing or select the correct URL from the drop-down AutoComplete list (**Figure 11.43**).

## Multimedia settings

*Always show Internet Explorer Radio bar.* If you frequently use the new radio bar (**Figure 11.44**), check this option. Doing so will save you the trouble of having to enable the radio bar each time by choosing View > Toolbars > Radio.

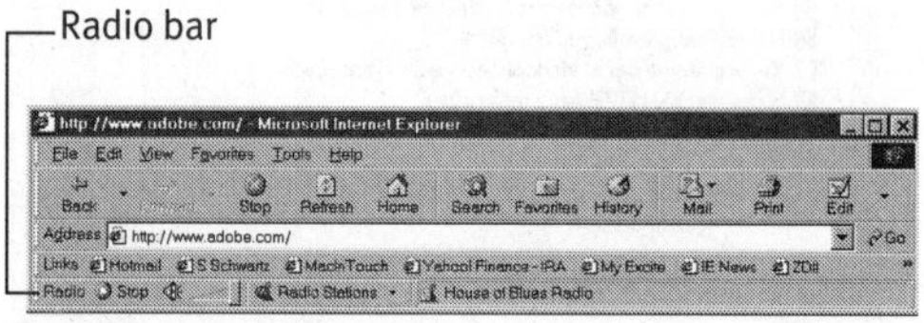

*Play animations, Play sounds, Play videos,* and *Show pictures.* If you have a slow connection or a slow modem, you can speed up the display of pages by turning off some of these multimedia options. Because graphics are plentiful on the Web, removing the check mark from *Show pictures* will have the most pronounced effect on your Internet sessions.

## Printing settings

*Print background colors and images.* By default, page backgrounds are not printed. While you will probably want to leave this option unchecked, you can temporarily turn it on in those instances when you want to include a page background in a printout.

## Search from the Address bar settings

*When searching...* As in Internet Explorer 3 and 4, you can perform searches by typing a search string in the Address bar (see Chapter 5). Choose an option to specify what you want to happen after executing such a search.

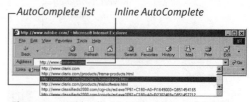

AutoComplete list          Inline AutoComplete

**Figure 11.43** With Inline AutoComplete enabled, IE5 attempts to complete URLs as you type them. If multiple matches are available, a drop-down list is also presented.

Radio bar

**Figure 11.44** If you have a reasonably speedy Internet connection, you can use the radio bar to listen to music as you browse.

## Security settings

*Check for publisher's certificate revocation, Check for server certificate revocation,* and *Warn about invalid site certificates.* The presence of a valid certificate makes the site—and material that you download from it—more trustworthy. You may want to enable all three of these options.

*Do not save encrypted pages to disk* and *Empty Temporary Internet Files folder when browser is closed.* If others share your computer, you can enable these options to reduce the likelihood that someone will be able to read private material you have downloaded or track your browsing activity. Note, however, that emptying the Temporary Internet Files folder after each session will slow down subsequent visits to the same Web sites. Pages will have to be downloaded fresh each session, even if nothing has changed since your last visit.

*Warn if forms submittal is being redirected.* Leave this option checked. When submitting data via a form, you will receive a warning if the data will be transmitted to a different Web site.

## ✔ Tips

- To learn more about any of the Advanced options, click the question mark icon in the upper-right corner of the dialog box and then click the option you want to understand.

- If you're unsure about the changes you've made, you can click Restore Defaults to reset the Advanced options to their original settings.

- If Show Pictures or Play Videos is not checked, you can still view a graphic or video by right-clicking its placeholder icon and choosing Show Picture.

---

## IE5 Easter Eggs!

Programmers are notorious for hiding amusing bits of code (called *Easter eggs*) in programs. And Internet Explorer 5 is no exception. Try the following:

### Programmer fireworks display

1. Open Notepad.

2. Type:
   ```
   <!-- introducing the Trident
   team -->
   ```

3. Save the file as `test.htm`.

4. Open test.htm in IE5.

### New search options

1. Run IE5.

2. Choose Tools > Internet Options.

3. In the General section, click the Languages button.

4. Click Add, type: `ie-ee`, and click OK.

5. Move *User Defined [ie-ee]* to the top of the list.

6. Click OK twice to close the dialog box.

7. Click the Search button to reveal a *new* Search Assistant.

# PART 2

# OUTLOOK EXPRESS: EMAIL AND NEWSGROUPS

# INTRODUCING
# OUTLOOK EXPRESS

# 12

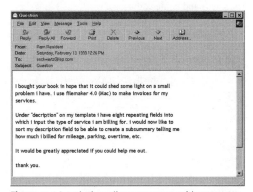

Figure 12.1 A typical email message resembles a memo.

*News servers*

*Subscribed to newsgroups*

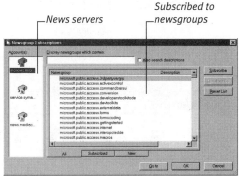

Figure 12.2 You can subscribe to as many newsgroups as you like.

Outlook Express provides email- and news-group-handling features in a single program. You can easily switch between reading, reply-ing to, and composing new email messages and reading, replying to, and composing new newsgroup messages—without leaving Out-look Express. And because Outlook Express is integrated into Internet Explorer, you can send messages and Web page addresses to people without leaving IE5.

## About email

An *email message* is an electronic note sent from one person to another (**Figure 12.1**). Email can be transmitted within a company (over a LAN) and between BBS or information service subscribers (such as America Online). If you have Internet access—as is the case with virtually everyone reading this book—you can send email to anyone on the Internet. It doesn't matter where in the world they are or whether they have an *ISP* (Internet Service Provider) or use an information service.

## About newsgroups

*Newsgroups* are collections of messages from people who share an interest in a topic, such as cars, Amiga computers, or flower arrang-ing. Most news servers carry messages (called *articles*) from thousands of newsgroups (**Figure 12.2**). Newsgroup topics can be very broad (e.g., rec.crafts), narrowly focused (e.g., alt.games.duke3d), or anything in between. You're free to select, read, and post to all newsgroups that interest you.

## Outlook Express features

In addition to making it easy to send and receive email and keep up with your favorite newsgroups, Outlook Express has lots of special features. You can:

◆ Customize the interface and toolbar.

◆ Use the address book (**Figure 12.3**) to record detailed background information about each contact person.

◆ Address outgoing email by typing part of the recipient's name or by choosing it from a list.

◆ Send and receive formatted messages that contain fonts, styles, and backgrounds (**Figure 12.4**). You can also send and receive entire Web pages.

◆ Create new folders to store different classes of mail, such as Budget Project, Business Correspondence, and Sales Leads.

◆ View graphic files that are attached to email and newsgroup messages.

◆ Automate the way that incoming mail is handled.

◆ Compose and send email from within Internet Explorer (**Figure 12.5**).

◆ Click the address to launch IE5 and visit the page if an email message contains an address for a Web page.

◆ Manage multiple email accounts and multiple users.

In this chapter, I briefly explain the functions of the mail window components and help you set up your email and newsgroup accounts.

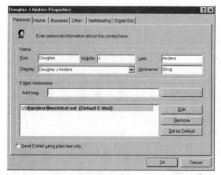

**Figure 12.3** You can record detailed information about any contact in your address book, such as multiple email addresses, phone numbers, and business and home addresses.

*Background image* — *Font menu*

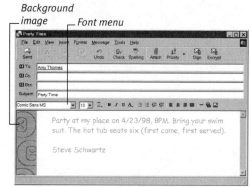

**Figure 12.4** Outlook Express lets you send and receive formatted messages as well as plain text ones.

*Mail menu*

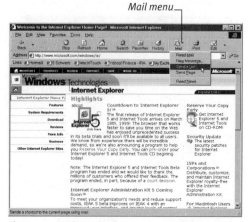

**Figure 12.5** IE5 has a Mail menu you can use to launch your email program, create a new message, send a URL or a complete Web page, or read your newsgroups.

Outlook bar        Folder bar

Folder list    Toolbar      Message list

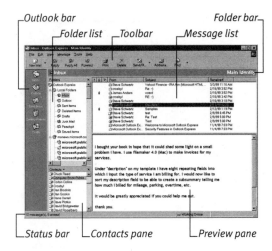

Status bar    Contacts pane     Preview pane

**Figure 12.6** The Outlook Express window.

Links

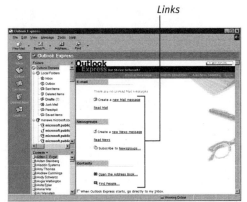

**Figure 12.7** You can perform many common actions (such as creating messages and opening the address book) by clicking text links in the Outlook Express pane. This pane is visible whenever you launch the program or select Outlook Express in the folder list.

# Parts of the Outlook Express Window

The Outlook Express window is divided into eight parts (**Figure 12.6**).

◆ *Toolbar*. Contains buttons for common email and newsgroup functions.

◆ *Folder bar*. Shows the name of the currently active (selected) folder—and the user name, if there are multiple users.

◆ *Outlook bar*. Provides shortcuts to frequently used folders.

◆ *Folder list*. Shows all email folders, news servers, and newsgroup folders.

◆ *Message list*. Displays basic information (called a *header*) for each message.

◆ *Preview pane*. Shows the text of the message that is selected in the message list.

◆ *Contacts pane*. Shows the name of every person in your address book.

◆ *Status bar*. Displays messages concerning the current activity and your connection status.

When you launch Outlook Express, the message list and preview pane are not visible. Instead, the Outlook Express pane is displayed, enabling you to perform common activities by merely clicking a text link (**Figure 12.7**). As soon as you select an email folder, newsgroup folder, or news server in the folder list, the message list and preview pane appear (refer to **Figure 12.6**).

## Toolbar

Many email and newsgroup functions can be performed by clicking toolbar buttons. The toolbar buttons automatically change to reflect the type of folder currently selected in the folder list; that is, email or newsgroup. You can customize the toolbar by adding and removing buttons, as desired.

## Folder bar

Beneath the toolbar is the folder bar. The folder bar has no function other than to remind you of the currently selected folder.

## Outlook bar

The Outlook bar contains buttons that you can click to quickly open frequently used folders. As you customize Outlook Express by creating new folders to better organize your messages, you may wish to add some of these folders to the Outlook bar.

The default folders in the Outlook bar are:

◆ *Inbox*. Contains incoming messages.

◆ *Outbox*. Contains outgoing messages that are waiting to be sent (that is, new out-going messages, forwarded messages, and replies). After the messages have been sent, they are moved to the Sent Items folder.

◆ *Sent Items*. Contains copies of messages that you previously sent.

◆ *Deleted Items*. Contains messages that you have marked for deletion.

◆ *Drafts*. Contains incomplete messages that you have created but elected not to send yet.

## Folder list

Messages are organized in folders by type. To view a given class of email messages, select a message folder from the folder list. Select a newsgroup name to view messages from that newsgroup. Select a news server to view the list of newsgroups to which you have subscribed.

## Message list

The message list contains message headers that correspond to the currently selected email folder or newsgroup. To read, reply to, forward, or delete a message, you always begin by select-ing its header. The message text appears in the preview pane—below the message list.

**Figure 12.8** Graphic attachments to email messages can often be viewed from within Outlook Express.

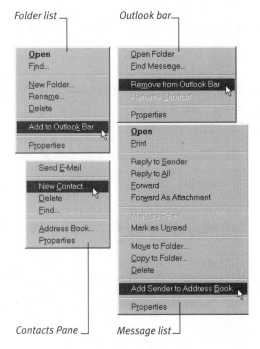

**Figure 12.9** You can perform many commands by right-clicking folders, contact persons, and messages headers.

You can select messages with the mouse or use any of the following keys to move through the message list: (Home), (End), (Pg Up), (Pg Dn), (↑), or (↓).

You can open any email or newsgroup message in its own window (refer to **Figure 12.1**). On the other hand, messages that you *create* (including new messages, replies, and forwarded messages) are *automatically* displayed in a separate window.

## Preview pane

The preview pane displays the text of the selected message. You can read any message in the preview pane, regardless of the folder in which it is stored.

## Contacts pane

The Contacts pane shows the names of all persons for whom you have created records in your address book. You can double-click a person's name to address a new message to him or her. If you want to work with the address book, right-click anyone's name and choose Address Book from the menu that appears. The address book is fully explained in Chapter 13.

## Status bar

The status bar displays messages to indicate when you are online and offline.

## ✔ Tips

- If a message contains an attached JPEG or GIF graphic image, you can view it in the preview pane (**Figure 12.8**).

- Many powerful—and otherwise hidden— features can be found by right-clicking items within the panes (**Figure 12.9**).

- To learn how to customize the Outlook Express toolbar and display, as well as create additional folders to help you organize your messages, see Chapter 22.

**PARTS OF THE OUTLOOK EXPRESS WINDOW**

# Configuring for Multiple Users

If you share your computer with others (family members or co-workers, for example), you can configure Outlook Express so that each person's email and newsgroups are kept separate. To do this, you create new *identities*.

## To create a new identity:

1. Choose File > Identities > Add New Identity.
   The New Identity dialog box appears (**Figure 12.10**).

2. Enter a name for the identity (such as the person's name), and click OK.
   The Identity Added dialog box appears, asking if you wish to switch to the new identity.

3. Click Yes to switch to the new identity and complete the setup process. (If you click No, the setup will be postponed until the first time someone chooses the new identity.)
   The Switch Identity dialog box appears (**Figure 12.11**).

4. To use the same Internet connection for the new identity, click Yes. If the person uses his or her own connection (a different ISP, for example), click No.

5. If Outlook Express has not been designated as your default email program, the dialog box shown in **Figure 12.12** appears. Select the appropriate option.
   The Internet Connection Wizard appears (**Figure 12.13**).

6. If other email software is detected on this computer, you can use its settings (*Use an existing Internet mail account*). Confirm or change the existing settings. Click Next to continue. Go to Step 14.

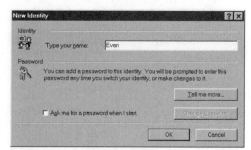

**Figure 12.10** Enter a name for the new identity.

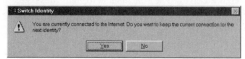

**Figure 12.11** If this identity uses the same dial-up settings as the current identity, click Yes. Otherwise, click No.

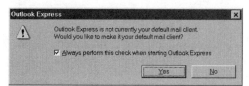

**Figure 12.12** If Outlook Express will be your main email program, click Yes.

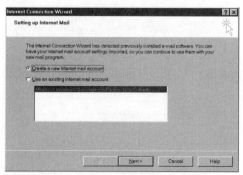

**Figure 12.13** The Internet Connection Wizard gathers the information necessary for the new identity to connect to your ISP and send/receive mail.

Incoming and outgoing mail server names

Incoming mail server type

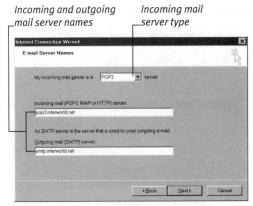

**Figure 12.14** Your ISP will provide you with the information needed to complete this dialog box.

User name

password

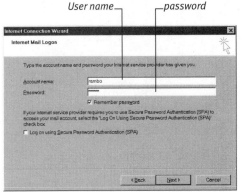

**Figure 12.15** In this dialog box, enter all the information required by your ISP to log onto your account.

Otherwise, choose *Create a new Internet mail account*. Click Next to continue.

7. Enter the name you want others to see when they receive messages from you. Usually, this will be your full name. (It need *not* be your user name.) Click Next to continue.

8. Enter your email address in the form *username@domain.name*. Click Next to continue.

9. Select the type of mail server your ISP has (POP3 or IMAP) and enter the names of the incoming and outgoing mail servers (**Figure 12.14**). Your ISP will provide you with this information (it is often `mail.domain.name`, `pop.domain.name` or `smtp.domain.name`). Click Next to continue.

10. Enter your logon information (**Figure 12.15**), consisting of your user name and password.

11. If you want to be able to automatically log on, click the option to *Remember password*. If you'd rather be prompted for your password at each logon, leave this option unchecked.

12. If your ISP requires Secure Password Identification, click the bottom checkbox.

13. Click Next to continue.

14. If an existing email program was found on your computer, you can optionally import its messages and address book. Choose the desired options and click Next. The import procedure commences.

15. Click Finish.

## Managing identities

Using the File > Identities > Manage Identities command, you can specify a default identity, set a startup identity, rename identities, and delete identities.

### To specify a default identity:

**1.** Choose File > Identities > Manage Identities. The Manage Identities dialog box appears (**Figure 12.16**).

**2.** Highlight the identity you wish to make the default and click Make Default.

**3.** Click Close to accept the new settings.

### To set a startup identity:

**1.** Choose File > Identities > Manage Identities. The Manage Identities dialog box appears.

**2.** If you always want Outlook Express to start with a particular identity, choose it from the *Startup using* list. If you want Outlook Express to prompt for an identity at each startup, choose *Ask Me*.

**3.** Click Close to accept the new settings.

### To rename an identity:

**1.** Choose File > Identities > Manage Identities. The Manage Identities dialog box appears.

**2.** Highlight the identity you wish to rename and click Properties. The Identity Properties dialog box appears.

**3.** Enter a new name for this identity and click OK.

**4.** Click Close to accept the new settings.

### To delete an identity:

**1.** Choose File > Identities > Manage Identities. The Manage Identities dialog box appears.

*Identities list*

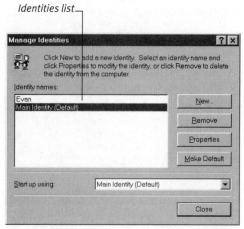

**Figure 12.16** You make changes to identities in the Manage Identities dialog box.

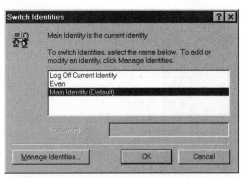

**Figure 12.17** The Switch Identities dialog box.

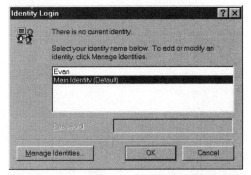

**Figure 12.18** If you chose "Ask Me," you will be asked to select a logon identity when you launch Outlook Express.

**2.** Highlight the identity you wish to delete and click Remove.

Note that you cannot delete the currently active identity. To do so, switch to another identity before performing this procedure.

**3.** Confirm the deletion and then click Close.

## Switching identities

While running Outlook Express, you can switch identities (to allow someone else to use the system), as well as log off as the current user. Here's what you should know:

◆ If you want to switch users, choose File > Switch Identity (**Figure 12.17**), select an identity, and click OK. The program closes and reopens using the new identity. If the new user has specified a different Internet connection, it is used rather than the current one.

◆ If you have set up multiple identities, the proper way to quit Outlook Express is by choosing File > Identities > Logoff *username*. The next time Outlook Express runs, the *Start up using* choice is invoked. If you chose *Ask Me*, you'll be asked to select an identity to use (**Figure 12.18**). If a specific identity was set, it is used.

◆ If a user quits Outlook Express without logging off, he or she automatically continues as the current user when the program next runs.

## ✔ Tips

■ Although most incoming mail servers use the POP3 protocol, your ISP may support IMAP. Check with your ISP if you aren't sure.

■ Although Outlook Express supports multiple identities, it doesn't stop one user from reading another's mail. To provide that level of security, you must set Windows for multiple users (see "multiple users of one computer" in Windows Help).

# Setting Up Mail and Newsgroup Accounts

If you have multiple email accounts (with one or more ISPs), you can use Outlook Express to handle them all. Similarly, although your primary news server will usually be one that is provided by your ISP, you can add other news servers as well. Microsoft and Symantec Corporation, for example, both maintain public news servers that anyone can use.

When you install Outlook Express or create new identities, a set-up wizard steps you through the process of entering the information needed to connect to a default mail and news server. To make changes to these account settings, choose Tools > Accounts, click the Mail or News tab, select the account, and click Properties.

To create an additional email account or add another news server, choose Tools > Accounts, click the Add button, and choose Mail or News. The Internet Connection Wizard will walk you through the setup process.

If you want to create a new Hotmail account (a free email account available from http://www.hotmail.com), the process is a little different.

## To create a new Hotmail account:

1. Choose Tools > New Account Signup > Hotmail.

   The Setup Hotmail Account wizard appears (**Figure 12.19**). Click Next to continue.

2. After agreeing to the Terms of Service, you will be asked to choose a login name and password (**Figure 12.20**).

3. Enter the additional information requested by the wizard.

   After completing the setup, the new account is added to the Folders list.

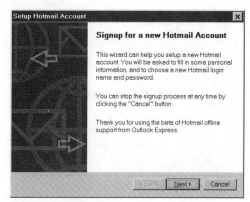

**Figure 12.19** The Setup Hotmail Account wizard.

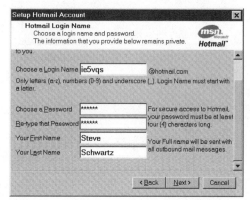

**Figure 12.20** Choose a login name and password for your new Hotmail account. Your email address will be *login name*@hotmail.com.

## You Can't Use Outlook Express Everywhere

Some Internet service providers (America Online, for example) require that all mail- and newsgroup-handling be done with *their* software. You may not be able to use Outlook Express to send and receive email from these accounts.

# USING THE
# ADDRESS BOOK

The Windows Address Book (used by Outlook Express) is the repository for email addresses of business associates, family, and acquaintances. After you have entered addresses in the Address Book, any message can be addressed by simply pointing and clicking.

# Address Book Features

You may notice that the Windows Address Book is similar in design and function to many stand-alone address book programs. In addition to storing email addresses, it can hold other information, such as company name, street address, phone numbers, Web site addresses, NetMeeting videoconferencing information, and notes (**Figure 13.1**). Other features of the Address Book include the following:

**Figure 13.1** The Address Book has many features found in stand-alone address book applications.

◆ You can record multiple email addresses for each contact, setting one as the default.

◆ You can create groups to organize contacts according to some common element.

◆ The address list can be displayed in a variety of formats and sort orders.

◆ You can print it in several formats.

◆ Other Windows programs can access it.

◆ You can create a business card that you can email to others.

◆ You can import address data from Microsoft Exchange, Netscape Communicator, and other address book programs.

Click this link

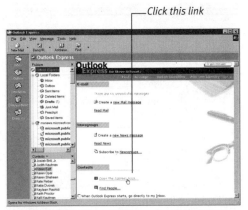

**Figure 13.2** The Outlook Express main window contains a link that you can click to open the Windows Address Book.

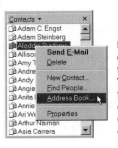

**Figure 13.3** Right-click any entry in the Contacts pane to open the Address Book. You can also address email to any contact by double-clicking the person's name or by right-clicking and choosing Send E-Mail.

Buttons

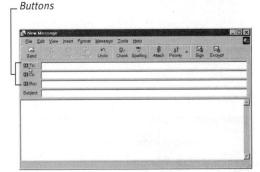

**Figure 13.4** The To, Cc, and Bcc labels in an outgoing message window are buttons. Click them to select recipients from your Address Book.

# Opening the Address Book

To work with your contact data, open the Address Book by doing one of the following:

♦ Click the Address Book button in the Outlook Express toolbar.

♦ Choose Tools > Address Book, or press Ctrl+Shift+B.

♦ Click the `Open the Address Book` link in the Outlook Express main window (**Figure 13.2**).

♦ Right-click a name in the Contacts pane of the Outlook Express window (**Figure 13.3**) and choose Address Book.

♦ Click the Address Book icon in the To, Cc, or Bcc line of a message window (**Figure 13.4**).

♦ Click Start > Programs > Accessories > Address Book.

## ✔ Tips

■ Other programs may also use the Windows Address Book. For example, Outlook 98 (another Microsoft email/contact manager) can also store and extract data from it.

■ Windows Address Book is resizable. To change its size, simply click and drag in the lower-right corner of the window.

■ To find a contact in the Address Book, you can scroll through the list, type part of the person's name in the *Type name or select from list* box, click the Find People button in the Address Book or the Find button in Outlook Express, choose Edit > Find People, or press Ctrl+E.

OPENING THE ADDRESS BOOK

# Creating New Records

When the Address Book is open, you can create new contacts, as well as edit or delete existing records. You can manually enter contact data or extract it from a received message.

## To manually create a new record:

1. Choose File > New Contact, press Ctrl+N, or click the New button or the down arrow at the top of the Contacts pane and choose New Contact.

   A blank Properties dialog box appears (**Figure 13.5**).

2. Fill in the fields. To move from field to field, press Tab.

3. To enter a person's email address, type or paste it into the E-Mail Address field and then click Add. The first email address that you enter is set as the person's default address.

   If the person has other email addresses, enter each one and click Add. To specify a new default email address, select it in the bottom window and click Set as Default.

4. *Optional*: Enter information in other sections of the dialog box (**Figure 13.6**).

5. Click OK to save the record.

## To create a new contact record from a received message:

1. Do one of the following:
   ◆ Right-click the message in the message list and choose Add Sender to Address Book.
   ◆ Select the message in the message list, and choose Tools > Add Sender to Address Book.
   ◆ Double-click the message line to open it in its own window, and choose Tools > Add to Address Book > Sender (**Figure 13.7**). This method offers greater control over the persons added.

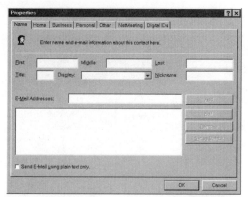

**Figure 13.5** Each address record has seven sections, indicated by the tabs at the top of the Properties dialog box.

*Click to see a street map in IE5* — *Click to go to the Web page* —

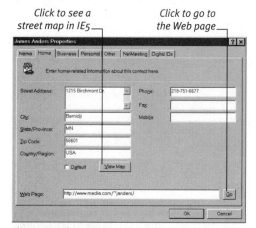

**Figure 13.6** If a complete street address and/or Web page is entered, you can summon a street map or visit the person's home page.

**Figure 13.7** Perhaps the easiest way to create a new contact record is by adding a received message's sender to the Address Book.

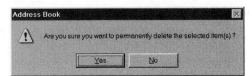

**Figure 13.8** Click Yes to confirm a record deletion.

You can also elect to add the recipient or all persons listed in the To line.

The Properties dialog box *may* appear. If so, the contact's name and email address are already filled in.

2. Complete other fields, as desired (opening the Address Book, if needed), and click OK.

Whether you want to correct a mistake or update a person's information, you can modify address records whenever you want.

## To edit a contact record:

1. Open the Address Book by using any of the methods previously mentioned.

2. Highlight the record in the address list.

3. Open the record using any of these methods:
   ◆ Double-click the record line.
   ◆ Click the Properties button.
   ◆ Choose File > Properties.
   ◆ Right-click the record line and choose Properties.
   ◆ Press [Enter] or [Alt]+[Enter].

4. Make the necessary changes. Click the tabs to view other sections of the record.

5. Click OK to save the changes.

## ✔ Tips

■ At a minimum, you must enter a contact name and an email address for each record.

■ The Address Book list only displays the name, email address, business phone, and home phone fields. Unless you intend to use it as your main address program, you may want to restrict entries to these fields.

■ To delete a contact record, select it in the address list and click Delete, choose File > Delete, or press [Del]. Confirm the deletion by clicking Yes (**Figure 13.8**).

# Creating Groups

If you sometimes send the same message to several contacts, you may find it helpful to define them as a *group*. Then the next time you need to send them all a message, you can simply address it to the group.

## To create a group:

1. Open the Address Book by using any of the methods previously mentioned.

2. Do one of the following:

   ◆ Choose File > New Group (or press [Ctrl]+[G]).

   ◆ Click the New button, and choose New Group.

   ◆ Right-click anywhere in the address list, and choose New > New Group.

   The Properties dialog box appears (**Figure 13.9**).

3. Enter a name for the group in the Group Name box.

4. You can use any of the following methods to add people to the group:

   ◆ Type the person's name and email address in the boxes at the bottom of the window, and then click Add.

   ◆ To simultaneously create a new contact card for a person and add him or her to the group, click the New Contact button.

   ◆ To add existing contacts to the group, click the Select Members button. The Select Group Members dialog box appears (**Figure 13.10**). Select a contact from the address list. Click Select or double-click the contact's record line to add the person to the group. Repeat this step to add other members. Click OK when you are done.

5. Click OK to save the new group.

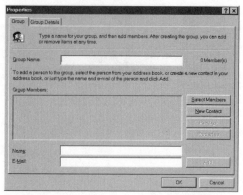

**Figure 13.9** Groups are defined in this version of the Properties dialog box.

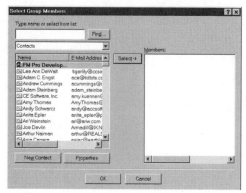

**Figure 13.10** You add group members in the Select Group Members dialog box.

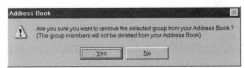

**Figure 13.11** Click Yes to confirm the deletion of the chosen group.

# Modifying a Group

You can modify any existing contact group by deleting it, changing its name, or changing its members.

## To delete a contact group:

1. Open the Address Book by using any of the methods previously mentioned.

2. Select the group name in the address list and do one of the following:
   - ◆ Click the Delete button.
   - ◆ Choose File > Delete.
   - ◆ Press (Del).
   - ◆ Right-click the group name, and choose Delete from the pop-up menu.

3. Confirm the deletion by clicking Yes in the dialog box that appears (**Figure 13.11**).

## To rename a contact group:

1. Open the Address Book by using any of the methods previously mentioned.

2. Select the group name in the address list, and then choose File > Properties, click the Properties button, double-click the group record, or press (Enter) or (Alt)+(Enter).

3. Type a new name in the Group Name box.

4. Click OK.

## To change a group's members:

1. Open the Address Book by using any of the methods previously mentioned.

2. Select the group name in the address list, and then choose File > Properties, click the Properties button, double-click the group record, or press (Enter) or (Alt)+(Enter).

**3.** To delete a member, select the member's name, and do one of the following:

- ◆ Click Remove.
- ◆ Right-click the member's name, and choose Remove from the pop-up menu that appears.
- ◆ Press the [Del] key.

Note that deletions are immediate; there is no opportunity for you to confirm or cancel the member's removal. If you delete a member by mistake, close the dialog box by clicking Cancel rather than OK.

**4.** To add a member, use any of the methods listed in Step 4 of "To create a group."

**5.** To save all changes, close the dialog box by clicking OK. If you want to leave the membership unchanged, click Cancel.

## ✔ Tips

- ■ When deleting a group, only the group definition is deleted—not the contact information for the group members.

- ■ To send email to all members of a group, you can do any of the following:

  - ◆ Type the group name in the To line of the message.
  - ◆ Click the To button in the email message, and choose the group name from the list presented in the Select Recipients dialog box (**Figure 13.12**). Group names are shown in bold type.
  - ◆ Double-click the group name in the Contacts pane. (Group names appear at the bottom of the contact list.) You can also right-click the group name, and choose Send E-Mail from the pop-up menu that appears.

*Send message to this group*

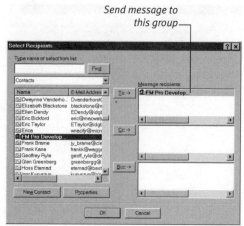

**Figure 13.12** If you don't remember the group name, you can choose it from the Select Recipients dialog box.

**Figure 13.13** Use the View menu to set a display format and sort order for the contact list.

*Double arrow*

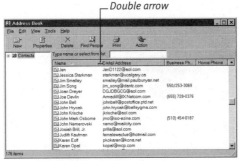

**Figure 13.14** You can change column widths in the Address Book by clicking between a pair of column headings and then dragging.

# Setting Display Options

You can't change the Address Book's toolbar or column headings, but you can set a display format and sort order. The standard display format is Details, which shows all four fields. In other views, only the contact name is shown.

To set a display format for the address list, choose Large Icons, Small Icons, List, or Details from the View menu.

Regardless of the view chosen, you can also specify a sort order for the address list, as follows:

◆ Select a sort order from the View > Sort By submenu (**Figure 13.13**). To choose between ascending and descending sorts, choose the appropriate option from the bottom of the Sort By submenu.

◆ In Details view, click a column heading to sort the list by that field. To change between ascending and descending sorts, click the same column heading again.

## ✔ Tips

■ If you only use the address list to choose email recipients, you may prefer the uncluttered look of Large Icons, Small Icons, or List view. You can still sort the list by first name, last name, or full name.

■ You can hide the toolbar, status bar, or the folder and group list by choosing View > Toolbar, Status Bar, or Folders and Groups. (When the element is visible, the command is preceded by a check mark.)

■ You can widen, shrink, or hide columns in Details view. Move the pointer between any pair of columns until it changes to a double arrow (**Figure 13.14**). Then drag to widen or shrink the column on the left.

■ You can change the order in which columns are displayed by dragging them to different positions.

# Printing the Address Book

If you need a paper copy of your address information, you'll find that Windows Address Book is more than up to the task.

## To print the Address Book:

1. Open the Address Book by using any of the methods previously mentioned.

2. Address records print in the sort order that is in effect at the time the Print command is issued. Sort the records by choosing View > Sort By, followed by the sort field.

3. Choose View > Sort By > Ascending or View > Sort By > Descending.

   An *ascending sort* lists the records in alphabetical order (A to Z); a *descending sort* is in reverse alphabetical order (Z to A).

4. *Optional*: If you want to print only selected records, choose them by Shift-clicking or Ctrl-clicking (**Figure 13.15**).

5. Choose File > Print (or press Ctrl+P). The Print dialog box appears (**Figure 13.16**).

6. Select an installed printer from the Name drop-down list. To view or change print settings for this printer, click Properties.

7. To print only the currently select record(s), click Selection in the Print Range section of the dialog box. To print all records in the Address Book, click All.

8. Choose a print layout (Memo, Business Card, or Phone List) from the Print Style section of the dialog box.

9. *Optional*: To print more than one copy of the records, enter a number greater than 1 in the Copies box.

10. Click OK to begin printing.

*Selected records*

**Figure 13.15** You can restrict a printout to the currently selected records by selecting them prior to issuing the Print command.

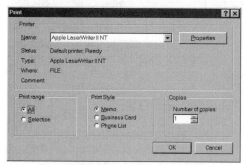

**Figure 13.16** The Print dialog box.

*Supported formats*

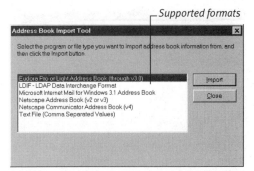

**Figure 13.17** The Address Book Import Tool lists all file formats that can be imported into your Address Book.

*Importing an address book*

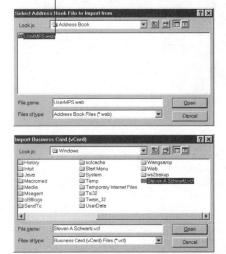

**Figure 13.18** Importing an Address Book file.

**To Share or Not to Share**

By default, data stored in your primary Windows Address Book file is accessible to all Windows applications that want to use it. If you prefer to keep Outlook Express' data separate from that of other programs, open Address Book, choose Tools > Options, and select the "Do not share..." option. Note that the business card import and export capabilities are available only when the Address Book data is not shared.

# Importing and Exporting Contact Information

You can import address data into Windows Address Book, as well as export it in a form that can be interpreted by other Address Book programs. And the new vCard business card file format makes it easy to exchange individual contact records with other users.

## To import address data:

1. Do one of the following:
   ◆ Choose File > Import > Address Book (WAB) to import an existing copy of Windows Address Book (a .wab file).
   ◆ To import an address book from Eudora Pro or Lite, Microsoft Internet Mail for Windows 3.1, Netscape or Netscape Communicator, or one in LDIF–LDAP or comma-delimited format, choose File > Import > Other Address Book. The Address Book Import Tool dialog box appears (**Figure 13.17**). Select a format, and click Import.

2. When importing a Windows Address Book file, a standard file dialog box appears (**Figure 13.18**), asking you to locate the file to import. Select the file, and click Open.

   *or*

   When importing another type of address book, Windows automatically searches your attached disk drives for the file.

**IMPORTING/EXPORTING INFO**

## To export address data from Windows Address Book:

1. Launch Outlook Express.

2. Choose File > Export > Address Book. The Address Book Export Tool dialog box appears (**Figure 13.19**).

3. Select a format and click Export. The CSV Export wizard appears (**Figure 13.20**).

4. Enter a path and filename, or click the Browse button to select a path. Click Next.

5. Enter checkmarks in the fields you wish to export (**Figure 13.21**). Click Finish. The file is exported to disk.

6. Select another export file format, if desired; or click Close to dismiss the dialog box.

## ✔ Tip

- As long as Address Book is set so it isn't sharing its data with other programs (Tools > Options > Do not share…), you can also import and export data directly from Address Book. Choose File > Import or File > Export. If Address Book *is* sharing its data, the Import and Export commands are disabled.

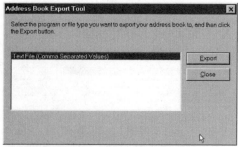

**Figure 13.19** Select a file format for the exported Address Book data from the list in the Address Book Export Tool dialog box.

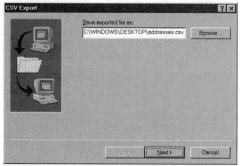

**Figure 13.20** Specify a path and filename for the exported data.

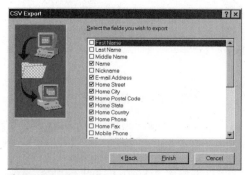

**Figure 13.21** Check all fields that you want to export.

IMPORTING/EXPORTING INFO

**Figure 13.22** Choose a location on disk to which your business card will be exported.

**Figure 13.23** Find the business card (.vcf) file that you want to send as an email attachment.

## Working with business cards

If many of your associates and friends are Windows users, you'll find that one of the simplest ways to give them your contact data is by creating a Business Card file and emailing it as an attachment. Once received, it's easy for others to import your information into their Windows Address Book. And they can quickly send you their contact data in the same manner.

### To create a business card:

1. Open the Address Book by using any of the methods previously mentioned.

2. Create a new record for yourself, including all contact information you want to share.

3. Choose File > Export > Business Card (vCard).

   An Export dialog box appears (**Figure 13.22**).

4. Save the card in a location where you can easily find it. The file will be named *yourname*.vcf.

### To email your vCard to others:

1. Create an email message.

2. Click the Attach button in the toolbar, or choose Insert > File Attachment.

   The Insert Attachment dialog box appears (**Figure 13.23**).

3. Navigate to the drive and folder that contains your business card file, select the file, and click Attach.

## Adding a received card to the Address Book:

1. When an email message with an attached vCard is received by Outlook Express, it is shown as an ordinary attachment. (It is marked with a paper clip icon.) Double-click the message to open it (**Figure 13.24**).

   If a vCard is attached, an Address Book icon is displayed at the right side.

2. Click the Address Book icon, and choose Open.

   The Open Attachment Warning appears (**Figure 13.25**).

3. Click Open it, and then click OK.

   The contact record for the individual appears (**Figure 13.26**).

4. To add the record to your Address Book, click Add to Address Book.

## ✔ Tip

- If you send a vCard to someone who doesn't use Windows Address Book, they may not be able to import it into their address book. However, they can still view the data. Tell them it is an ordinary text file that can be opened in any word processing program or text editor.

**Figure 13.24** A message with an attached business card is denoted in Outlook Express by a tiny business card icon.

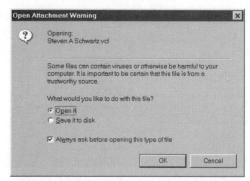

**Figure 13.25** You can either open the attached business card or save it on disk in a location of your choosing.

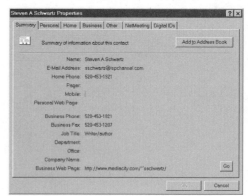

**Figure 13.26** To add a received business card to Windows Address Book, click the Add to Address Book button.

# COMPOSING AND SENDING EMAIL

The first thing you need to know about email is that every person with Internet access has a unique *email address*. When you send a message, you indicate the intended recipient by specifying his or her email address.

An email address has two parts: a *user name* and a *domain name* (the service on which the person has an account). The service might be an ISP (networx.net), a company (global.com), an information service (aol.com), or an educational institution (hnrc.tufts.edu).

Every domain name has a suffix (also called a *zone*) that indicates what kind of organization it is. Common suffixes include:

- com (commercial).
- net (network).
- org (organization).
- edu (educational).
- gov (government).

User names are either created by the individual or assigned by their service or institution. User names can include letters, numbers, and special characters, such as underscores and periods. Spaces are *not* allowed. Although hundreds of people on the Internet may have the same user name, there can be only one person with a given user name in a domain.

The user and domain names are separated by an @ character. Here are some typical email addresses:

- spatterson@aol.com
  (America Online address).

- johnadams@postoffice.ptd.net
  (ISP address).

- dave73@eng.uchicago.edu
  (educational address).

As you can see, you may or may not be able to determine a person's name from an email address.

To make it easy to deal with complex, lengthy addresses, most email programs provide an *address book* in which to record addresses (see Chapter 13). Every address is linked to the person's full name, company, and other identifying data (**Figure 14.1**). When addressing email, you can choose the recipient's name from the address book (**Figure 14.2**). Thus, after recording an address, you'll never have to type it again.

## ✔ Tips

- If you are allowed to pick your user name, create one that readily identifies you. Unless you want to remain relatively anonymous, sschwartz and steveschwartz are better choices than roadhog or dude1.

- Although letter case does not matter when addressing Internet email, the convention is to enter email addresses in all lowercase. It's easiest, for one thing.

- Include your email address on letterhead, business cards, and fax forms. When making new business contacts, it's important to provide as many convenient ways to contact you as possible.

- If you change ISPs, inform everyone in your address book of your new email address. (It changes when you switch providers.)

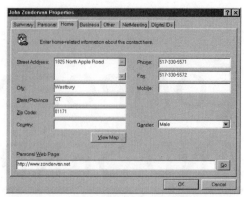

**Figure 14.1** In addition to each person's name, you can enter other useful information in a contact record, such as phone numbers and Web page URLs.

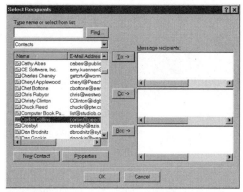

**Figure 14.2** You can select mail recipients from the address book.

*Message body*  *Subject of message*
*Toolbar*  *Carbon copy recipient(s)*  *Main recipient(s)*

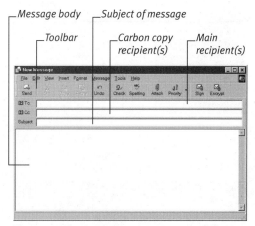

**Figure 14.3** The parts of the New Message window.

**Figure 14.4** The Contacts pane contains the names of all persons in your address book.

*Email address*

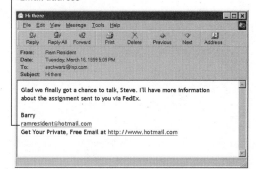

**Figure 14.5** Since many people include their email address in the body of their messages, you can quickly create a new message to them by clicking the address.

# Composing Email

There are three types of messages that you can create in Outlook Express:

◆ *New messages.* Messages that you compose from scratch.

◆ *Replies.* Responses to received messages.

◆ *Forwarded messages.* Received messages that you are forwarding to someone else.

All messages—whether new messages, replies, or forwarded—are composed in a New Message window (**Figure 14.3**).

The New Message Window contains two main parts: the message header (the To, Cc, and Subject lines) and the message body (the text of the message). Note that the window title differs for each message type, showing New Message for an original message, Re: for a reply, and Fw: for a forwarded message.

The first step in creating a message is to open a New Message window. The procedure differs depending on the type of message you are creating.

## To open a New Message window for a new message:

◆ Click the New Mail button in the toolbar, choose File > New > Mail Message, choose Message > New Message, or press Ctrl+N.

◆ Click the link to *Create a new Mail message* (when Outlook Express is selected in the Folders pane).

◆ Double-click a name in the Contacts pane, or right-click a name and choose *Send E-Mail* (**Figure 14.4**).

◆ Click an email address in the body of a received message (**Figure 14.5**).

**171**

◆ Click a mailto link (a link to an email address) on a Web page.

*or*

◆ Click the Mail button in IE5 and choose New Message (**Figure 14.6**).

## To open a New Message window for a reply:

◆ Click the Reply button.

*or*

◆ Choose Message > Reply to Sender or press [Ctrl]+[R].

It is customary to quote relevant parts of the message to which you are replying (**Figure 14.7**). To automatically insert a copy of the original message into your reply, choose "Include message in reply" in the Send section of the Options dialog box. You can edit the quoted text as necessary.

## To open a New Message window for a forwarded message:

◆ Click the Forward button.

*or*

◆ Choose Message > Forward, or press [Ctrl]+[F].

You can edit forwarded messages, as well as enter additional text.

## ✔ Tip

■ You'll note that Outlook Express has two Reply commands in the Message menu, as well as two Reply buttons. The Reply to All command and button are meant for replying to newsgroup messages, as well as to "group" emails—messages sent to three or more people at once. For group emails, Reply to All sends your reply to everyone at once. In the case of a newsgroup message, choosing Reply to All sends two copies of your message: one to the original author's email address and another to the newsgroup in which the message originated.

**Figure 14.6** You can create new email messages without leaving IE5—simply click the Mail button in the toolbar.

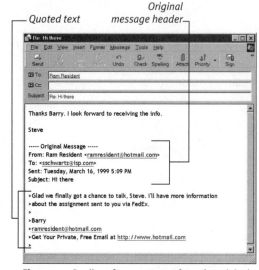

**Figure 14.7** Replies often quote text from the original message.

**Figure 14.8** The Edit menu.

_Find options_

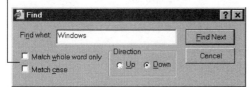

**Figure 14.9** Use the Edit > Find > Text in this message command to locate a text string in the message. If it is found, the window scrolls to display the string. Click Find Next to search for additional instances.

_Choose a default message format_

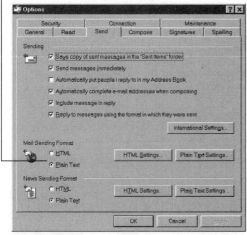

**Figure 14.10** Click a radio button to set the default message format.

# Writing a Message

When you're writing messages, Outlook Express works like a typical word processing program or text editor. Words automatically wrap from one line to the next. You only have to press (Return) when you want to start a new paragraph.

Similarly, the standard editing commands are available. You can choose the following commands from the Edit menu (**Figure 14.8**), or you can use these keyboard shortcuts:

◆ *Undo* ((Ctrl)+(Z)). Undo the most recent edit or command.

◆ *Cut* ((Ctrl)+(X)). Delete the selected text and place a copy of it on the clipboard (making it available for pasting).

◆ *Copy* ((Ctrl)+(C)). Copy the selected text to the clipboard (making it available for pasting).

◆ *Paste* ((Ctrl)+(Y)). Paste text from the clipboard at the cursor location.

◆ *Select All* ((Ctrl)+(A)). Select all text in the document.

◆ *Find text in this message* ((F3)). Find text in the message body (**Figure 14.9**).

## ✔ Tips

■ You can select a word by double-clicking anywhere within the word. Triple-click to select an entire paragraph.

■ If Microsoft Office is installed, the Spelling ((F7)) command and button are enabled.

## Formatting a message

Outlook Express can create plain text and rich text (HTML-formatted) messages. Options for the two formats differ significantly.

You can set a default message format in the Send section of the Options dialog box (**Figure 14.10**). Regardless of the default setting,

**WRITING A MESSAGE**

you can select a format for each outgoing message from the Format menu (**Figure 14.11**).

## Plain Text formatting

Plain Text messages are formatted with a single font and point size. There is no style support (such as boldface or italic) and no paragraph alignment commands. Tabs can be included, but are treated as strings of spaces. To ensure compatibility with other mail programs and computer systems, most messages you send and receive will probably be Plain Text.

## Rich Text (HTML) formatting

HTML messages can contain multiple fonts, sizes, styles, and colors. You can set paragraph alignments (left, right, and centered) and create bulleted lists.

To set formatting for selected text or the current paragraph, you can choose options from the format toolbar (**Figure 14.12**) or the Format menu.

## ✔ Tips

- HTML formatting is visible only in HTML-capable mail programs and browsers. Not all mail programs can display HTML. If you don't know what email program an intended recipient uses, stick to Plain Text messages.

- You can also add a decorative background and separator lines (rules) to HTML-formatted messages. To add a background, choose Message > New Message Using, and then select a design (**Figure 14.13**). To add a rule, choose Insert > Horizontal Line.

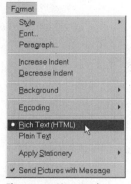

**Figure 14.11** You can choose Rich Text (HTML) or Plain Text format. The chosen format is marked with a bullet.

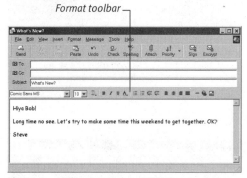

**Figure 14.12** When creating an HTML message, a format toolbar (similar to the ones found in many word processing programs) can be used to apply text and paragraph formatting.

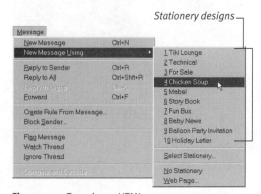

**Figure 14.13** To make an HTML message even more eye-catching, choose a stationery design.

**Figure 14.14** Select a text file to insert into the message from the Insert Text File dialog box.

*Hypertext links*

**Figure 14.15** Hypertext links to Web pages, email addresses, and the like can be added to the body of your message.

## Inserting a text file

There are two ways to insert text from other documents into a message. One way is to copy the text in the other document (Ctrl+C), and then paste it into the message (Ctrl+V). The other method is to insert a text file directly from disk.

## To insert a text file into the current message:

1. Position the cursor where you want to insert the text file.

2. Choose Insert > Text from File.

   The Insert Text File dialog box appears (**Figure 14.14**).

3. Select a text (.txt) file to insert and click Open.

## ✔ Tip

■ Only text files can be inserted. To insert a word processing file, you must first save a copy of it as ASCII, Plain Text, or a similar format. (Note that the file's extension *must* be .txt.)

## Adding hypertext links

Hypertext links, such as Web page URLs and email addresses, can be added to the body of any message (**Figure 14.15**). If the recipient has Outlook Express, Microsoft Outlook, Eudora, or a similar email client, the embedded hypertext links are *clickable*. That is, when clicked, the user's browser launches automatically and fetches the designated Web page; the email client launches and creates a blank message addressed to the email hypertext link; and so on.

You can add hypertext links by typing them directly into the body of the message or by choosing the Insert > Hyperlink command (**Figure 14.16**). Note that the Hyperlink command is available only when creating a Rich Text message. However, you can manually type such links into either Plain Text or Rich Text messages.

## Adding a signature

Optionally, a message can end with a *signature* (one or more lines that provide your name and postal address, Web site URL, phone number, or a brief note).

To add a signature to the current message, do one of the following:

◆ Choose Insert > Signature followed by the signature you want to use.

◆ To automatically add your signature to every outgoing message, check *Add signature to end of all outgoing messages* (**Figure 14.17**) in the Signature section of the Options dialog box.

Signature text is designated in the Signature section of the Options dialog box. To learn more about signatures, see "Signature Options" in Chapter 16.

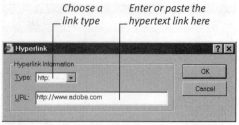

Figure 14.16 Links can be typed or pasted directly into the message body, or you can specify them in the Hyperlink dialog box.

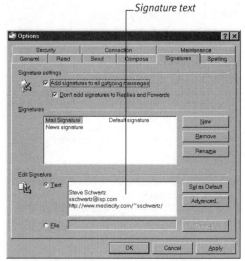

Figure 14.17 You can specify default email and newsgroup signatures in the Options dialog box.

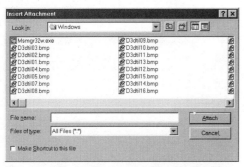

**Figure 14.18** Choose files to attach from this dialog box. Any type of file can be an attachment, such as sounds, graphics, movies, spreadsheets, or programs.

*Attachments*

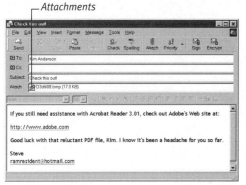

**Figure 14.19** Attachments are listed in the Attach line of the message window.

*Select a picture*

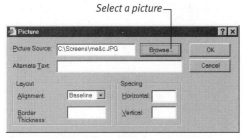

**Figure 14.20** The ability to include a picture in the body of a message (rather than as an attachment) is a new feature in Outlook Express. To locate the picture, click the Browse button.

# Adding Attachments

One popular use of email is to transmit formatted documents, graphic images, and programs along with a message. Such files are called *attachments*.

## To add an attachment:

1. Choose Insert > File Attachment or click the Attach button on the message toolbar.

   The Insert Attachment dialog box appears (**Figure 14.18**).

2. Select a file, and click Attach.

   The filename is added to the Attach box (**Figure 14.19**).

You can select additional attachments by repeating these steps. To remove an attachment, select it in the message window and press Del.

## ✔ Tips

■ Attachments are encoded using *MIME* (Multipurpose Internet Mail Extensions). To decode them, the recipient must have a mail program or utility that can handle this task.

■ Although pictures are generally sent as attachments, Outlook Express will also let you embed pictures in the body of a Rich Text (HTML) message. Place the cursor where you want the picture to be inserted, choose Insert > Picture, and select a picture from your hard disk (**Figure 14.20**).

## Adding a business card

A business card (also known as a *vCard*) is a special type of attachment that contains your contact information, such as your email address, home page URL, street address, phone numbers, and so on. By attaching a business card to all or some of your outgoing messages, you can quickly convey all of your essential contact information to others. If the recipient uses Outlook Express, Microsoft Outlook, or another program that understands the vCard file format, they can then add your contact information to their address book.

To learn how to create a business card, see Chapter 13.

## To attach a business card:

1. Choose Insert > File Attachment, or click the Attach button on the message toolbar.
   The Insert Attachment dialog box appears (**Figure 14.21**).

2. Select the business card file from its location on your hard disk (such as Steven Schwartz.vcf) and click Attach.
   An icon for the file is added to the Attach box.

## ✔ Tips

■ Even if the recipient doesn't have an email client that recognizes business cards as a special type of attachment, the vCard file can be opened and viewed in any text editor, such as Notepad.

■ Business cards are a relatively new addition to the world of email. Since many recipients will have no idea what they are or what they should do with them, you may want to ask first rather than automatically attaching your business card to all messages.

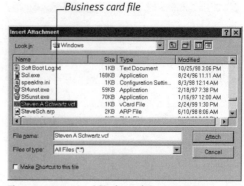
Business card file

**Figure 14.21** A vCard file (*.vcf) is a special type of attachment that you use to send address book information about yourself to others.

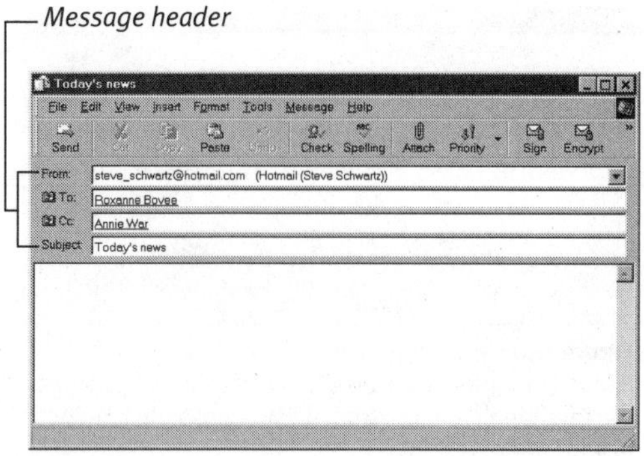

*Message header*

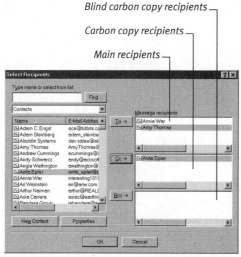

**Figure 14.22** The message header lists all intended recipients and a subject line.

*Blind carbon copy recipients*

*Carbon copy recipients*

*Main recipients*

**Figure 14.23** One way to address an outgoing message is by choosing names from the address book.

*Recipients*

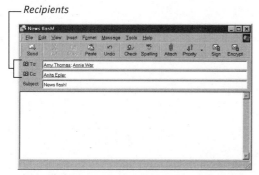

**Figure 14.24** This message will be sent to Amy Thomas and Annie War. A copy of it will be sent to Anita Epler.

# The Message Header

Before sending a message, you must enter information in the header (**Figure 14.22**). Every message header contains four lines: To, From, Cc, and Subject. The Priority button is used to set an optional priority for the message. If you have only one email account, the From line is omitted.

## Addressing a message

The names or addresses of the primary recipients are entered in the To line. Use the Cc line to specify recipients of a "carbon copy" of the message. A short title or explanation of the subject matter is entered in the Subject line. At a minimum, there must always be an entry in the To line.

Outlook Express provides several ways for you to select message recipients, as described below.

## To select an address from the address book:

1. Click the To, Cc, or Bcc icon in the header or choose Tools > Select Recipients.

   The Select Recipients dialog box appears (**Figure 14.23**).

2. Do one of the following:
   - ◆ Select a name from the contact list and click the To, Cc, or Bcc button to add it to the appropriate recipient list.
   - ◆ Type a full or partial name in the *Type name or select from list* box. As you type, the closest matching contact is highlighted. Click To, Cc, or Bcc icon to add it to the appropriate recipient list.

3. Click OK to close the dialog box, accepting the recipient list. The chosen name or names appear in the message header (**Figure 14.24**).

THE MESSAGE HEADER

## Manually entering a recipient

You can also type or paste a name or an email address into the To, Cc, or Bcc lines of the message header.

♦ If the contact isn't in the address book, type or paste the person's full email address into the To, Cc, or Bcc line (e.g., sox@lox.net).

♦ If the contact is in your address book, type all or part of his or her name in the To, Cc, or Bcc line (e.g., Steve, Simms, or Steve Simms). When you send the message, Outlook Express prompts for the correct recipient, if necessary (**Figure 14.25**).

## ✔ Tips

■ The message header can be expanded to include a *Bcc* line (blind carbon copy). Recipients entered in the Bcc line will receive the message, but their names will not be visible to recipients in the To or Cc lines. To add the Bcc line, choose View > All Headers.

■ The To, Cc, and Bcc lines can contain *multiple* recipients. Separate recipients with a semicolon, such as:

gjames@aol.com; roadie@inter.net

■ Web pages often contain mail-to links that when clicked instruct your default email program to address a letter to that person or company.

**Figure 14.25** If a name typed into the To, Cc, or Bcc line is ambiguous, Outlook Express asks you to select the intended recipient from a list of possible matches in your address book.

**Figure 14.26** You can email a hypertext link to the current Web page or the actual page itself by choosing a command from IE5's Mail button.

# Other Message Options

There are other message options that you may sometimes want to use, as described below.

## Sending to a group

Messages—as well as attachments—can be sent to a group. Rather than picking individual recipient names from the address book, select the name of their group. See Chapter 13 for help with creating groups.

## Sending a Web page

You can email a link to a Web page or the page itself from within Internet Explorer. IE5 uses your default email client (Outlook Express) to mail the link or page to others.

## To email a link to a Web page or a complete Web page:

1. Visit the page in IE5.

2. In IE5, click the Mail button and choose Send a Link or Send Page (**Figure 14.26**).

3. An email message window appears, containing either a hypertext link to the page or the page itself.

4. Address the message, and click Send.

## ✔ Tip

■ Not all email clients can display Web pages. It is often more useful to send the hypertext link (the URL), rather than the actual page.

## Setting a message priority

You can set a priority for an outgoing message to indicate its level of importance. Setting a priority, however, has no impact on the manner in which it is delivered, and many mail programs do not recognize or use priorities.

## To set a priority for a message:

1. Create the message in its own window.

2. Click the Priority button (**Figure 14.27**), or choose Message > Set Priority.

3. Choose a priority: High, Normal, or Low.

## ✔ Tips

- By default, all outgoing messages are sent Normal priority. Unless you want to set the priority to High or Low, you do not need to use the Set Priority command.

- If the recipient's email client recognizes priorities, a prioritized message will be marked as you designated. (For example, Outlook Express denotes a high priority message with an exclamation point and a low priority message with a down-arrow.)

## Sending secure messages

Outlook Express supports two features that can help assure that your messages have not been tampered with en route. First, by obtaining and using a *digital ID*, recipients can be assured that you really sent a given message. Second, if both you and your recipient have a digital ID, you can exchange *encrypted* email—assuring both parties that no one else will be able to read your messages. (At this writing, VeriSign offers free personal digital IDs for a 60-day trial period.)

## To obtain a digital ID:

1. Choose Tools > Options.
   The Options dialog box appears.

2. Click the Security tab at the top of the dialog box (**Figure 14.28**).

3. Click the Get Digital ID button.
   IE5 launches, and displays a page from Microsoft's Web site.

4. Click the VeriSign link and follow the instructions to apply for and install your personal digital ID.

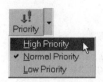

**Figure 14.27** You can quickly set a priority by clicking the Priority button.

*Click to apply for a digital ID*

**Figure 14.28** You can get information about or apply for a digital ID by clicking this button in the Options dialog box.

*Click to reveal the menu*

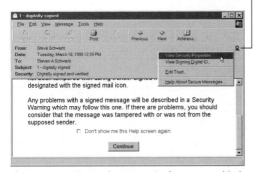

**Figure 14.29** To learn about security features enabled for an incoming message, click the security icon to the right of the message header.

*Add ID to your address book*

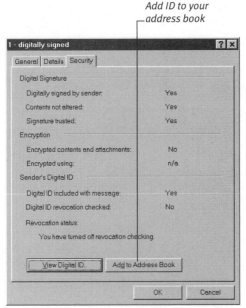

**Figure 14.30** In general, you'll want to record the digital IDs from most incoming messages.

## To sign all outgoing messages with your digital ID:

1. Choose Tools > Options.

   The Options dialog box appears.

2. Click the Security tab (refer to **Figure 14.28**).

3. Add a checkmark for the option to *Digitally sign all outgoing messages.*

4. Click OK.

## ✔ Tip

- If you do not instruct Outlook Express to digitally sign all outgoing messages, you still can digitally sign selected outgoing messages by clicking the Sign button or by choosing Tools > Digitally Sign.

## To add a received digital ID to your address book:

1. Double-click the received message to open it in its own window.

2. Click the digital signature icon to the right of the message header.

3. In the pop-up menu that appears (**Figure 14.29**), choose View Security Properties.

   The digitally signed dialog box appears (**Figure 14.30**).

4. Click the Add to Address Book button.

5. Click OK.

## ✔ Tip

- If you prefer to have all received digital IDs automatically added to the address book, choose Tools > Options, click the Security tab, click the Advanced button, and make sure that the option to *Add senders' certificates to my address book* is enabled.

# Sending Messages

To send an individual message, click the Send button in the New Message window, choose File > Send Message, or press [Alt]+[S].

If the option to *Send messages immediately* has been checked in the Send section of the Options dialog box, the message is immediately transmitted to your mail server. Otherwise, it is held in the Outbox and will be sent the next time mail is exchanged with the server.

To send and receive all waiting messages, click the Send/Receive button (in the main mail window), choose Tools > Send and Receive > Send and Receive All, or press [Ctrl]+[M].

If you have defined multiple email accounts, you can send and receive from any single account by choosing the account name from the Send and Receive submenu.

As mentioned earlier, Outlook Express can also send encrypted messages.

## To send an encrypted message:

1. With the message window open, click the Encrypt button or choose Tools > Encrypt.

2. Click the Send button—or use any of the other Send options discussed in this section.

   Note that unless both you and the recipient(s) have a digital ID recorded in your address book, you will not be allowed to send the message in its encrypted form.

## ✔ Tip

- To force an outgoing message to be temporarily stored in your Outbox (rather than being sent immediately), choose File > Send Later.

# RECEIVING MAIL

There's more to receiving mail than simply opening and reading it. In this chapter, you'll learn how to manage incoming mail, print messages, handle attachments and encrypted messages, and import and export messages.

# Checking for New Mail

You can check for new mail manually or automatically. (Note that whenever you check for mail, messages in the Outbox are also sent.)

## To manually check for new mail:

1. Switch to the mail window.

2. Do one of the following:

    ◆ Click the Send/Receive button to send and receive for all email accounts.

    ◆ Click the down-arrow beside the Send and Receive button. Choose Send and Receive All, Receive All, or the name of a specific email account (**Figure 15.1**).

    ◆ Choose Tools > Send and Receive > Send and Receive All, Receive All, or the name of a specific email account.

    ◆ Press [Ctrl]+[M] to send and receive for all email accounts.

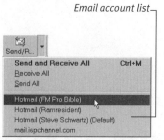

*Email account list*

**Figure 15.1** To manually send and receive mail, you can choose an option from the Send/Receive button's menu.

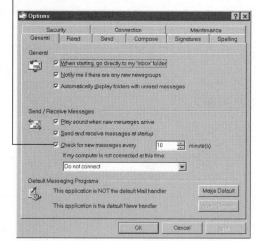

*Automatic mail checking*

**Figure 15.2** To automatically send and receive at regular intervals, check this option in the General Section of the Options dialog box.

*Include or exclude this account*

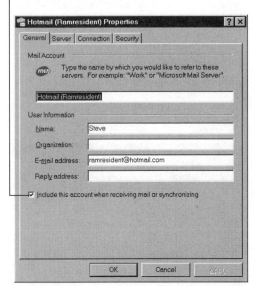

**Figure 15.3** Whether an account is included in Send and Receive All commands and automatic mail checking depends on this setting. If unchecked, you must specifically choose its account name when you want to receive and send email.

## To automatically check for mail:

1. Choose Tools > Options.

   The Options dialog box appears, open to the General Tab (**Figure 15.2**).

2. Set the option for *Check for new messages every* xx *minute(s)* and set the number of minutes you want to wait between checks.

3. Click OK.

   Whenever Outlook Express is running, it will now send and receive messages for all email accounts at the designated intervals. (And you can still do manual send/receives.)

## ✔ Tip

■ To prevent mail for an account from being automatically retrieved, choose Tools > Accounts, select the email account, click Properties, and remove the checkmark from the option at bottom of the General section (**Figure 15.3**).

## What About Identities?

As explained in Chapter 12, you can create multiple *identities* so you can share Outlook Express with others, while keeping your email private. You can create additional identities for other family members or to keep business and home email activities separate, for example.

As long as each user remembers to switch to his or her identity at the start of every Outlook Express session, only their new email will be retrieved when executing a Send and Receive All.

CHECKING FOR NEW MAIL

# Reading Messages

When mail arrives, it is announced by a sound effect and a new mail icon in the Taskbar (**Figure 15.4**). You can read mail in the preview pane or in individual message windows.

## To read a message:

1. In the Folders pane, select the folder in which the message is stored (**Figure 15.5**). Incoming mail is normally found in the Inbox folder.

2. Select the message in the message list. The message text appears in the preview pane at the bottom of the mail window. Read the message in the preview pane, scrolling as required.

   *or*

   To read a message in its own window (**Figure 15.6**), double-click its header in the message list or select it and choose File > Open.

## ✔ Tips

- As long as a message is stored in one of the mail folders, it can be read—regardless of whether the message is new or old. This includes mail in the Deleted Items folder.

- If you have created message rules to automatically handle incoming mail (see "Creating Message Rules" later in this chapter), some messages may be routed to folders other than the Inbox. If this is the case, you should periodically check for unread messages in other folders. New messages are indicated by showing the folder name in boldface followed by the number of unread messages, such as Friends (2).

*New mail icon*

**Figure 15.4** When new mail arrives, an icon appears near the end of the taskbar. The icon remains until you read the new messages or mark them as read.

*Selected folder*  *Messages from selected folder*

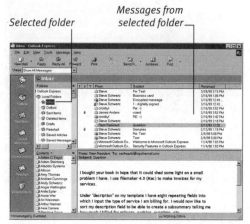

**Figure 15.5** To view the messages in any folder, begin by selecting the folder in the Folder pane.

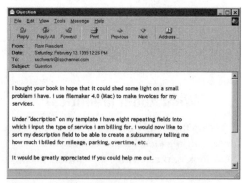

**Figure 15.6** You can view any message in its own window.

READING MESSAGES

**Figure 15.7** One of the easiest ways to change the status of a message is to right-click its header and choose a command from the pop-up menu.

## Read and unread messages

When a message arrives, its header in the message list is shown in boldface (indicating that it has not been read). After selecting the header, the boldface is removed (indicating that the message has been read).

## To manually change the read/unread status of a message:

1. Select one or more messages from the message list. (To choose additional messages, [Ctrl]-click them.)

2. Choose Edit > Mark as Read, right-click the message and choose Mark as Read, or press [Ctrl]+[Q] or [Ctrl]+[Enter].

   *or*

   Choose Edit > Mark as Unread, or right-click the message and choose Mark as Unread (**Figure 15.7**).

## ✔ Tips

■ Marking messages as read or unread is a convenience option. It does not affect the handling of the messages in any way. Read messages are not automatically moved to the Deleted Items folder, for example.

■ One reason to mark an unread message as having been read is so you can ignore it. This procedure is handy for dealing with unwanted or junk email.

## Finding messages

If a folder contains many messages, you can use the Find command to help locate the one(s) of interest.

## To find a message in the current folder:

1. Select a folder in the Folders pane.

2. Choose Edit > Find > Message in this Folder, select this command from the

Find button menu (**Figure 15.8**), or press [Shift]+[F3].

The Find dialog box appears (**Figure 15.9**).

**3.** Enter the search text. (Outlook Express will examine the message headers for the search text.)

**4.** *Optional:* To search the message bodies as well as the headers, check the option to *Search all the text in downloaded messages.*

**5.** Click Find Next.

If a matching message is found, it is highlighted in the message list.

**6.** To look for additional matches, choose Edit> Find > Find Next or press [F3].

## To perform an advanced search:

**1.** Select a primary folder in the Folders pane.

**2.** Choose Edit > Find > Message, click the Find button, select this command from the Find button menu, or press [Ctrl][Shift]+[F].

The Find Message dialog box appears (**Figure 15.10**).

**3.** Enter the search criteria.

**4.** *Optional:* If you want to search in subfolders of the current folder, be sure that *Include subfolders* is checked.

**5.** Click Find Now.

Matches are displayed at the bottom of the Find Message window (**Figure 15.11**).

**6.** Double-click any match to view the message in its own window, right-click a match for additional options, or select a match and then choose an appropriate menu command.

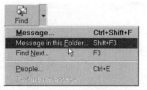

**Figure 15.8** Now that the Find menu is available on the toolbar, you no longer have to hunt for it or remember arcane keyboard shortcuts.

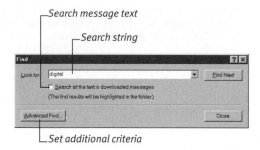

*Search message text*

*Search string*

*Set additional criteria*

**Figure 15.9** When you choose Find Message in this Folder, the Find dialog box appears.

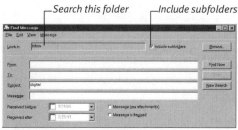

*Search this folder*   *Include subfolders*

**Figure 15.10** Enter search criteria in the Find Message dialog box.

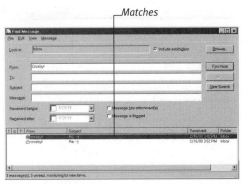

*Matches*

**Figure 15.11** Matches appear at the bottom of the Find Message dialog box.

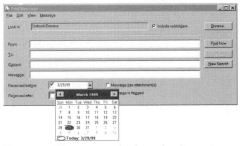

**Figure 15.12** The pop-up calendar makes it easy to choose search dates.

*Click to display list*

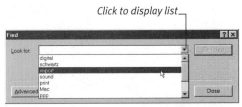

**Figure 15.13** To repeat a Find Message in this Folder search, click the arrow at the end of the text box and select the appropriate search string.

## ✔ Tips

■ If you execute the Find Message in this Folder command and decide that you want to search multiple folders or specify additional criteria, click the Advanced Find button (refer to **Figure 15.9**). The dialog box that appears is the same one that is used to perform a Find Message command.

■ Each Find begins its search from the current position in the message list. If the message is not found, you are given an opportunity to continue the search from the beginning of the message list.

■ Each Find command identifies only those messages that match *all* of the criteria. Specifying fewer criteria will result in more potential matches.

■ Date-based searches can be facilitated with a pop-up calendar that you can use to specify dates (**Figure 15.12**). To use the calendar, click the pop-up indicator to the right of the Received Before or Received After date box. To search for a message between two dates, enter date criteria for *both* Received Before and Received After.

■ If you begin a Find Message search by selecting the Outlook Express folder and checking the *Include subfolders* option, the search will encompass all mail folders and subscribed-to newsgroups.

■ You can restrict a search to all folders for a single email account. Select the Local Folders icon (or the name of the email account), choose Edit > Find > Message, and checking the option to *Include subfolders*.

■ It's easy to repeat a Find Message in this Folder command. Click the button at the end of the Look for box and choose a previously used search string (**Figure 15.13**).

# Managing the Mail

Outlook Express offers many features to help you organize and manage your messages.

## Deleting messages

Perhaps the simplest way to manage received mail is by deleting any messages you do not want to save.

To delete messages, select one or more messages in the message list and do one of the following:

◆ Click the Delete button in the toolbar.

◆ Choose Edit > Delete.

◆ Press Del or Ctrl+D.

The selected messages are moved to the Deleted Items folder. To permanently delete these items, you can any of the following:

◆ Open the Deleted Items folder, select the message(s) to delete, and press Del. Click Yes in response to the dialog box that appears (**Figure 15.14**).

◆ Choose Edit > Empty 'Deleted Items' Folder.

◆ In the Maintenance section of the Options dialog box, click the option to *Empty messages from the 'Deleted Items' folder on exit*. Each time you quit Outlook Express, the deleted messages are removed.

## ✔ Tip

■ Until a message has been permanently deleted from the Deleted Items folder, it can be read or moved to another folder.

## Using folders

Outlook Express has five default folders: *Inbox* (received messages), *Outbox* (outgoing messages), *Deleted Items* (messages marked for deletion), *Sent Items* (messages moved to

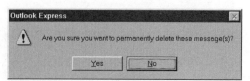

**Figure 15.14** Click Yes to permanently delete the selected messages, or click No to cancel.

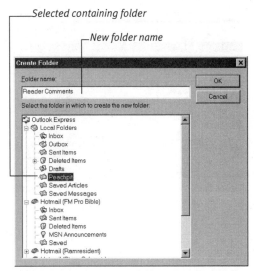

Selected containing folder

New folder name

**Figure 15.15** To create a new folder, select a containing folder and enter a name.

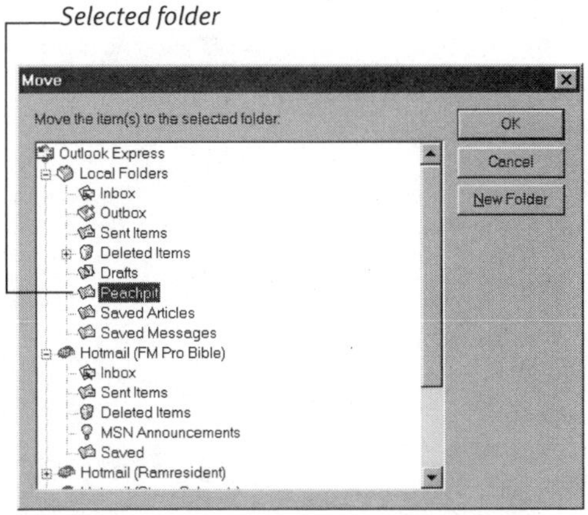

Selected folder

**Figure 15.16** To move or copy a message to another folder, select the folder and click OK.

this folder after having been sent), and *Drafts* (messages that have been partially or completely composed but not sent).

To help further organize your email, you can create new folders; move or copy messages between folders; and compact, move, and delete folders.

You can create as many message folders as you like. With separate folders, you can organize messages by project or subject, for example.

## To create a new message folder:

1. Choose File > New > Folder, File > Folder > New, or press Ctrl Shift + E.

   The Create New Folder dialog box appears (**Figure 15.15**).

2. Name the folder, select a containing folder, and click OK.

Messages can be moved between folders, copied to new folders, or saved on disk as new files.

## To move or copy a message:

1. Open the folder where the messages are stored. To select multiple messages, Ctrl - click each one. (You can only select messages in one folder at a time.)

2. To move the messages to another folder, drag them onto the destination folder's icon in the Folders pane. As an alternative, you can choose Edit > Move to Folder, and then select a destination folder in the Move dialog box (**Figure 15.16**).

3. To place a copy of the selected message(s) in another folder, choose Edit > Copy to Folder, and select a destination folder from the Copy dialog box.

   The selected messages are moved or copied, as directed.

**MANAGING THE MAIL**

## ✔ Tip

- You can automatically move various types of incoming messages to specific folders by creating message rules, as explained later in this chapter.

## To save a message as a file:

1. Select the message in the message list, and choose File > Save As.

   The Save Message As dialog box appears (**Figure 15.17**).

2. *Optional*: Rename the message.

3. Select a format for the message. Choose Mail (.eml) to save it as an Outlook Express file. Choose Text (.txt) to save it as an ordinary text file.

4. Click Save.

## ✔ Tip

- The file type you should select when saving depends on what you intend to do with the message. To save the message in a form that can be read by any text editor or word processing program, choose Text. To move the message to another computer that has Outlook Express, choose Mail.

## Compacting folders

Compacting folders is an easy way to reclaim wasted disk space without deleting messages. All messages are retained, but they take up less space.

## To compact a folder:

1. In the Folders pane, select the folder you want to compact.

2. Choose File > Folder > Compact.

   *or*

   To compact all folders (including newsgroup message folders), choose File > Folder > Compact All Folders.

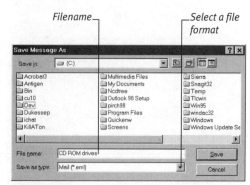

*Filename*      *Select a file format*

**Figure 15.17** You can save any message as a separate file in the Save Message As dialog box.

## Moving folders

Since Outlook Express is fully *drag-and-drop enabled*, the easiest way to reorganize your folders is to simply drag them within the Folders pane. To move a folder into another folder, for example, just drag the folder onto the destination folder.

## Deleting folders

Any folder that you create for storing messages can be deleted. (But you cannot delete the default folders.) Deleting a folder is one of the fastest ways to delete many messages at once. You can then recreate the folder, if desired.

To delete a folder, select the folder in the Folders pane and choose File > Folder > Delete. You must then click Yes in the confirmation dialog box that appears. You can also delete folders by right-clicking them in the Folders pane and choosing Delete.

## Printing messages

You can print any message. Select the message in the mail window, or open it in its own window. Then choose File > Print, click the Print button, or press Ctrl+P. Individual message windows also have a Print button.

## ✔ Tip

- You cannot print a message that you are still writing. After you have marked it for sending or have sent it, though, you can select the message in the Outbox or Sent Items folder, and then print it.

MANAGING THE MAIL

# Working with Attachments

When you receive a message with one or more attached files, you can open the attachments and/or save them to disk.

### To open an attachment:

1. In the message list, select the message with the attachment.

2. Click the paper clip icon above the preview pane. A pop-up menu appears (**Figure 15.18**).

3. Click the filename.

   The Open Attachment Warning appears (**Figure 15.19**).

4. Click *Open it* and click the OK button.

   If you have a program that is associated with the file, the file opens.

### ✔ Tips

- If no program on your hard disk is associated with the attachment's file type, you will not be able to open the attachment in this manner. Obtain the necessary program, and use it to open the attachment.

- Choosing to save an attachment to disk (rather than opening it) enables you to specify a location for storing the received file or program. You can then open or run it at your leisure.

*—Message with an attachment*

*Attachment pop-up menu —*

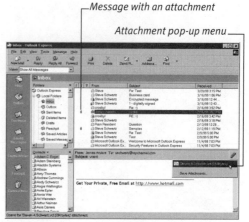

**Figure 15.18** In the message list, a message with an attachment is marked with a paper clip icon. Click the paper clip icon above the preview pane to open or save the attachment.

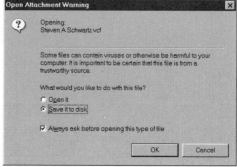

**Figure 15.19** The Open Attachment Warning gives you a choice. You can open the file now or save it to disk.

Destination          Selected        Choose a different
directory        attachment(s)           directory

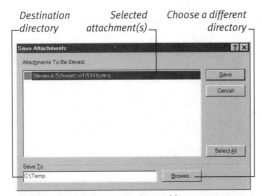

**Figure 15.20** Select the attachment(s) you want to save, choose a destination directory, and click Save.

**Figure 15.21** You can view common types of graphic attachments without leaving Outlook Express.

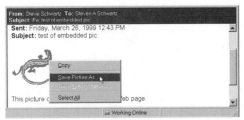

**Figure 15.22** You can save an embedded image by right-clicking it and choosing Save Picture As.

## To save an attachment:

1. Select the message in the message list, click the paper clip icon above the preview pane, and choose Save Attachments from the pop-up menu that appears (refer to **Figure 15.18**). Or you can also choose File > Save Attachments.

   The Save Attachments dialog box appears (**Figure 15.20**).

2. Select the attachments you want to save (messages can contain *multiple attachments*), click the Browse button to select a location for the file(s), and click Save.

## To view and save attached JPEG or GIF images:

1. JPEG and GIF graphic attachments are automatically displayed at the bottom of the message (**Figure 15.21**). If there are multiple attachments, click the Next and/or Previous buttons to view them.

2. To save an attached graphic, right-click the picture and choose Save As. (Or follow the directions in "To save an attachment," above.)

## ✔ Tip

■ Outlook Express users can now embed graphics in the message body (in addition to sending them as attachments). To save an embedded image in a received message (**Figure 15.22**), right-click it and choose Save Picture As.

**WORKING WITH ATTACHMENTS**

# Odds and Ends

This section offers several additional techniques for handling messages. You'll learn how to:

- ◆ Determine a sender's email address.

- ◆ Forward an email message as an attachment.

- ◆ View encrypted messages.

- ◆ Create rules for automatically handling incoming messages.

- ◆ Import and export messages.

## Determining a sender's email address

Most mail programs display the sender's email address in the message header—but Outlook Express doesn't. Although you can store the address in your address book (see "To create a new record from a received message" in Chapter 13), there's another way to learn the sender's address.

### To determine a sender's address:

1. Right-click the message in the message list.

2. Choose Properties from the pop-up menu that appears.

   You can see the sender's email address in either the General or Details section of the dialog box that appears (**Figure 15.23**).

## Forwarding an email message as an attachment

You can forward a message as an attachment to a new message, rather than forwarding it as quoted text (as is done when you use the Forward command).

Email address

**Figure 15.23** Open the Properties dialog box for a message to view the sender's email address.

*Attached message*

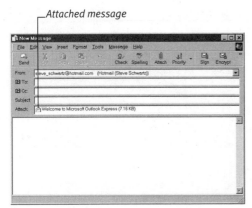

**Figure 15.24** An attached email message is denoted by a letter icon in the Attach box.

**Figure 15.25** This help screen explains that the selected message is encrypted.

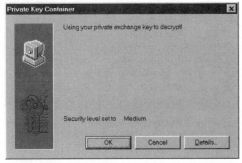

**Figure 15.26** To decode the message, simply click OK.

## To forward a message as an attachment:

**1.** Select the message to forward from the message list.

**2.** Choose Message > Forward as Attachment.

A New Message window opens, and the selected message is added to the Attach box (**Figure 15.24**).

**3.** Compose and address the message, and then click the Send button.

## Viewing encrypted messages

Outlook Express 5 users can exchange encrypted messages with others. The only requirement is that you both must have a *digital ID* (discussed in Chapter 14).

When you receive an encrypted message, each time you attempt to view it (in the preview pane or in its own window), a Help message appears (**Figure 15.25**). Click Continue. The Private Key Container dialog box appears (**Figure 15.26**). Click OK to decode the message.

## Creating message rules

By defining message rules, you can instruct Outlook Express to automatically perform certain actions on some types of email. For example, I could create a rule that causes all email received from peachpit.com to be stored in my Peachpit folder.

## To create a message rule:

**1.** Choose Tools > Message Rules > Mail. The Message Rules dialog box appears.

**2.** Click the New button to create a new message rule. (To edit an existing rule, select the rule and click Modify.)

The New Mail Rule dialog box appears (**Figure 15.27**).

**3.** Set criteria in section 1 of the dialog box.

**4.** In section 2, specify one or more actions that should be taken when the criteria in section 1 are met for a message.

**5.** As necessary, modify the rule description in section 3 by clicking the blue underlined text strings.

**6.** In section 4, name the rule.

**7.** Click OK to save the rule.

Once saved, the rule is automatically applied to incoming messages. **Figure 15.28** shows a completed rule definition.

## ✔ Tips

■ Message rules cannot be applied to IMAP or HTTP (such as Hotmail) accounts.

■ You can temporarily disable a message rule by removing its checkmark in the Message Rules dialog box.

■ The usefulness of your rules is limited only by your creativity. With little effort, you can create a rule to deal with junk mail (those with the word "Sex" or "$$" in the Subject line, for example), another to ignore or delete messages from certain senders, and one to flag all messages from family members or route them to a given folder.

## Importing and exporting email messages

If you previously used another email program, your old messages can be imported into Outlook Express. And if you also use Microsoft Exchange or Microsoft Outlook, you can export your Outlook Express messages to either program. Choose File > Import > Messages or File > Export > Messages, and then follow the prompts.

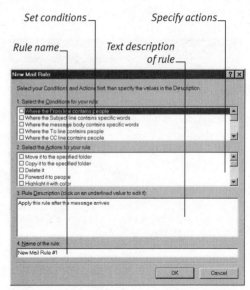

Set conditions — Specify actions —

Rule name — Text description of rule —

**Figure 15.27** Rules are defined in the New Mail Rule dialog box.

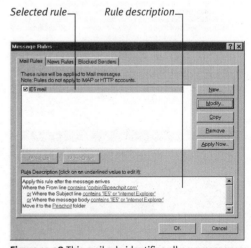

Selected rule — Rule description —

**Figure 15.28** This mail rule identifies all new messages that are related to this book and automatically routes them to the Peachpit folder.

**ODDS AND ENDS**

# SETTING MAIL OPTIONS

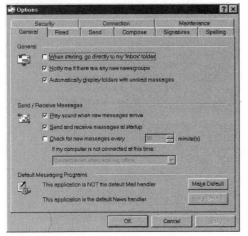

**Figure 16.1** Click the tabs at the top of the Options dialog box to set mail and newsgroup preferences.

## Two Functions, One Dialog Box

Email and newsgroup preferences are both set in the Options dialog box. Only options that are relevant to email are discussed in this chapter. Refer to Chapter 21 for information about setting newsgroup options and to Chapter 22 for assistance in customizing Outlook Express.

Like IE5, you can customize Outlook Express by setting preferences in the Options dialog box. Although the default settings will suffice for most users, you should glance through this chapter to learn about options that can make your computing sessions more productive.

To set options, choose Tools > Options. The Options dialog box appears (**Figure 16.1**). There are nine option categories that correspond to the tabs at the top of the dialog box:

- ◆ *General*. Startup actions and procedures for sending and retrieving messages.

- ◆ *Read*. Time interval after which a message is automatically marked as read; default fonts for displaying messages.

- ◆ *Send*. Settings and formats for sending messages.

- ◆ *Compose*. Default fonts, stationery, and business cards used with new messages.

- ◆ *Signatures*. Specifying a signature line or file to be appended to outgoing messages; managing multiple signatures.

- ◆ *Spelling*. Spell checking conventions.

- ◆ *Security*. Security zones, digital IDs, and encryption options.

- ◆ *Connection*. Specifying a connection method for sending and retrieving mail.

- ◆ *Maintenance*. Managing the message caches.

# General Options

You can set the following email-related preferences in the General section of the Options dialog box (**Figure 16.1**).

## General

*When starting, go directly to my 'Inbox' folder.* Set this option to cause Outlook Express to select the Inbox folder of your default email account on startup, rather than the Outlook Express main folder.

*Automatically display folders with unread messages.* When checked, and you receive email, the Inbox is automatically selected and the first new message is highlighted in the message list. (Unless you spend a lot of time browsing newsgroups and don't want to lose your place, check this option.)

## Send/Receive Messages

*Play sound when new messages arrive.* When checked, new messages are announced by playing the sound file specified for New Mail Notification in the Sounds control panel (**Figure 16.2**).

*Send and receive messages at startup.* When checked, Outlook Express scans all email accounts for new messages each time the program is launched.

*Check for new messages every* xx *minutes.* When set, Outlook Express automatically checks all email accounts for new messages at the designated interval. (Note that Outlook Express must be running.)

If you are not connected to the Internet at the designated interval, the setting below (*If my computer is not connected at this time...*) determines the circumstances under which the program initiates a connection.

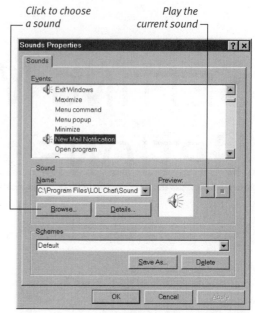

Click to choose a sound

Play the current sound

**Figure 16.2** To change the sound that plays when mail arrives, select the New Mail Notification event and click Browse to choose a different .wav file.

*Clear checkmark for manual receiving*

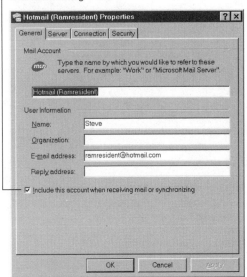

**Figure 16.3** You can set account-specific settings in the account Properties dialog boxes.

## Default Messaging Programs

*This application is (is NOT) the default Mail handler.* Click the Make Default button to make Outlook Express your primary mail program. When you perform an email activity in another program (such as sending a message from your browser), the default mail program is used.

### ✔ Tips

- You can change the mail notification sound by opening the Sounds control panel, scrolling to the Windows section of the list, selecting *New Mail Notification*, and clicking Browse to choose a WAV file from your hard disk (refer to **Figure 16.2**).

- If you have multiple email accounts and elect to automatically check for new messages at startup, you can exclude some of your accounts by clearing the checkmark for *Include this account when receiving mail or synchronizing* (**Figure 16.3**). To set this and other properties for an email account, choose Tools > Accounts, click the Mail tab, select the account, and click Properties.

# Read Options

Read options (**Figure 16.4**) apply to reading and displaying incoming mail.

## Reading Messages

*Mark message read after displaying for* xx *seconds.* Unread messages are shown in boldface, so they can easily be identified. If a message is selected in the message list for longer than the specified time, it is marked as *read;* i.e., the boldface is removed.

If you remove the checkmark, a message is only marked as read if you open it, scroll the preview pane while the message is selected, or issue the Edit > Mark as Read command.

## Fonts

*Click here to change the fonts and default encoding used when reading messages.* Click the Fonts button to select the fonts used to display proportional text and fixed-width text, and specify a font size (**Figure 16.5**). The chosen fonts and size will be used to display all received Plain Text messages. (Rich Text messages will retain their original formatting.)

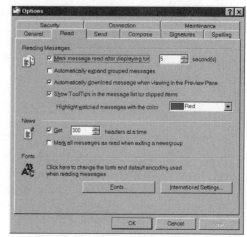

**Figure 16.4** Read options.

**Figure 16.5** The Fonts dialog box.

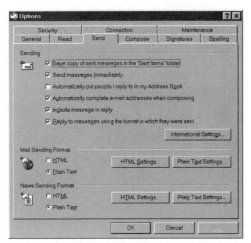

**Figure 16.6** Send options.

Original message header

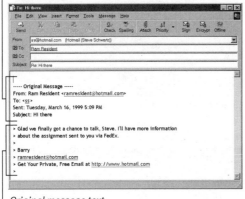

Original message text

**Figure 16.7** When sending a reply, it is an accepted convention to quote the original message. If only portions of the original message are relevant to your reply, you should delete the extraneous material.

# Send Options

Send options are set in the Send section of the Options dialog box (**Figure 16.6**).

## Sending

*Save copy of sent messages in the 'Sent Items' folder*. Check this option to store copies of outgoing messages.

*Send messages immediately*. When checked, outgoing messages are sent the moment you issue the Send Message command. Otherwise, they are held in the Outbox until the next scheduled send or until you issue the Send and Receive command.

*Automatically put people I reply to in my Address Book*. When checked, the name and email address of every new person to whom you reply is added to your address book. (Since replies are often one-time contacts, most people will want to leave this option unchecked.)

*Automatically complete e-mail addresses when composing*. When checked, as you type a name in the To, Cc, or Bcc lines of the message header, Outlook Express attempts to complete the name for you by selecting potential matches from your address book.

*Include message in reply*. When checked, a copy of the message to which you are replying is automatically inserted at the bottom of the message (**Figure 16.7**).

*Reply to messages using the format in which they were sent*. When checked, your replies will use the format (HTML or Plain Text) that the sender used. To ensure compatibility, you will probably want to check this item. (You can still override this setting on a message-by-message basis.)

**SEND OPTIONS**

## ✔ Tips

- You can also create copies of outgoing messages by including your mail address in the To or CC lines.

- If you elect to save copies of sent messages, you may need to think about wasted disk space. Periodically, you can open the Sent Items folder and delete any message that you don't want to keep.

## Mail Sending Format

Click the radio button for HTML or Plain Text to select a default format for outgoing messages. (You can still override this setting on a message-by-message basis.)

- *HTML*. Messages formatted with HTML (Hypertext Markup Language) can contain paragraph alignments, fonts, sizes, styles, and colors (**Figure 16.8**). Such formatting, however, is visible only to users who use HTML-capable mail programs or when the message is viewed in a browser. Individuals without such a program see the message as ordinary text with an HTML attachment.

- *Plain Text*. Currently, most messages are still plain, unformatted text. Choosing this option assures you of compatibility with all mail systems and computer platforms.

To specify settings for HTML or text messages, click the associated Settings button and pick options from the dialog box that appears (**Figures 16.9** and **16.10**).

**Figure 16.8** HTML (or Rich Text) messages can include multiple fonts, sizes, and colors, as well as colorful stationery backgrounds.

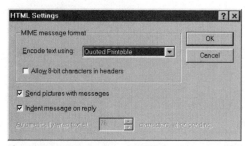

**Figure 16.9** HTML Settings dialog box.

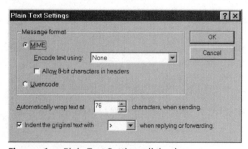

**Figure 16.10** Plain Text Settings dialog box.

*Quoted material (indented)*

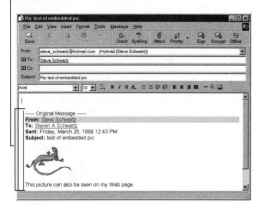

**Figure 16.11** Quoted material (indented)

*Quoted material (no indent)*

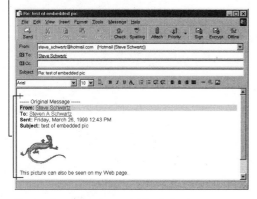

**Figure 16.12** Quoted material (no indent)

# HTML Settings

*Encode text using.* All HTML messages are sent as MIME (Multipurpose Internet Mail Extensions) files. Choose Quoted Printable to send text files that optionally can contain upper ASCII characters. Choose Base64 to send binary files as text.

*Allow 8-bit characters in headers.* These are upper ASCII characters, such as foreign language letters, bullets, and so on. Some mail readers may not be able to interpret these characters.

*Send pictures with messages.* In addition to sending pictures as attachments, you can insert pictures into the body of an HTML message. When this option is checked, a copy of the picture is automatically sent with the message (ensuring that the recipient can see it). If the pictures you normally insert are available on the Web (rather than on your hard disk), you can clear the checkmark.

*Indent message on reply.* When set, the quoted original text is indented (**Figure 16.11**). Otherwise, it is printed flush left (**Figure 16.12**).

*Automatically wrap text at...* This option can only be set when *Encode text using* is None. It specifies the number of characters per line.

## Plain Text Settings

*MIME format: Encode text using.* When sending ordinary text, choose None. For a discussion of the other options, refer to "HTML Settings" earlier in this section.

*MIME format: Allow 8-bit characters in headers.* Refer to the discussion of this option in "HTML Settings" earlier in this section.

*Uuencode.* Uuencode is a common format for sending binary files, such as graphic images and programs, as ordinary text within the body of a message. (Leave unchecked unless a recipient requires this format.)

*Automatically wrap text at* xx *characters when sending.* Some mail systems limit the length of message lines. It is best to wrap lines at fewer than 80 characters.

*Indent the original text with > when replying or forwarding.* This is the standard way to quote a message when replying or forwarding a message (refer to **Figure 16.7**). If you prefer, you can pick a different character or no character to mark the quoted text.

## ✔ Tip

- If the *Include message in reply* option is not checked, the setting for *Indent the original text with...* is irrelevant.

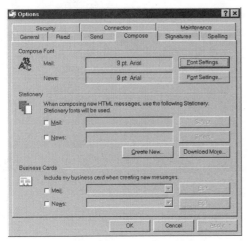

**Figure 16.13** Compose options.

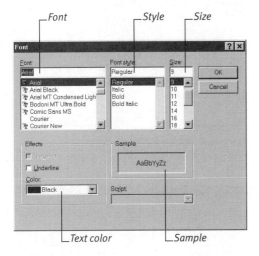

*Font* ─── *Style* ─── *Size*

*Text color* ─── *Sample*

**Figure 16.14** Choose a display font to use when composing new messages.

# Compose Options

Compose settings (**Figure 16.13**) affect the creation of new messages.

## Compose Font

The font and size listed (e.g., 9 pt. Arial) is what is displayed onscreen when you compose a message.

## To select a different font or size:

1. Click the Font Settings button.

   The Font dialog box appears (**Figure 16.14**).

2. Select a font, style, size, and color. A sample of the chosen settings is shown in the Sample box.

3. When you are satisfied with your choices, click OK.

## ✔ Tip

■ The font settings are only for displaying messages on *your* screen. When you create a Plain Text message, it doesn't matter which font or color you've chosen—the message is delivered as a one-font, uncolored text file.

   On the other hand, when you compose an HTML message, the default font is used to format the message (unless you override it by choosing other fonts, sizes, styles, and colors).

## Stationery

If you intend to send HTML-formatted messages, you can select a default stationery image to use. (If you pick a default stationery, Outlook Express assumes that you wish *all* new messages to be HTML-formatted. However, you can override this setting by choosing Format > Plain Text for any new message.)

COMPOSE OPTIONS

## To select a default stationery image:

1. Click the Mail checkbox in the Stationery section of the dialog box.

2. Click the Select button.

   The Select Stationery dialog box appears (**Figure 16.15**).

3. Select one of the provided stationery files. (If Show Preview is checked, the stationery is displayed in the Preview box.)

4. *Optional*: To create your own stationery file, click Create New.

   The Stationery Setup Wizard appears (**Figure 16.16**). Select a picture from your hard disk to serve as the stationery. You can also select a background color, if you wish.

5. Click OK to dismiss the Select Stationery dialog box.

## ✔ Tips

■ If you are comfortable working directly with HTML code, you can modify a stationery file by clicking the Edit button in the Select Stationery dialog box.

■ If you receive a message on impressive stationery, you can save the stationery by choosing File > Save as Stationery.

■ Occasionally, Microsoft releases additional stationery files. To check for new ones, click the Download More button.

## Business Cards

If you want to make your contact information readily available to the persons with whom you exchange messages, click the Mail checkbox in the Business Cards section of the Option dialog box. Then choose your contact card from the scrolling list (**Figure 16.17**). If you do not already have a business card, all you need to do is create a new contact for yourself in the Address Book (see Chapter 13).

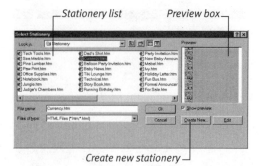

*Stationery list*  *Preview box*

*Create new stationery*

**Figure 16.15** You can select or create stationery in the Select Stationery dialog box.

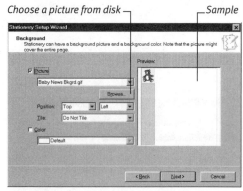

*Choose a picture from disk*  *Sample*

**Figure 16.16** Use the Stationery Setup Wizard to design a new stationery file.

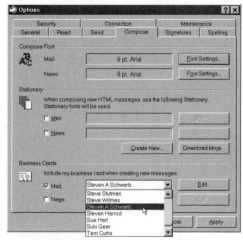

**Figure 16.17** Your Address Book contact card becomes your business card.

**Figure 16.18** Signatures options.

*Signature*

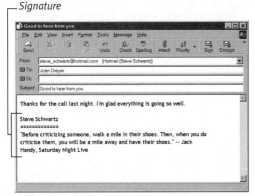

**Figure 16.19** A signature can be appended to outgoing messages.

# Signatures Options

A *signature* is an optional tag line used to conclude messages. A signature can convey a personal message, offer a bit of humor, or explain your philosophy of life. It is also common to cite a mailing address, phone numbers, or a URL for a personal Web page in a signature.

The Signature Options are shown in **Figure 16.18**. A sample message with a signature is shown in **Figure 16.19**. Outlook Express allows you to create multiple mail and news signatures. However, you can only have one default signature.

## Signature Settings

*Add signature to all outgoing messages.* When checked, your signature is automatically appended to all new messages.

*Don't add signature to Replies and Forwards.* This setting works in conjunction with the previous setting. When this setting is checked, your signature is only added to new messages. When it is not checked, the signature is added to *every* type of outgoing message.

## Signatures

This section of the dialog box lists the names you have assigned to signatures and shows which one (if any) is the default signature.

### To create a new signature:

1. Select Mail Signature or News Signature in the Signatures section of the dialog box or click New to create a signature with a different name.

**2.** Click the Text radio button in the Edit Signature section and type or paste the signature text into the box.

*or*

Click the File radio button and then click the Browse button to locate the text file on disk that you want to use as a signature.

**3.** *Optional*: If you want the current signature to be used by default, click the Set as Default button.

Because you may have multiple email accounts and news servers, you can optionally associate different signatures with each of them. Select a signature, click the Advanced button, and then enter a checkmark for each email account and/or news server you want to use the signature with (**Figure 16.20**).

## ✔ Tips

■ You can edit any signature by selecting its name in the Signatures box and then changing the typed text or the file with which it is associated.

■ Add a blank or dashed line at the beginning of a signature to separate it from the message text.

■ When *Add signature to all outgoing messages* is not checked, you can still include a signature in the current message by choosing Insert > Signature, followed by the specific one you want to use (**Figure 16.21**).

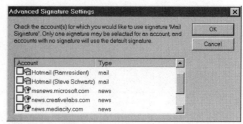

**Figure 16.20** Choose the email accounts and news servers with which you want to associate this signature.

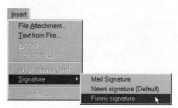

**Figure 16.21** Use the Insert > Signature command to choose a signature to add to the current message.

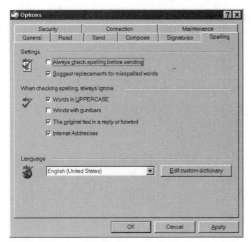

**Figure 16.22** Spelling options.

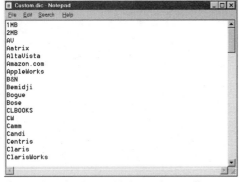

**Figure 16.23** The Custom Dictionary is an ordinary, alphabetized text file with one word per line.

*Click to add word to the custom dictionary*

*Unknown word*

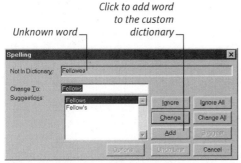

**Figure 16.24** If the flagged word is correct and you want its spelling to be remembered in future sessions, click the Add button.

# Spelling Options

You set spell-checking options in the Spelling section of the Options dialog box (**Figure 16.22**). If you don't have Microsoft Office or one of its components installed on your computer, the Spelling option won't be available.

## Settings

*Always check spelling before sending.* When checked, a spelling check is initiated automatically when you send a message. Otherwise, you will have to choose Tools > Spelling, click the Spelling button in the message toolbar, or press F7.

*Suggest replacements for misspelled words.* Unless you want to make all changes manually, leave this option checked.

*When checking spelling always ignore...* Add a checkmark for every condition that you want the spelling checker to ignore.

## Language

Select a language to use when conducting a spelling check. For U.S. users, there may be only one choice: English (United States).

You can create a custom dictionary that stores the spellings of words not found in the standard dictionary, such as proper names, industry-specific terms, and so on. Click the Edit Custom Dictionary button to edit the dictionary in Notepad (**Figure 16.23**).

## ✔ Tip

■ You can use the Edit Custom Dictionary feature to quickly make many changes to the custom dictionary: removing words that were added by mistake, correcting spellings, or adding a series of new terms. The other way to add words is to click the Add button when a correctly spelled word is questioned (**Figure 16.24**)

# Security Options

Security zones, digital IDs, and message encryption settings are managed in the Security section of the Options dialog box (**Figure 16.25**).

## Security Zones

The security zone setting determines whether active content can be run in received HTML messages. For most users, *Internet zone* is the best choice. It enables active content to run.

## ✔ Tip

- The security zone settings in IE5 (in the Security section of the Internet Options dialog box) are applied to Outlook Express.

## Secure Mail

If you want message recipients to be certain that mail originated from you, you can obtain a *digital ID* and use it to sign your messages. If both you and the recipient have digital IDs, you can also exchange *encrypted messages* that cannot be read by others.

To apply for a digital ID, click Get Digital ID. (Refer to "Sending secure messages" in Chapter 15 for instructions.) To digitally sign all outgoing messages, click this option at the bottom of the dialog box. To view all stored digital IDs, click the Digital IDs button.

Click *Encrypt contents and attachments for all outgoing messages* to automatically send encrypted messages. Normal messages will be sent to those without digital IDs.

## ✔ Tip

- If you do not set these options as defaults for outgoing messages, you can digitally sign selected messages by clicking the Sign button or by choosing Tools > Digitally Sign. You can encrypt selected messages by clicking the Encrypt button in the message toolbar or by choosing Tools > Encrypt.

**Figure 16.25** Security options.

Figure 16.26 Connection options.

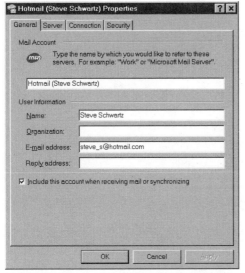

Figure 16.27 You can view or change dialup settings for a particular email account in its Properties dialog box.

# Connection Options

The Connection options (**Figure 16.26**) specify the manner in which you connect to your mail server to send and receive email.

*Ask before switching dial-up connections.* Check this box if you have multiple dial-up networking connections that you can use to access the Internet. If there are problems with the current connection, Outlook Express will offer to change to another connection.

*Hang up after sending and receiving.* Check this option to automatically close the connection after sending and receiving mail. Do not check it if you normally keep the connection open (enabling you to continue checking for mail and using other Internet programs, such as IE5).

Outlook Express uses the dial-up networking settings from Internet Explorer 5. If you want to examine or change these settings, click the Change button.

## ✔ Tips

- For help in configuring a dial-up networking connection, see "Connection Options" in Chapter 11.

- When you create an email account, you specify connection settings for the account. To view or change the settings for a particular account, choose Tools > Accounts, click the Mail tab at the top of the Internet Accounts dialog box, select an account, and click Properties (**Figure 16.27**).

# Maintenance Options

Most of the options in the Maintenance section (**Figure 16.28**) of the Options dialog box apply only to newsgroup messages. The following items are relevant to mail functions.

## Cleaning Up Messages

*Empty messages from the 'Deleted Items' folder on exit.* When this option is checked, all messages marked for deletion are removed from the Deleted Items folder when you quit the program. If you do not check this option, you must manually delete the messages in the Deleted Items folder.

*Purge deleted messages when leaving IMAP folders.* If one or more accounts uses an IMAP mail server, setting this option causes deleted messages to be immediately removed when you leave the IMAP folders.

## Troubleshooting

If you have difficulty sending or receiving messages from a particular mail server, enter a checkmark for each server type that you use. Outlook Express will create an activity log that may help you discover the source of the problem.

Enter a checkmark for *Mail* if your ISP uses a POP3 server; check *IMAP* if an IMAP server is used; and check *HTTP* if you are using Outlook Express to send and receive mail from a Hotmail account.

**Figure 16.28** Maintenance options.

## ✔ Tips

- The troubleshooting log files can be found in the following folder: `C:\WINDOWS\Application Data\ Microsoft\Outlook Express\`

- Each troubleshooting file has a .log extension. The HTTP log is named HTTPMail.log, for example. Because each log is an ordinary text file, it can be opened and viewed in Wordpad or any other text editor.

- If you create log files, you should periodically check their sizes and/or delete them. After less than a week, my HTTP log file had grown to over 1MB.

# NEWSGROUP ESSENTIALS

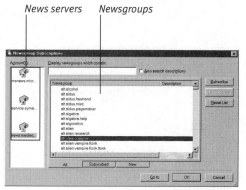

*News servers*   *Newsgroups*

**Figure 17.1** This ISP carries almost 40,000 newsgroups.

Usenet newsgroups are collections of messages from people who share an interest in a topic, such as cars, Amiga computers, hang gliding, or flower arranging. Most news servers carry messages (called *articles* or *posts*) from thousands of newsgroups (**Figure 17.1**).

Newsgroup topics can be extremely broad (such as `rec.crafts`), narrowly focused (such as `alt.games.duke3d`), or anywhere in between. You're free to select, read, and post to every newsgroup that interests you. On some of the most popular newsgroups, hundreds of new messages are generated every day.

As mentioned elsewhere in this book, Outlook Express serves as both your email program and newsgroup reader. You can use Outlook Express to read the posts of others, as well as compose your own posts and replies.

# About Newsgroups

Following are some important general facts about newsgroups.

## Subscribing to newsgroups

If you find a newsgroup that you want to read and participate in, you can *subscribe* to it. Subscribing is a news reader software feature, rather than a formal declaration of interest. When subscribing to a newsgroup, you are simply instructing your newsreader to keep track of new posts in that newsgroup.

## Article types

Although the majority of articles are text messages, they can contain *attachments* (**Figure 17.2**). There are graphics newsgroups, for example, filled with image files, such as photographs and drawings. When you post an article with an attachment, it is automatically encoded by Outlook Express prior to being sent to the news server.

## Article threads

Articles for a newsgroup are grouped in *threads*, a series of messages in response to a post. Every new article can conceivably be the start of a new thread (**Figure 17.3**).

For example, I might send a message named "My Collie." Responses with the title "Re: My Collie" would be part of the message thread. You can configure your newsreader to group articles by thread, so you can easily find all the articles on a topic that interests you.

## Posting to a newsgroup

Although you can gain a lot of information from reading articles, you can actively participate in newsgroups by posting new articles and responding to others. An article (**Figure 17.4**) can be sent to the newsgroup (where it can be viewed by everyone), it can be sent privately to the article's author (as e-mail), or both.

*Attachment Icon*

**Figure 17.2** Articles larger than a few hundred lines frequently contain binary encoded attachments, such as this clip art file.

*A message thread*

**Figure 17.3** To make it easy to follow a topic, articles can be grouped into threads. In Outlook Express, articles in a thread are marked with a plus sign.

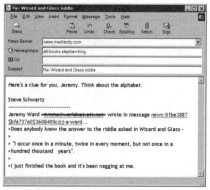

**Figure 17.4** Composing an article is the same as composing email. You can address it to one or more newsgroups or to an individual whose post you're responding to.

Microsoft newsgroups

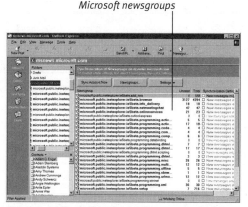

**Figure 17.5** Microsoft maintains its own news server.

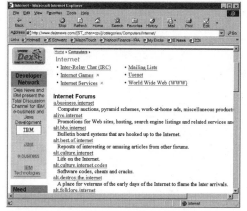

**Figure 17.6** At Deja News, you can select newsgroups and articles to view by simply clicking links.

**Figure 17.7** Don't post test articles to normal newsgroups. You can find many newsgroups that are intended for test posts, such as microsoft.test.

# About News Servers

A news server is responsible for tracking the newsgroups it carries. As new articles arrive from around the world, the news server makes them available to you and other users.

Many news servers track thousands of newsgroups. Some, on the other hand, handle only a small set of newsgroups. For example, Microsoft and Intel each has its own news server that covers company business and discussions about new hardware and software (**Figure 17.5**).

Your primary news server is usually the one provided by your ISP. In addition, there are many public news servers that you can use to gain access to newsgroups which are not carried by your ISP.

## ✔ Tips

■ If your news server doesn't carry the newsgroups you want (or you don't *have* a news server), visit Deja News (http://www.dejanews.com), as shown in **Figure 17.6**. Or you can use one of the Internet search sites to look for other public news servers, such as the list available from Yahoo! at:

http://dir.yahoo.com/Computers_and_Internet/Internet/Usenet/Public_Access_Usenet_Sites/

Note that all public news servers allow you to read articles, but not all let you post.

■ When learning about newsgroups, you may want to make some test posts. Look for a newsgroup with test in its name. Such newsgroups were specifically created for testing (**Figure 17.7**). To avoid warnings from the server when testing, include the word ignore somewhere in the Subject line of each test message.

# About Outlook Express

Outlook Express provides all the capabilities that most users will ever need to read and participate in newsgroups. Here are some of the major features and where you can learn about them:

- Subscribe to newsgroups on multiple news servers (Chapter 18).

- Search for newsgroups by keyword (Chapter 18).

- View all articles, only unread articles, or only responses to your posts (Chapter 18).

- Sort the articles by the contents of any column in the article list (Chapter 18).

- Encode and decode binary attachments (Chapter 18).

- Combine and decode multi-part posts (Chapter 18).

- Unscramble ROT13 articles (Chapter 18).

- Post replies to the newsgroup, the author, or both (Chapter 19).

- Cancel personal posts (Chapter 19).

- Work offline, marking articles for downloading from multiple newsgroups (Chapter 20).

- Customize the message display and tool-bar (Chapters 21 and 22).

- Automatically download all or a specified number of new article headers each time you connect (Chapter 21).

# READING AND MANAGING ARTICLES

If you're like most people, you'll spend much of your time in the news section of Outlook Express in an endless cycle of clicking headers, waiting for the message text to appear, and reading. However, there are a few preparatory steps you must take before launching into this routine.

# Adding a News Server

Outlook Express can accommodate multiple news servers and subscribed-to newsgroups. Although you can add more servers whenever you want, the first step is to specify at least *one* news server. Normally, this is done when you install Outlook Express.

## To add a news server:

1. Choose Tools > Accounts.

   The Internet Accounts dialog box appears (**Figure 18.1**).

2. Click the Add button and choose News from the pop-up menu that appears.

   The Internet Connection Wizard appears (**Figure 18.2**).

3. Enter a *display name* (the name you want others to see when you post messages). Click Next.

4. Enter the email address you want people to use when replying to you via email concerning your posts (**Figure 18.3**). Click Next.

5. Enter the name of the news server (**Figure 18.4**). News server names are generally in the form news.*domain.name*.

   If this news server requires you to log on (specifying an account name and password), click the check box and then fill in the Logon settings on the screen that follows (**Figure 18.5**). Click Next.

6. Click Finish.

   The Internet Accounts dialog box appears again and includes the news server you just added.

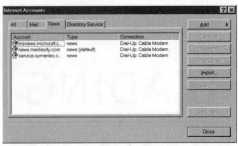

**Figure 18.1** News servers are added and listed in the Internet Accounts dialog box.

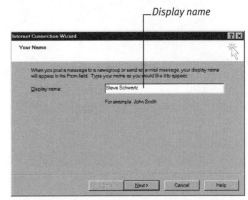

**Figure 18.2** The Internet Connection Wizard walks you through the process of adding a news server. Begin by entering the name you want your messages to display.

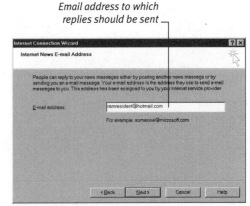

**Figure 18.3** Enter the email address to which responses to your articles should be mailed.

_News server name_

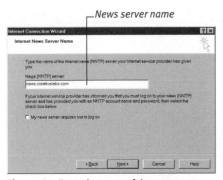

**Figure 18.4** Enter the name of the server.

_Account name_   _Logon password_

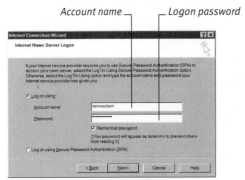

**Figure 18.5** If you are required to log onto the news server with a user name and password, enter them in this dialog box.

**Figure 18.6** Before you can subscribe to newsgroups on this server, you must download the newsgroup list. Click Yes.

_Newsgroups available from_
_News servers_   _the selected news server_

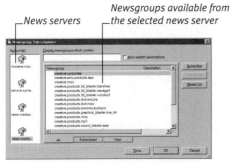

**Figure 18.7** Choose newsgroups to which you want to subscribe.

**7.** If you would like to view or change any of the settings for the news server (such as the displayed connection method), select the news server in the list and click Properties. Otherwise, click the Close button or close box to dismiss the dialog box.

A prompt appears (**Figure 18.6**), asking if you'd like to download the list of newsgroups available from this news server.

**8.** Click Yes.

The Newsgroup Subscriptions dialog box appears (**Figure 18.7**).

**9.** You can subscribe to newsgroups now, if you want (see the section "Subscribing to Newsgroups" later in this chapter). When you're done, click OK.

## ✔ Tips

- When adding a news server, you don't need to use your real name or primary email address. Companies that specialize in mass mailings frequently grab email addresses from newsgroup posts, making your designated email account a prime candidate for junk email. It is often preferable to use a fake email address or a secondary one, such as those you can create for free at services such as Hotmail.com.

- Most public news servers don't require you to supply a user name and password when logging on. Unless you're told otherwise (as may be the case with your ISP's news server), assume they aren't required.

**ADDING A NEWS SERVER**

# Subscribing to Newsgroups

You may want to follow many newsgroups. But to read them regularly, you have to *subscribe* to them.

## To subscribe to a newsgroup:

**1.** Click the Newsgroups button in the toolbar, or choose Tools > Newsgroups.

The Newsgroup Subscriptions dialog box appears (refer to **Figure 18.7**).

**2.** Select a news server from the list on the left. (Only servers that you have added will appear in the list.)

**3.** Click the All tab.

All newsgroups available on the selected server are displayed in an alphabetical list.

**4.** Select a newsgroup that interests you and click Subscribe.

An icon is added to the left of the newsgroup name indicating that you now subscribe to this group.

**5.** To unsubscribe from a newsgroup, select any newsgroup marked with the subscribed icon and click Unsubscribe.

**6.** When you're done, click OK.

## ✔ Tips

- Double-clicking a newsgroup name in the Newsgroup Subscriptions dialog box toggles its status between subscribed and unsubscribed.

- To quickly finding newsgroups of interest, type a keyword (such as auto or explorer) in the box at the top of the Newsgroup Subscriptions dialog box. All newsgroup names that contain the keyword will be displayed.

_Download newsgroup descriptions_

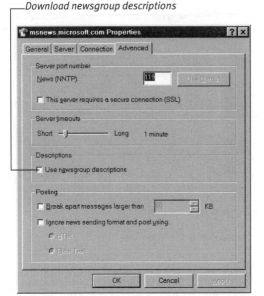

**Figure 18.8** To display descriptions for newsgroups on this news server, click the _Use newsgroup descriptions_ checkbox.

- When selecting and managing newsgroups, you can restrict the list to only subscribed groups (click the Subscribed tab) or recently added newsgroups (click the New tab). Note that after the new groups have been viewed, they are merged with the All list.

- You can also download newsgroup _descriptions_ if you set that option for a news server (**Figure 18.8**). If you set the option _after_ adding the news server, click the Reset button in the Newsgroup Subscriptions dialog box to download a fresh list of newsgroups and descriptions. (Note that many newsgroups have no descriptions.)

- After examining a newsgroup, you may decide you no longer want to follow it. Its contents may not suit your needs or there may be too few messages, for example. You can quickly unsubscribe from a newsgroup by right-clicking its name in the Folders pane and choosing Unsubscribe.

- You can view the messages of any newsgroup _without_ subscribing to it. Click the Newsgroups button in the toolbar or choose the Tools > Newsgroups command. Select a newsgroup, and click the Go to button. When you exit from the newsgroup, you will be asked if you want to subscribe.

- To make it easy to find a favorite newsgroup, right-click its name in the Folders pane and choose _Add to Outlook Bar_. The newsgroup icon appears in the Outlook bar. You can change its position by clicking and dragging up or down. If you later want to remove the icon, right-click the icon and choose _Remove from Outlook Bar_.

# Reading Articles

After you've chosen one or more newsgroups, you're ready to start reading articles. (Note that the terms *article*, *message*, and *post* are all used to mean newsgroup messages.)

## To read articles in a newsgroup:

1. Select a newsgroup in the Folders pane of the main window. Or choose a news server from the Folders list and double-click a newsgroup in the pane to the right (**Figure 18.9**).

   The list of article headers is displayed (**Figure 18.10**).

2. If you are already connected to the Internet, the article list will update to reflect the new articles. If you are not connected or are working offline, connect as you normally do or choose File > Work Offline (to remove the checkmark), respectively.

3. Click to select an article that interests you. The text of the article is downloaded to the cache, the header is marked with a new icon, and the article appears in the preview pane.

   After an article has been read, the boldface is removed from the header and the icon turns white.

To read other articles in the current newsgroup, repeat Step 3. To read articles in other newsgroups, start again from Step 1.

## ✔ Tips

- You can continue clicking and reading articles as others download.

- To view any article in a separate window (**Figure 18.11**), double-click its header.

- If additional articles are available on the server for the current newsgroup, you can choose Tools > Get Next 300 Headers to retrieve them.

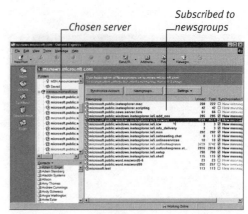

*Chosen server*     *Subscribed to newsgroups*

**Figure 18.9** To see a list of all newsgroups you've subscribed to on a given news server, select the news server in the Folders list.

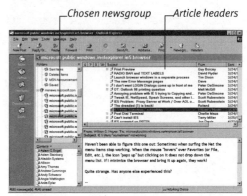

*Chosen newsgroup*     *Article headers*

**Figure 18.10** Article headers are displayed in the message list.

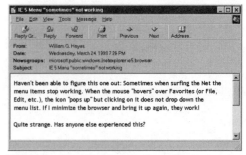

**Figure 18.11** If you find it easier to read that way, you can open any article in its own window.

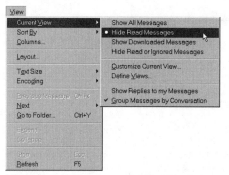

**Figure 18.12** Choose a command from the View > Current View submenu to display only the messages that you want to see.

**Figure 18.13** You can sort the message list by choosing a menu command or by clicking column headers.

**Figure 18.14** If you are viewing only unread articles, you can manually mark the ones that don't interest you as already read.

# Article Selection Tips

There are several techniques and procedures that you can use to help select and read articles:

◆ Don't use the up- and down-arrow keys to scroll through the article list. Each article that you highlight will be downloaded. Instead, choose articles with the mouse.

◆ Choose View > Current View > Hide Read Messages (**Figure 18.12**) to limit the list to unread articles.

◆ To see all current articles (including ones you've read), choose View > Current View > Show All Messages.

◆ Some conversations (called *threads* in other programs) will be of no interest to you. To ignore a conversation, select its main header and choose Message > Ignore Conversation. Then to eliminate these conversations from the message list, choose View > Current View > Hide Read or Ignored Messages.

◆ You can also lessen the clutter in the article list by choosing Hide Read Messages, and then periodically choosing View > Refresh. Articles read during the current session will be removed from the list.

◆ If you have recently posted an article, you can view all replies to it by choosing View > Current View > Show Replies to my Messages.

◆ You can sort the article list by any column. Click a column heading to sort by that column. Click it again to toggle between an ascending and a descending sort. You can also choose sort commands from the View > Sort By submenu (**Figure 18.13**).

◆ If the article list contains unread and read articles, you can move to the next unread article in the list by choosing View > Next > Next Unread Message or Next Unread Conversation.

- To move to the next or previous article (regardless of whether it has been read), choose View > Next > Next Message or View > Previous Message.

- To make it easy to follow article threads, select View > Current View > Group Messages by Conversation. Otherwise, the articles will be scattered throughout the list, according to the current sort order.

- To expand or collapse a conversation, click the + or - symbol to the left of the article header. You can automatically expand all conversations by setting *Automatically expand grouped messages* in the Read section of the Options dialog box.

- It's easier to spot important articles when you keep the article list to a reasonable size. Eliminate articles that don't interest you by selecting them and choosing Edit > Mark As Read (**Figure 18.14**) or Edit > Mark Conversation as Read.

- You can also mark messages as read by right-clicking them (**Figure 18.15**) or using keyboard shortcuts: Mark as Read ([Ctrl]+[Q]) and Mark Conversation as Read ([Ctrl]+[T]).

- To mark *all* messages in a newsgroup as read, choose Edit > Catch Up.

- To view a previously read article, choose View > Current View > Show All Messages, select the article, and choose Edit > Mark as Unread. When you switch back to Hide Read Messages view, the article will be visible.

- To ignore all messages from a person, select any message from him/her and choose Message > Block Sender.

- You can use the Find command to search for messages. Open a newsgroup, and choose Edit > Find > Message (**Figure 18.16**) or Edit > Find Message in this Folder (**Figure 18.17**).

**Figure 18.15** If you can't remember the keyboard shortcuts for marking messages as read, you can choose commands from this popup menu.

Criteria     Matches     Newsgroup to search

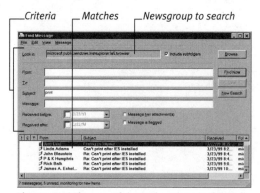

**Figure 18.16** The powerful search options in the Find Message dialog box make it easy to find a specific article or all articles that mention a given topic. Double-click any match to view the article.

Set additional options and criteria

Keyword

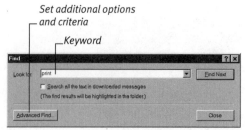

**Figure 18.17** Choose Edit > Find Message in this Folder to search article headers for a keyword. Press [F3] to search for additional matches.

Description of view    View conditions    View name

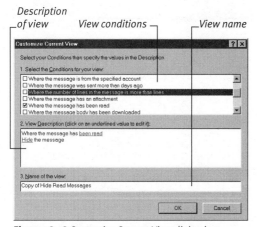

**Figure 18.18** Customize Current View dialog box.

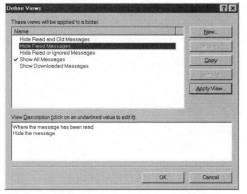

**Figure 18.19** You can create and manage custom views in the Define Views dialog box.

**Figure 18.20** Click any underlined text string to alter its setting.

# Creating Custom Views

Outlook Express 5 offers many useful View settings, but you can also create and manage *custom* views.

## To create a custom view:

1. To base the view on an existing view, select it from the View > Current View submenu, and then choose View > Current View > Customize Current View. The Customize Current View dialog box appears (**Figure 18.18**).

   To base the view on an existing view, choose View > Current View > Define Views. The Define Views dialog box appears (**Figure 18.19**). Select a view and click Copy. Then select the copy and click Modify. The Edit View dialog box appears.

   To create a view from scratch, choose View > Current View > Define Views. The Define Views dialog box appears. Click New. The New View dialog box appears.

   Note that Customize Current View, Edit View, and New View dialog boxes are identical (except for their titles).

2. Select conditions in section 1 of the dialog box by adding and removing checkmarks.

   The selected conditions appear in section 2 of the dialog box.

3. Modify the conditions as necessary by clicking any of the underlined text strings in section 2 of the dialog box. An appropriate dialog box appears (**Figure 18.20**).

4. Enter a new name for the view in section 3 of the dialog box.

5. Click OK to accept the new view definition.

   The new view is added to the View > Current View submenu and becomes the current view.

## To manage existing views:

1. Choose View > Current View > Define Views.

   The Define Views dialog box appears (refer to **Figure 18.19**).

2. You can do any of the following:

   ◆ To design a new view from scratch, click New.

   ◆ To change a custom view's name or criteria, select the view and click Modify.

   ◆ To delete a custom view, select the view and click Remove.

   ◆ To apply a view to the current news-group folder or all folders, select the view and click Apply View.

   ◆ To create a new view based on another view, select the view and click Copy.

3. Click OK to dismiss the dialog box, accepting all changes.

## ✔ Tip

■ You cannot modify or delete the four standard views (Show All Messages, Hide Read Messages, Show Downloaded Messages, and Hide Read or Ignored Messages). To base a new view on one of these views, you must copy the view. There are two ways to accomplish this:

   ◆ Switch to the standard view you want to modify by choosing its name from the View > Current View submenu. Then choose View > Current View > Customize Current View. A copy is automatically created.

   ◆ Choose View > Current View > Define Views, select a standard view, and click the Copy button.

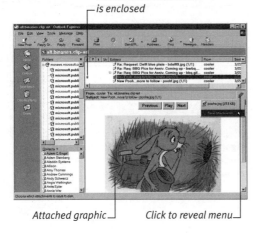

*Indicates an attachment
— is enclosed*

*Attached graphic* ⌐     *Click to reveal menu* ⌐

**Figure 18.21** You can view and save most graphic attachments without changing programs.

# Attachments and Encoded Articles

Some articles contain more than a text message. Each requires a procedure to decode or use the non-text material, as explained below.

## Article attachments

Like email messages, articles can contain binary attachments, such as graphic files, word processing documents, or computer programs. For assistance in opening an attachment, see "Working with Attachments" in Chapter 15.

Note that some types of attachments, such as JPEG and GIF graphic files can be viewed without leaving Outlook Express (**Figure 18.21**). If there are multiple graphic attachments, click the Next and Previous buttons above the image.

To save such a graphic file, click the paperclip symbol, choose Save Attachments, and select a location on disk to store the file. (You can also save a graphic attachment by right-clicking the image and choosing Save Picture As.)

## Unscrambling ROT13 articles

To make an article difficult to decipher, authors occasionally scramble the text using a simple protocol called ROT13. Letters in the message are shifted by 13 characters. To decode the scrambled text, select the article in the article list and choose Message > Unscramble (ROT13).

## Multi-part articles

Because of the size limits imposed on articles by many servers, you'll sometimes encounter an article than has been split into two or more parts. This is most common when sending large graphics, programs, movies, and .ZIP files. The article parts are usually listed as (1/2) and (2/2), for example.

## To combine a multi-part article:

1. Download all of the article parts.

2. Select the article parts in the article list by Ctrl-clicking.

3. Choose Message > Combine and Decode. The Order for decoding dialog box appears (**Figure 18.22**).

4. Arrange the parts in the correct order, lowest to highest. (You can move parts by dragging them or by clicking the Move Up and Move Down buttons.)

5. Click OK.

   The parts are combined and decoded. The article opens in a new window. The non-text material is displayed as an attachment at the bottom of the window. (If the file is a graphic, the image itself is displayed.) For help opening the attachment, refer to "Working with Attachments" in Chapter 15.

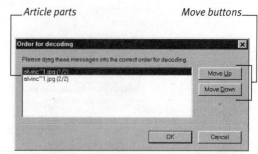

Figure 18.22 Use the Order for decoding dialog box to specify the order in which the article parts are to be arranged.

## ✔ Tips

- A downloaded article that contains one or more attachments has a paper clip symbol to the left of its header in the message list.

- ROT13 messages are rare. While ROT13 may fool Internet novices, it is no substitute for encryption. If you're interested in real security, buy an encryption program or use the encryption features of Outlook Express (see Chapters 14–15).

- There are several ways to tell if an article contains an attachment. First, look for a file name in the article header, such as boat.jpg or turkey.gif. Second, check the file size. Larger files frequently contain an attachment. To make it easy to spot such files, you can sort by the Size column or rearrange the display, making Size the first column.

ATTACHMENTS AND ENCODED ARTICLES

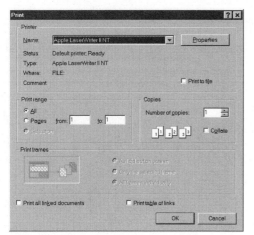

**Figure 18.23** Prior to printing, you can set print options in the Print dialog box.

*Filename* — *Click to select a file type*

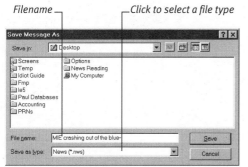

**Figure 18.24** Articles can be saved in Outlook Express (.nws) or text (.txt) format.

# Managing Articles

After downloading articles and reading them, there are several actions you can take to manage the new information.

## Printing articles

You can print any article that you've downloaded. Select the article in the article list or open it in its own window, and choose File > Print (or press Ctrl+P). Set options in the Print dialog box (**Figure 18.23**), and click OK.

## Saving articles

You can save important articles to disk as News (.nws) or Text (.txt) files. Select the article in the message list or open it in its own window, choose File > Save As, select a location and file type (**Figure 18.24**), and click Save. (News files can be opened in Outlook Express; Text files can be opened in any text editor or word processing program.)

Another way to save articles is to drag them to a folder in the Folders pane or the Outlook bar. You can also copy an article to a folder by highlighting the article header and choosing Edit > Copy to Folder. (You can also choose this command by right-clicking any message header.)

## Marking articles

You've probably noticed that four tiny columns precede headers in the message list. From left to right, the columns are:

◆ *Paper Clip.* If a paper clip is shown, the article contains one or more attachments, such as a graphic or text file.

◆ *Flag.* If a flag appears, the article has been manually marked by you or by applying a message rule.

◆ *Download.* If a down-arrow appears, the article has been marked for downloading (for offline reading).

◆ *Watch.* If a pair of glasses appears, the conversation of which this article is a part has been manually marked by you or by applying a message rule. It signifies that you want to follow this conversation. Conversely, a ⊘ symbol in this column indicates that you want to ignore the conversation.

You can click in the Flag or Watch column of any article to mark it with a flag, watch, or ignore symbol. Use this technique to mark articles and conversations—making them easier to find or to serve as a reminder to read them later. To quickly locate all such marked articles, click the flag or watch column header to sort by that column (**Figure 18.25**).

To cycle through the available symbols for a Flag or Watch column, click repeatedly. For the Watch column, the first click sets the watch symbol, a second click sets the ignore symbol, and a third click clears the symbol. For the Flag column, the first click sets the flag symbol and the second click removes it.

## Removing articles

Although you can't delete messages from the article list, you can request that an article you personally posted to a newsgroup be removed from news servers around the world. To remove an article, select the article in the message list, and choose Message > Cancel Message.

**Figure 18.25** Important articles and conversations can be marked with the flag and/or watch symbols.

Specify conditions —                    — Set actions

Rule name —                    — Text description of the rule

**Figure 18.26** You create message rules in the New News Rule dialog box.

— Automatically compact                    Compact now —

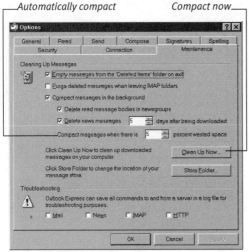

**Figure 18.27** To set cache management options, go to the Maintenance section of the Options dialog box.

# Setting message rules

You can automate the manner in which newly downloaded messages are handled by creating *message rules*.

## To create a message rule:

1. Choose Tools > Message Rules > News. The New News Rules dialog box appears (**Figure 18.26**).

2. Set criteria in section 1 of the dialog box.

3. In section 2, specify one or more actions that should be taken when the criteria in section 1 are met for a message.

4. As necessary, modify the rule description in section 3 by clicking the blue underlined text strings.

5. In section 4, name the rule.

6. Click OK to save the rule.

# Cleaning up the cache

There are two ways to free up disk space that Outlook Express uses to store article headers and bodies:

◆ *Save space automatically*. As shown in the Maintenance section of the Options dialog box (**Figure 18.27**), Outlook Express can automatically compact the caches whenever a specified percentage of disk space is wasted.

◆ *Save space manually*. Click Clean Up Now in the Maintenance section of the Options dialog box. The Local File Clean Up dialog box appears, enabling you to compact the caches, delete article bodies, or delete headers and bodies. See Chapter 21 for details.

## ✔ Tips

■ By default, message rules only apply to new articles. To apply a rule to articles that you've already downloaded, choose Tools > Message Rules > News, select the rule, click Apply Now (**Figure 18.28**), choose the newsgroup you wish to apply it to (by clicking the Browse button), and click Apply Now (**Figure 18.29**).

■ You can quickly create a message rule that applies to the author of an article by selecting the article in the message list and then choosing Message > Create Rule from Message. Then pick an action and name the rule. The new rule will be applied to any new articles posted by that individual.

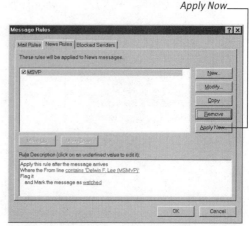

Apply Now

**Figure 18.28** Click Apply Now to apply this rule to previously downloaded message headers.

Selected newsgroup

Click to choose a newsgroup

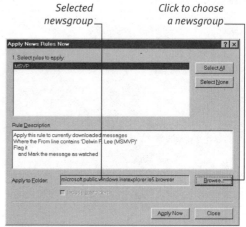

**Figure 18.29** Click the Browse button to pick a newsgroup to which the rule will be applied, and then click Apply Now.

# POSTING TO NEWSGROUPS

Header

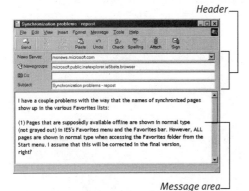

Message area

**Figure 19.1** Compose a new article for a news-group in a normal message window.

If you want to *participate* in a newsgroup (rather than only reading other people's articles), you can post new articles or reply to articles written by others.

All articles are composed in an Outlook Express message window (**Figure 19.1**). You can post any of the following types of articles:

◆ *A new article to a newsgroup*. The article is listed in the article list for the news-group and can be read by anyone.

◆ *A reply to an existing article*. The article becomes part of a thread.

◆ *A direct reply to an individual, sent as e-mail*. Only the author of the original arti-cle sees the reply, not the newsgroup.

In addition, you can forward any article that you read in a newsgroup as an e-mail message.

## ✔ Tips

■ When posting articles, send them only to appropriate newsgroups. An article about gardening problems will not be well received in a computing newsgroup. Read a group for awhile before posting to it.

■ You can add attachments to an article by clicking the Attach button in the toolbar or by choosing Insert > File Attachment.

# Composing and Posting Articles

The process of composing and posting articles varies somewhat, depending on whether you are sending a new message, replying to an existing article, replying directly to the author of an article, or forwarding an article as e-mail.

## To post a new article:

1. Click the New Post button, choose File > New > News Message, choose Message > New Message, press Ctrl+N, or click *Create a new News message* in the main Outlook Express window (**Figure 19.2**).

   A New Message window appears (refer to **Figure 19.1**).

   *or*

   To add a decorative background to your article, click the down arrow beside the New Post button and choose a stationery format (**Figure 19.3**).

   *or*

   To send a Web page as an article, click the down arrow beside the New Post button, choose Web Page, and type or paste the URL into the Send Web Page dialog box.

2. Fill in the necessary lines in the message header. See "Addressing the Article," later in this chapter.

3. Compose the article.

4. Click the Send button, choose File > Send Message (**Figure 19.4**), or press Alt+S.

Click to create an article

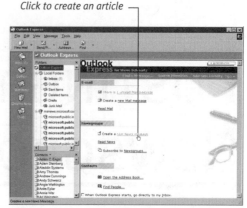

**Figure 19.2** You can create a new article from the Outlook Express main window.

**Figure 19.3** If you like, you can choose a decorative stationary background for your message.

**Figure 19.4** Choose File › Send Message to post your article to the newsgroup(s).

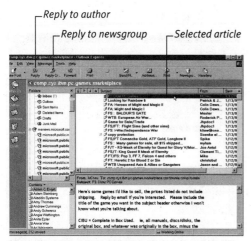

*Reply to author*

*Reply to newsgroup*       *Selected article*

**Figure 19.5** To reply to an article, select it and click the Reply to newsgroup button.

## To post a reply to a newsgroup:

**1.** Select an article in the message list to which you want to reply (**Figure 19.5**) or open the article in its own window.

**2.** Click Reply Group, choose Message > Reply to Group, or press Ctrl+G.

**3.** Fill in the necessary lines in the header.

**4.** Compose the article.

**5.** Click the Send button, choose File > Send Message, or press Alt+S.

## To reply directly to an individual:

**1.** Select an article in the message list to which you want to reply or open an article in its own window.

**2.** Click Reply in the toolbar, choose Message > Reply to Sender, or press Ctrl+R.

**3.** Fill in the necessary lines in the header. Compose the article.

**4.** Click the Send button, choose File > Send Message, or press Alt+S.

## To forward an article as e-mail:

1. In the message list, select the article that you want to forward or open the article in its own window.

2. Click the Forward button in the toolbar, choose Message > Forward, or press Ctrl+F.

3. Fill in the necessary lines in the header.

4. Add any necessary comments to the forwarded article.

5. Click the Send button, choose File > Send Message, or press Alt+S.

## ✔ Tips

■ To add your signature to an article, choose Insert > Signature.

■ To create or edit your signature(s), choose Tools > Options and click the Signatures tab in the Options dialog box (**Figure 19.6**). You can specify that a particular signature should automatically be added to each outgoing message by checking *Add signature to all outgoing messages*. Click the Advanced button to link a particular signature to specific news servers (**Figure 19.7**).

■ You can also forward an article as an email attachment. Select the article in the message list and choose Message > Forward as Attachment.

*Add a signature to all messages*

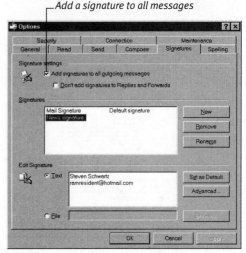

**Figure 19.6** Setting signature options.

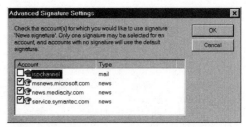

**Figure 19.7** The Advanced Signature Settings dialog box enables you to set a different default signature for e-mail and news servers.

### Plain Versus Formatted Text

Like e-mail messages, newsgroup articles can be created as ordinary text or formatted text. Outlook Express users can view either type of article. Older newsreaders, on the other hand, may limit the user to viewing articles formatted only as plain text.

By default, new messages are formatted according to the text specifications set in the Send section of the Options dialog box. To select a different formatting option for the current message, choose Format > Plain Text or Format > Rich Text (HTML).

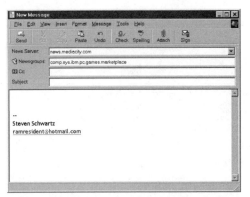

**Figure 19.8** A new message with standard header lines.

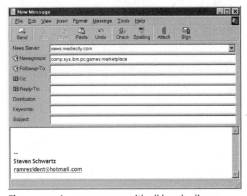

**Figure 19.9** A new message with all header lines.

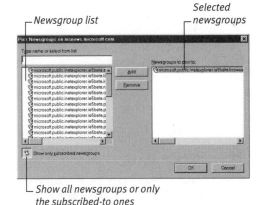

*Newsgroup list*

*Selected newsgroups*

*Show all newsgroups or only the subscribed-to ones*

**Figure 19.10** Select one or more newsgroups to which the message will be posted.

# Addressing the Article

When readying an article for posting, you must fill in some lines in the message header. The number of lines shown depends on whether All Headers is chosen in the View menu of the message window (**Figures 19.8 and 19.9**). There are also minor differences between posting or replying to a group, and replying to or forwarding an article to an individual.

The lines of the message header are as follows:

◆ *News Server* This is the news server to which the article will be posted. It is automatically filled in for you, based on the newsgroup you are currently viewing. If you are not viewing a newsgroup, your default news server is used.

◆ *Newsgroups* Appears when posting a new article or a reply to a newsgroup. Enter the names of the newsgroup(s) to whom the article will be sent, separated by commas. If you are currently viewing a newsgroup, its name is automatically entered. You can choose other newsgroups by clicking on the word *Newsgroups* in the message header (**Figure 19.10**).

◆ *To* Appears when replying to or forwarding an article to an individual. Enter the names of the individuals to whom the article will be sent, separated by semicolons. You can choose names from your address book by clicking the word *To* in the message header.

◆ *Followup-To* An entry in this line specifies the newsgroup to which follow-up articles to your article should be posted. Normally, this line contains the name of the original newsgroup, but it can be used to redirect the discussion to another newsgroup.

◆ *Cc* Enter the names of individuals to whom a copy of the article will be sent. You can pick names from your address book by clicking the word *Cc* in the message header.

◆ *Bcc* Appears when replying to an individual or forwarding an article. Enter the names of individuals to whom a copy of the article will be sent. Bcc stands for *blind carbon copy*; other recipients will not see the names of the individuals to whom you've sent a blind carbon copy. You can pick names from your address book by clicking the word *Bcc* in the message header.

◆ *Reply-To* If you want replies sent to a different e-mail address than your usual one, enter the address here. To select an address from your address book, click the word *Reply-To* in the message header.

◆ *Distribution* Any entry found in this line is used to restrict the areas of the country or world to which the article is made available. You might enter Dallas, for example, to restrict distribution to the Dallas area.

◆ *Keywords* Some newsreaders are able to sort or find articles based on keywords that have been assigned by the author. Commas must separate keywords.

◆ *Subject* Enter a descriptive title for the article.

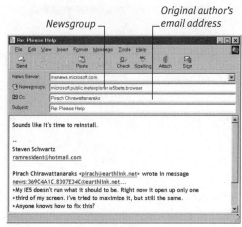

**Figure 19.11** When replying to "All," the message is sent to the newsgroup, and a copy is emailed to the message's author.

## ✔ Tips

- When replying to or forwarding an article, some header lines will be filled in for you.

- To make sure that an author sees your reply, choose Message > Reply to All or press Ctrl+Shift+R (**Figure 19.11**). Choosing this command addresses the message to the current newsgroup and also emails a copy of it to the original author.

- You *can* post an article to several newsgroups, although usually it's not a good idea, and it only works if they are on the same news server. To post to newsgroups on different servers, you must send a copy of the article to each news server.

**ADDRESSING THE ARTICLE**

# Canceling an Article

Normally, when you post an article, it is available to newsgroup subscribers throughout the world until deleted from their news server. If, however, you discover an error in the article or no longer seek replies to it, you can cancel the article—removing it from all news servers entirely.

To cancel an article that you posted to a newsgroup, select it in the message list and choose Message > Cancel Message (**Figure 19.12**).

**Figure 19.12** You can cancel any of your posts to a newsgroup.

# WORKING OFFLINE

In addition to working interactively with Outlook Express (reading and replying to news articles while online), you can also do much of your newsgroup work offline.

# Reading News Offline

The process is straightforward.

## To read news offline:

1. While online, select a news server and its newsgroups that interest you.

2. Instruct Outlook Express to synchronize those newsgroups by downloading new headers. Then disconnect from the Internet by choosing File > Work Offline. When prompted, click Yes (**Figure 20.1**).

3. Examine the new headers (while offline), and mark the articles that you want to read.

4. Instruct Outlook Express to connect again, download the articles to your hard disk, and disconnect again.

5. Read the articles at your leisure.

If you pay for Internet access based on connect time, this process keeps online time to a minimum. Rather than wasting billable minutes reading messages online, connect time is devoted to downloading headers and articles.

## ✔ Tip

■ If your goal is to minimize online time, be sure to check the status bar. It should read *Working Offline* (**Figure 20.2**) while you are picking newsgroups to update and marking messages. If not, choose File > Work Offline.

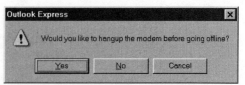

**Figure 20.1** You can work offline with or without disconnecting the modem. If you're interested in saving connect charges, choose Yes.

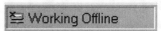

**Figure 20.2** Check the status bar at the bottom of the Outlook Express window to determine if you are on- or offline.

Selected news server — Newsgroups to which you're subscribed —

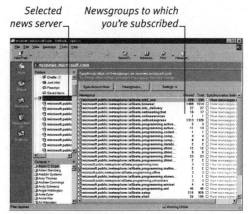

**Figure 20.3** To view or alter the synchronization settings for individual newsgroups, select a news server in the Folders pane.

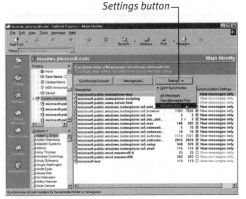

Settings button

**Figure 20.4** Click the Settings button to choose a sync setting for the currently selected newsgroup(s).

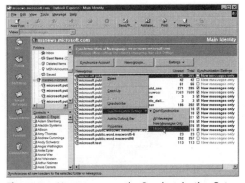

**Figure 20.5** You can access the Synchronization Settings menu by right-clicking any newsgroup name.

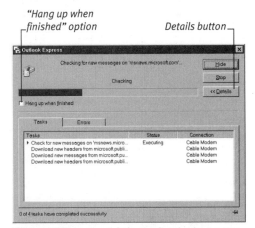

"Hang up when finished" option

Details button

**Figure 20.6** You can watch the synchronization progress by keeping this dialog box open. Click Details to see the specifics of what is occurring.

# Downloading New Headers

Unless you routinely read all articles posted to a given newsgroup, the first step in offline work is to download the new article headers. That way, your list of available articles will match that of your news server. This is referred to as *synchronizing* a newsgroup.

## To download new article headers:

1. Choose a news server in the Folders pane.

   The list of subscribed newsgroups for that news server appears in the right side of the window (**Figure 20.3**).

2. Select each newsgroup you want to synchronize, click the Settings button (**Figure 20.4**), and choose New Headers Only. Alternatively, you can right-click the newsgroup and choose the same command from the pop-up menu (**Figure 20.5**).

   Be sure that each selected newsgroup has a checkmark in the Synchronization Settings column. Only checked newsgroups will be synchronized.

3. To download the new headers from the selected newsgroups on the chosen news server, click Synchronization account. Or to download headers from all selected newsgroups on all news servers, choose Tools > Synchronize All.

   A dialog box appears (**Figure 20.6**), and the newsgroups are synchronized.

4. Unless you want to remain online, click the option to *Hang up when finished.*

## ✔ Tip

- You can simultaneously set synchronization options for multiple newsgroups by Shift- or Ctrl-clicking them, and then choosing an option.

# Downloading Articles

You can use the offline capabilities of Outlook Express to download:

◆ All new articles from selected newsgroups (on one or all news servers).

◆ Specific articles from selected newsgroups.

The procedure for downloading all new articles from one or more newsgroups is done in the same manner as downloading new headers. In Step 2 of "To download new article headers:" specify New Messages Only for each newsgroup of interest. Or if you want to be sure that you haven't missed any older articles, choose All Messages instead.

Unless you prefer to read every article in a newsgroup, you can download the ones that interest you—just as you do when you are working online. Instead of clicking and reading, however, you mark the messages you want and then send the list to the news server.

## To download selected articles:

1. Choose File > Work Offline (if you are currently online).

2. Select a subscribed newsgroup from the list in the Folders pane (**Figure 20.7**). The message list for the newsgroup appears in the right side of the window.

3. Select a message to download, and choose Tools > Mark for Offline > Download Message Later. You can also choose this command by right-clicking the message (**Figure 20.8**).

   Note that you can simultaneously mark multiple messages by Shift- or Ctrl-clicking them and choosing Download Message Later.

Selected newsgroup | Text of currently selected message | Message list

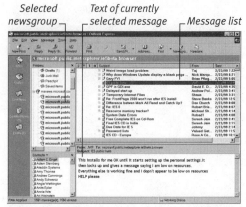

**Figure 20.7** Select a newsgroup whose messages you want to mark for later downloading.

**Figure 20.8** Although you can mark messages for downloading by choosing a command from the Tools menu, the quicker way is to right-click the message and choose a command from the pop-up menu.

Marked for
downloading    Not downloaded

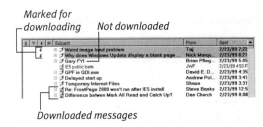

Downloaded messages

**Figure 20.9** A text document icon indicates a message that is already downloaded. Messages that have not been downloaded are shown as blank pieces of paper. A curved down arrow indicates a message marked for later downloading.

**4.** To mark a message *conversation* for downloading (messages preceded by a + sign), select the outermost message and choose Tools > Mark for Offline > Download Conversation Later.

**5.** To download all visible messages in the current newsgroup, choose Tools > Mark for Offline > Download All Messages Later.

**6.** If you change your mind about downloading some of the marked articles, select them again and choose Tools > Mark for Offline > Do Not Download Message.

**7.** Repeat Steps 2 through 6 for additional newsgroups, as desired.

**8.** When you're ready to retrieve the selected articles, choose File > Work Offline (to remove its checkmark and return to online mode), and choose Tools > Synchronize All.

Retrieved articles are indicated in the message list by the icon shown in Figure **20.9**.

## ✔ Tips

- You can mix synchronization settings as needed. For instance, if you routinely read all messages from a few newsgroups, set those newsgroups for New Messages Only or All Messages, leaving the others initially set for Headers Only.

- You can select contiguous groups of articles by Shift-clicking the first and last article.

- You can quickly assign the same synchronization setting to all newsgroups on a server. Select the server in the Folders pane, select any newsgroup, press Ctrl+A (to select *all* newsgroups), and then choose a synchronization setting.

- You can synchronize a single newsgroup by opening that newsgroup and choosing Tools > Synchronize Newsgroup.

# Composing and Posting Messages Offline

While offline, you can also create new messages for newsgroups and write replies to messages (see Chapter 19). Rather than send them immediately, Outlook Express holds them in your Outbox until the next connection with the news server is made.

## To post articles:

1. Create the message while offline.

2. Choose File > Send Message ([Alt]+[S]), choose File > Send Later, or click the Send button.

   The message is stored in your Outbox.

3. When you are ready to connect to your server, choose Tools > Send and Receive > Send and Receive All, choose Tools > Send and Receive > Send All, or click the Send/Receive button and choose one of these commands (**Figure 20.10**).

   The Outlook Express dialog box appears (**Figure 20.11**).

4. Click Yes to go online.

   All outgoing messages are sent.

## ✔ Tip

■ You can save more time by combining posts and downloads in the same synchronization session. Prepare your outgoing messages, mark articles for retrieval, and then choose Tools > Synchronize All.

**Figure 20.10** Click the Send/Receive button to choose a Send command.

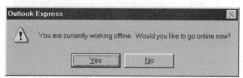

**Figure 20.11** Choosing Yes removes the checkmark from the File > Work Offline command. If you do not automatically reconnect to the Internet, you may also have to run your dialer program (typically, this is Dial-up Networking).

# SETTING NEWS OPTIONS

21

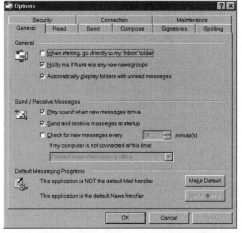

**Figure 21.1** Click the tabs at the top of the Options dialog box to set mail and newsgroup preferences.

You can customize the news portion of Outlook Express by setting preferences in the Options dialog box. Although the default settings will suffice for most users, you should glance through this chapter to learn about options that can make your newsgroup sessions more productive.

To set options, choose Tools > Options. The Options dialog box appears (**Figure 21.1**). There are nine option categories that correspond to the tabs at the top of the dialog box: General, Read, Send, Compose, Signatures, Spelling, Security, Connection, and Maintenance.

As you will discover, you set email and newsgroup preferences in the same dialog boxes. This chapter discusses only those options that are related to newsgroup usage. Refer to Chapter 16 for instructions on setting email preferences and for an explanation of options that affect both email and newsgroups.

### ✔ Note

- The following Options sections are *only* discussed in Chapter 16 (although the explanations also apply to newsgroups): Compose, Signatures, Spelling, Security, and Connection.

# General Options

You can set the following newsgroup-related preferences in the General section of the Options dialog box (refer to **Figure 21.1**).

## General

*Notify me if there are any new newsgroups.* Periodically, news servers increase their coverage by adding newsgroups. Check this option if you want to be notified when new newsgroups are added (**Figures 21.2–21.3**).

*Automatically display folders with unread messages.* When checked and you receive email, the Inbox is automatically selected and the first new message is highlighted in the message list. If you spend a lot of time browsing newsgroups and don't want to lose your place, do not check this option.

## Default Messaging Programs

*This application is (is NOT) the default News handler.* Click the Make Default button to make Outlook Express your primary newsgroup reader. When you perform a newsgroup-related activity in another program—such as choosing Tools > Mail and News > Read News in Internet Explorer—the default newsgroup reader is used.

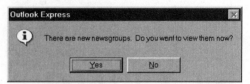

**Figure 21.2** Newsgroups are periodically added by most news servers. Click *Yes* to view them now or *No* to view them later.

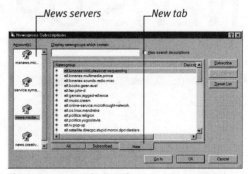

**Figure 21.3** To see the list of new newsgroups, click the Newsgroups button, select a news server, and then click the New tab.

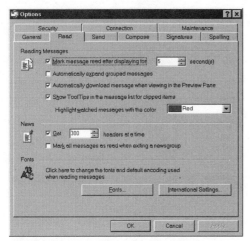

**Figure 21.4** Read options.

# Read Options

Read options (**Figure 21.4**) apply to reading and displaying newsgroup messages.

## Reading Messages

*Mark message as read after displaying for* xx *seconds*. Unread messages are shown in boldface, so they can easily be identified. If a message is selected in the message list for longer than the specified time, it is marked as read; i.e., the boldface is removed.

If you remove the check mark, a message is only marked as read if you open it, scroll the preview pane while the message is selected, or issue the Edit > Mark as Read command.

*Automatically expand grouped messages*. Newsgroup messages can generate replies from other users. Outlook Express groups these messages together into *conversations* and marks them with a plus symbol. If you enable this option, all messages in a conversation are automatically displayed/expanded. (When expanded, the symbols turn to minus signs.) If this option is unchecked, you can manually expand or collapse a conversation by clicking the plus and minus symbols.

*Automatically download messages when viewing in the Preview Pane*. When enabled, if you click a message header or select it with the cursor keys, its message is automatically downloaded and displayed in the preview pane. If you find that you are inadvertently downloading messages that don't interest you, disable this option. To download a message, select its header and press (Spacebar).

*Highlight watched messages with the color.* If you want to follow a conversation (reading all contributions and subsequent replies), you can mark it as *watched.* You can click in the Watch (eyeglasses) column of any message header in the conversation, select a header and choose Message > Watch Conversation, or design a message rule that automatically marks certain conversations as watched (**Figure 21.5**). To make all watched messages stand out, you can choose a color for them (**Figure 21.6**).

## News

*Get* xxx *headers at a time.* Specify the number of message headers to be downloaded from a newsgroup each time you choose the Tools > Get Next Headers command. When unchecked, all message headers from the newsgroup are downloaded.

*Mark all messages as read when exiting a newsgroup.* If you always want to read only the newest messages in each newsgroup, enable this option and choose View > Current View > Hide Read Messages (or Hide Read or Ignored Messages). Enabling this option is the same as choosing Edit > Mark All Read or Edit > Catch up.

## Fonts

*Click here to change the fonts and default encoding used when reading messages.* Click the Fonts button to select the fonts used to display proportional text and fixed-width text, and specify a font size (**Figure 21.7**). The chosen fonts and size will be used to display all received Plain Text messages. (Rich Text messages will retain their original formatting.)

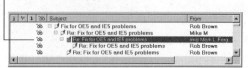

Watched messages

**Figure 21.5** To watch a conversation, click once in the Watch column of any message header in the conversation.

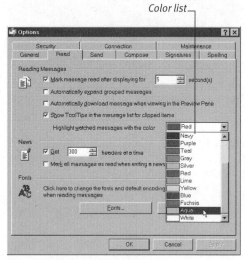

Color list

**Figure 21.6** To make them easier to spot, you can choose a special color that will automatically be applied to all watched conversations.

**Figure 21.7** Select fonts to use when displaying messages onscreen.

READ OPTIONS

**Figure 21.8** Send options.

# Send Options

Send options are set in the Send section of the Options dialog box (**Figure 21.8**). The majority of the Send options apply equally to email and newsgroup messages. Refer to Chapter 16 for a discussion of these options.

## News Sending Format

Click the radio button for *HTML* or *Plain Text* to select a default format for outgoing news messages. (You can still override this setting on a message-by-message basis.)

◆ *HTML*. Messages formatted with HTML (Hypertext Markup Language) can contain paragraph alignments, fonts, sizes, styles, and colors. Such formatting, however, is visible only to users who have HTML-capable newsreaders or when the message is viewed in a browser. Individuals without such a program see the message as ordinary text with an HTML attachment.

◆ *Plain Text*. Currently, most messages are still plain, unformatted text. Choosing this option assures you of compatibility with all mail systems and computer platforms.

To specify settings for HTML or text messages, click the associated Settings button. See Chapter 16 for a discussion of the Settings options.

## ✔ Tip

■ In general, you should restrict newsgroup posts to Plain Text format. If you want to send HTML-formatted messages to a particular newsgroup, scan some of the recent messages first and see if others are also posting formatted messages.

# Maintenance Options

The Maintenance options (**Figure 21.9**) specify the conditions under which old news messages are deleted and compacted (to avoid wasting disk space).

## Cleaning Up Messages

*Compact messages in the background.* Check this option if you want to be able to continue working in Outlook Express while it compacts messages.

*Delete read message bodies in newsgroups.* Check this option if you want messages to automatically be removed after they've been read. (To reread a deleted message, you'll have to download it again.) Click the Clean Up Now button to manually delete message bodies.

*Delete news messages* xx *days after being downloaded.* When checked, message bodies are automatically deleted after so many days have passed. Unless you tend to reread messages, set this to a low number.

*Compact messages when there is* xx *percent wasted space.* Set a percentage at which Outlook Express will automatically compact messages. The lower the percentage, the more frequently messages will be compacted.

*Clean Up Now.* To eliminate wasted space, click Clean Up Now. The Local File Clean Up dialog box appears (**Figure 21.10**). Execute clean-up options by clicking buttons.

*Store Folder.* If you like, you can change the hard disk and/or folder in which Outlook Express stores messages. Click Store Folder, click Change, and then select a new location in the Browse for Folder dialog box.

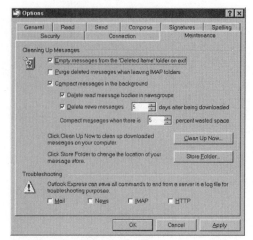

**Figure 21.9** Maintenance options.

**Figure 21.10** Click buttons to compact the message list or remove message headers and bodies.

## ✔ Tips

- Surprisingly, you don't save disk space by clicking the Remove Messages button or the Delete button (refer to **Figure 21.10**). To reclaim wasted space, you must also follow up by clicking the Compact button.

- By default, cleanup affects all Outlook Express folders. If you want to be more selective in this process, click the Browse button (refer to **Figure 21.10**) to select a particular email account, email folder, news server, or newsgroup.

## Troubleshooting

If you have difficulty downloading news messages from a news server, enter a checkmark for News. Outlook Express will create an activity log that may help you discover the source of the problem. The troubleshooting log files can be found in the following folder:

`C:\WINDOWS\Application Data\Microsoft\Outlook Express`

Each troubleshooting file has a .LOG extension. For example, the HTTP log is named `HTTPMail.log`. Because logs are ordinary text files, they can be opened in any text editor or word processing program.

**MAINTENANCE OPTIONS**

# CUSTOMIZING OUTLOOK EXPRESS

22

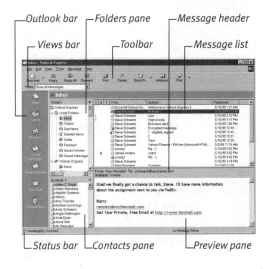

*Outlook bar* — *Folders pane* — *Message header*

*Views bar* — *Toolbar* — *Message list*

*Status bar* — *Contacts pane* — *Preview pane*

**Figure 22.1** The parts of the Outlook Express window.

Although the standard display and features of Outlook Express will suffice for many users, there are also several ways that you can customize the program:

♦ *Customize the display.* Change the size and orientation of the message list and preview panes; rearrange, resize, and change the column headings; set a sort order for the message list; and show or hide parts of the display (**Figure 22.1**).

♦ *Customize the toolbar.* Add or remove buttons, display buttons with or without labels, change the placement of the toolbar, and hide sections or the entire toolbar.

♦ *Add folders.* Create new folders to handle special classes of messages, adding them to the Folders pane and/or the Outlook bar.

♦ *Automate the handling of mail and newsgroup messages.* Depending on the criteria that you set, different types of messages can automatically be placed in particular folders.

Additional customization options are discussed in Chapter 16, "Setting Mail Options" and Chapter 21, "Setting News Options."

# Customizing the Display

The message list and preview pane can be changed in several ways by dragging, clicking, and choosing commands.

## Modifying the message list and preview pane

The message list and preview panes can be modified in the following ways:

◆ To change the orientation of the message list and preview pane, choose View > Layout, and click the radio button for *Below messages* or *Beside messages* (**Figure 22.2**).

◆ You can change pane widths or heights by dragging the vertical or horizontal bar that separates any two panes. Drag up and down or left and right, depending on whether the panes are split horizontally or vertically. One area increases in size as the other decreases.

◆ You can display or remove the message header information that appears above the message displayed in the preview pane (refer to **Figure 22.1**). Choose View > Layout, and add or remove the checkmark from *Show preview pane header*.

◆ To eliminate the preview pane, choose View > Layout and remove the checkmark from *Show preview pane*. After doing so, you will have to read messages by opening them in their own windows. (Double-click a message header or select the message and choose File > Open.)

## Modifying column headings

You can use the View > Columns command or manually resize, rearrange, or change the column headings for the message list (**Figure 22.3**).

*Add or remove components*          *Modify the toolbar*

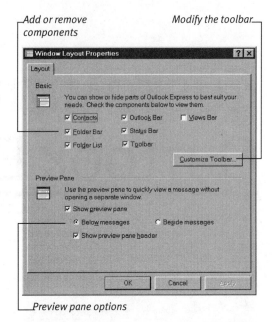

*Preview pane options*

**Figure 22.2** You can hide or show the various window components in the Basic section of the Window Layout Properties dialog box.

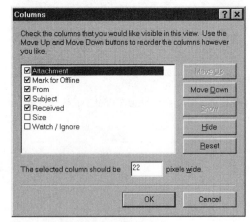

**Figure 22.3** The Columns dialog box.

### To resize column headings:

1. Move the pointer over the right edge of a column heading. The pointer changes to a double arrow.

2. Drag to the left or right to reduce or widen the column.

3. Release the mouse button when the column is the desired width.

### To resize column headings using the Columns command:

1. Choose View > Columns.

   The Columns dialog box appears (refer to **Figure 22.3**).

2. Select a column in the list.

3. Enter a number (in pixels) in the text box.

### To rearrange column headings by dragging:

1. Click to select a column heading.

2. Drag the heading to its new position and release the mouse button.

### To rearrange column headings using the Columns command:

1. Choose View > Columns.

   The Columns dialog box appears (refer to **Figure 22.3**).

2. Select a column to move.

3. Click Move Up or Move Down to change the column's position.

4. When all columns are arranged correctly, click OK.

### ✔ Tip

- To return the columns to their default positions, click Reset. Note, however, that if you have added or removed columns, those changes will also be reset.

**CUSTOMIZING THE DISPLAY**

## To add or remove column headings:

1. Choose View > Columns.

   The Columns dialog box appears (refer to **Figure 22.3**).

2. To add a column, enter a checkmark for any unused column heading. To remove a column, remove its checkmark.

3. To change the position of a new column, select it and click Move Up or Move Down.

4. Click OK to save your changes.

## ✔ Tip

■ To restore the default set of columns and their original positions, click Reset.

## Setting a sort order for the message list

You can set a sort order for the message list. The order you set remains until it is next modified.

◆ Select a sort column from the View > Sort By submenu (**Figure 22.4**). Choose Sort Ascending (for an A-Z sort) or Sort Descending (for a Z-A sort).

   *or*

◆ Click a column heading to sort the message list by the contents of that column. To change between ascending and descending sorts, click the same heading again.

## Showing or hiding display parts

You can selectively show or hide display parts via the View > Layout command. To add or remove parts, enter or remove checkmarks in the Basic section of the Window Layout Properties dialog box (refer to **Figure 22.2**).

## ✔ Tip

■ If you find yourself frequently switching views, add the Views bar (**Figure 22.5**).

**Figure 22.4** You can choose sort commands from the View > Sort By submenu.

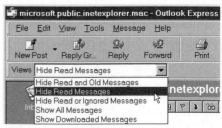

**Figure 22.5** The Views bar contains a drop-down list of all standard views, plus the ones you've created.

# Customizing the Toolbar

Customization options for the toolbar include rearranging and hiding the toolbar, changing its placement in the mail window, displaying small or large buttons, and adding and removing buttons.

## Rearranging the toolbar

You can rearrange the sections of the Outlook Express toolbar in the same way that you rearrange the IE5 toolbar. Click any vertical bar and drag up, down, left, or right. (Not all directions are possible at all times.) However, since there are only two possible sections— the toolbar and the Views bar—there isn't much to rearrange.

## Hiding the toolbar

To hide the toolbar, choose View > Layout, and remove the checkmark from *Toolbar*. You can also remove other components, such as the status bar. Another way to quickly hide or show the toolbar is to right-click to the right of the menus or the last toolbar button, and choose *Toolbar* (removing its checkmark)

## Modifying toolbar buttons

In addition to altering the appearance of the toolbar, you can change its functionality by adding or removing buttons, adding section separators, and changing button sizes and labels.

Note that Outlook Express has *many* toolbars. The toolbar changes as you select different types of folders (Outlook Express, email, and newsgroups) and create different types of messages (email and newsgroup articles). You can set different options for *each* of these toolbars.

## To add or remove buttons:

1. Right-click in a blank area of the toolbar. A pop-up menu appears (**Figure 22.6**). Choose Customize.

   *or*

   Choose View > Layout. The Window Layout Properties dialog box appears (refer to **Figure 22.2**). Click the Customize Toolbar button.

   The Customize Toolbar dialog box appears (**Figure 22.7**).

2. To add a button to the toolbar, select a function in the Available Buttons box, and click Add.

3. To remove a button from the toolbar, select a function in the Current Toolbar Buttons box and click Remove.

4. To change the order in which the buttons appear in the toolbar, select a function in the Current Toolbar Buttons section of the dialog box and click Move Up or Move Down.

5. To save the new toolbar, click Close.

## To set label and icon options:

1. Display the Customize Toolbar dialog box, as explained in the previous set of steps.

2. To set the size of the toolbar buttons, choose Large Icons or Small Icons from the Icon Options drop-down list.

3. To change the button labels, select an option from the Text Options drop-down list.

## ✔ Tips

- To restore the default buttons and reset the standard button order, click Reset.

- To create a dividing line between groups of buttons, add a separator or move one of the current separators by selecting it and clicking Move Up or Move Down.

**Figure 22.6** Right-clicking in the toolbar displays this pop-up menu.

— *Available buttons*    — *Buttons in use*

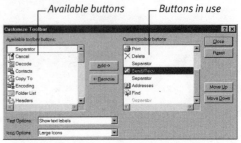

**Figure 22.7** The Customize Toolbar dialog box.

Select a containing folder

Folder name

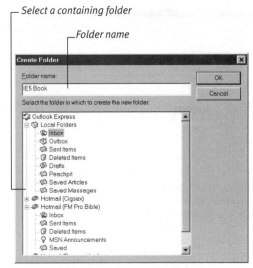

**Figure 22.8** The Create Folder dialog box.

# Adding Folders

One of the best ways to organize your email and newsgroup messages is by creating new folders in which to store them. For example, I routinely create a folder for each book I write, enabling me to store all incoming and outgoing messages concerning the book in one place. If I needed greater organization, I could create folders inside the main one, such as "Submissions," "Publisher Messages," and "Reader Comments." To make special folders such as these easily accessible, you can create copies of them in the Outlook bar.

Note that every folder you create must be a subfolder of another folder. Folders can be created with in Local Folders, an email account main folder, or any of the folders inside of these folders.

## To create a new folder:

**1.** Select any email folder in the Folders pane (other than Outlook Express) and choose File > Folder > New.

   *or*

   Right-click any email folder in the Folders pane (other than Outlook Express), and choose New Folder.

   The Create Folder dialog box appears (**Figure 22.8**).

**2.** Select a parent folder for the new folder; that is, the folder within which the new folder will be created.

**3.** Enter a name for the new folder.

**4.** Click OK.

## To store a message in a different folder:

**1.** Display the message list that contains the email or newsgroup message.

2. Select the message's header in the message list, and do one of the following:

♦ Choose Edit > Move to Folder or Edit > Copy to Folder. The Move or Copy dialog box appears (**Figure 22.9**). Select a destination folder and click OK.

♦ Drag the message to the desired folder in the Folders pane or the Outlook bar. (If the dragged message is email, the message is *moved* to the folder. If the message is a newsgroup article, it is *copied* to the folder.)

♦ Right-click the message and choose Move to Folder or Copy to Folder. The Move or Copy dialog box appears. Select a destination folder and click OK.

## To customize the Outlook bar:

1. To change the order of the folders in the Outlook bar (refer to **Figure 22.1**), drag the folder icon up or down to a new position.

2. To remove a folder from the Outlook bar, right-click the folder and choose Remove from Outlook Bar.

3. To add a folder icon to the Outlook bar, right-click the folder's name in the Folders pane and choose Add to Outlook Bar.

4. To change the size of the icons, right-click a blank spot at the bottom of the Outlook bar and choose Large Icons or Small Icons.

5. To remove the Outlook bar, right-click a blank spot at the bottom of the Outlook bar and choose Hide Outlook Bar.

## ✔ Tip

■ You can rename or delete any folder, as well as move a folder into another folder. Select the folder in the Folders pane and then choose the appropriate command from the File > Folder menu.

■ You can also hide or show the Outlook bar by choosing View > Layout.

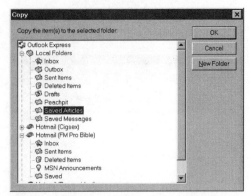

**Figure 22.9** The Move and Copy dialog boxes are identical. Choose a destination folder and click OK.

ADDING FOLDERS

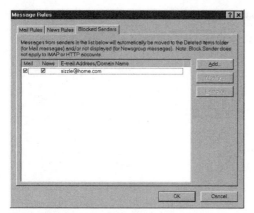

**Figure 22.10** You can add, remove, or modify persons in the Blocked Senders List.

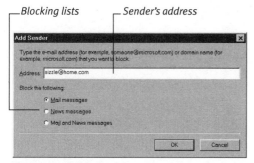

Blocking lists     Sender's address

**Figure 22.11** To block a person, you only need to know his or her email address.

# Automating Email and Article Handling

You can automate the handling of certain classes of incoming mail and newsgroup messages by creating message rules. (In previous versions of Internet Explorer, these were called Inbox Assistant rules.) Messages that meet your criteria are automatically routed to the folder of your choice. Email and newsgroup rules are created separately. For help creating message rules, refer to Chapters 15 and 18.

Outlook Express 5 also provides a new feature called the Blocked Senders List that makes it easy to ignore the messages or newsgroup articles from specific individuals.

## To add a person to the Blocked Senders List:

1. Choose Tools > Message Rules > Blocked Senders List.

   The Message Rules dialog box appears with the Blocked Senders tab chosen (**Figure 22.10**).

2. Click Add.

   The Add Sender dialog box appears (**Figure 22.11**).

3. Type or paste the individual's email address into the Address Box.

4. Choose Mail messages, News messages, or Mail and News messages (depending on where the person's messages are received).

5. To block additional senders, repeat Steps 2–4. Otherwise, click OK.

   The Message Rules dialog box reappears.

6. Click OK.

   Email messages received from blocked senders are automatically moved to the Deleted Items folder. Newsgroup articles created by blocked senders are automatically hidden.

# PART 3

# APPENDICES

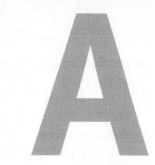

# GLOSSARY

If you're new to the Internet and the World Wide Web, you'll find that there's a whole new language for you to learn. This Glossary contains definitions for many of the terms and abbreviations you'll encounter.

**Active Desktop**　A system software component in Internet Explorer 4 and Windows 98 that integrates Internet functions into Windows.

**ActiveX component**　A software add-on to Internet Explorer that provides additional capabilities.

**address**　See **URL**.

**attachment**　A file—such as a text or word processing document, graphic image, or program—that is sent along with an email message (**Figure A.1**). See also **email**.

**BBS**　Abbreviation for *bulletin board system*; an electronic bulletin board where users can exchange messages and download files. BBSs are often run by individuals out of their homes or businesses and serve as online meeting places for computer users. Although frequently free, some BBSs charge a subscription fee based on usage or covering a period of time.

**bookmark**　Netscape Navigator's term for a favorite Web site. See also **favorite**.

**bps**　Abbreviation for *bits per second*; a measure of a modem's speed or file transmission rate (**Figure A.2**). A 33.3 modem, for example, can transmit up to 33,300 characters of data per second.

**browser**　A program, such as Internet Explorer 5 (**Figure A.3**), that enables you to view information on the World Wide Web. Browser features are often extended to enable email and newsgroup handling.

**chat**　Conversing with persons in real-time over the Internet via typing, microphones, desktop video cameras, or a combination of these mediums. See also **chat client** and **IRC**.

*Attachment icon*

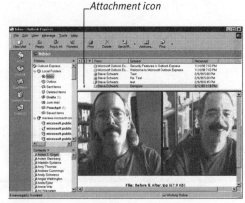

**Figure A.1** In Outlook Express, a paper clip icon indicates that a message contains attachments. Attached JPEG and GIF files can be viewed without changing programs.

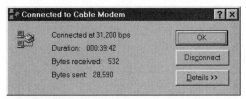

**Figure A.2** The Dial-Up Connection utility reports a modem's connect speed in bps.

**Figure A.3** A browser enables you to experience the complex multimedia that is now commonplace on the World Wide Web.

**Figure A.4** Microsoft Chat (formerly Comic Chat) turns IRC chat sessions into comic strips. Each participant can select his or her own character.

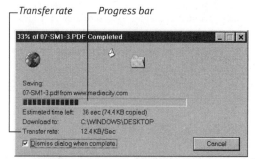

**Figure A.5** When downloading a file with Internet Explorer, a dialog box shows the progress of the download and the transfer rate.

**Figure A.6** Outlook Express enables you to exchange messages with friends and business associates.

**chat client**   A computer program, such as Microsoft Chat (**Figure A.4**), that enables you to participate in on-line, interactive chat sessions in which participants type messages to each other in real-time. See also **IRC**.

**compression, file**   Files downloaded from and uploaded to the Internet, information services, and BBSs are often compressed in order to reduce their size and transmission time. The most popular compression programs are PKZIP and WinZip (PC) and StuffIt Deluxe (Mac). See also **self-extracting archive** and **ZIP file**.

**download**   To retrieve a text, data, or program file from another person's computer, an information service, BBS, or a location on the Internet (**Figure A.5**). See also **upload**.

**duplex (half and full)**   Some applications, such as NetMeeting, enable individuals to talk to each other over the Internet by using a microphone and a sound card. If both individuals have full-duplex sound cards, they can simultaneously send and receive sound—as occurs during a normal telephone conversation. If either user's sound card is only capable of half-duplex, the individuals must take turns talking to one another.

**email**   Short for *electronic mail*; email messages are text notes created in an email program, a browser, text editor, or word processing program and then sent over the Internet (**Figure A.6**). Optionally, email can include attachments, such as text files, word processing documents, graphic images, or even programs. See also **attachment**.

**extension, file**   The three-character suffix for PC filenames that indicate a file type, such as *.zip* (a WinZip or PCZIP archive) or *.jpg* (a type of graphics file).

**GIF file** Abbreviation for *Graphic Interchange Format*; a popular format for creating compressed graphic files. GIF and JPEG are the two supported file formats for displaying graphics on the Web. See also **JPEG file**.

**favorite** A Web page that you visit frequently. Browsers typically provide features for remembering and organizing favorites (**Figure A.7**). Favorites are often referred to as *bookmarks* in other programs.

**folder** The Windows term for a directory on a disk; a container for files. Creating folders enables you to better organize your files.

**forward** To send a copy of a received email message to another user.

**freeware** Software that you may use for free. When redistributing such material, however, you must abide by the author's instructions. See also **shareware**.

**FTP site** The purpose of an FTP (File Transfer Protocol) site is to transmit and receive files (**Figure A.8**). When you click a link on a Web page to download a program, for example, you may note in the browser's status area that you are being transferred to an FTP site.

**helper application** A program that—when used in conjunction with a Web browser— enables particular types of files to be opened or otherwise handled. For example, you might configure a browser to automatically uncompress certain file types as they are received or to use a given graphics program to open JPEG files.

**home page** The first or starting page of a Web site; often referred to as the index page.

**HTML** Abbreviation for *Hypertext Markup Language*; the language used to create pages for the World Wide Web (**Figure A.9**).

Favorites bar

**Figure A.7** To quickly go to a favorite Web page, you can choose it from the Favorites bar or the Favorites menu.

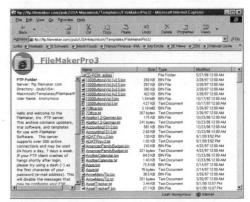

**Figure A.8** With IE5, you can work with files on an FTP site in the same manner that you work with files on your own hard disk.

**Figure A.9** If you'd like to see how a Web page was created, choose View > Source in IE5 to display the HTML code for the current page.

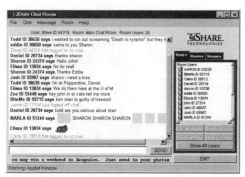

**Figure A.10** Web-based chat programs are frequently written in Java.

**Figure A.11** Movie files, such as this one showing some Frank Zappa concert footage, are readily available on the Web.

**Internet** The worldwide collection of interconnected computers.

**IRC** Abbreviation for *Internet Relay Chat*; a system that enables thousands of users to conduct chat sessions, typing messages to each other in real-time. See also **chat** and **chat client**.

**ISP** Abbreviation for *Internet Service Provider*; a company that provides access to the Internet, usually for a monthly or hourly fee.

**Java** A cross-platform programming language used to embed small programs (called *applets*) in Web pages (**Figure A.10**).

**JPEG file** Abbreviation for *Joint Photographic Experts Group*; a popular file format for creating compressed graphic files. See also **GIF file**.

**log on, log off** To connect or disconnect, respectively, from an information service, BBS, or Internet provider.

**movies** Motion picture files that can be downloaded from or played on the Web. Common movie file formats include AVI, MPEG, and QuickTime (MOV). Some browsers can automatically interpret and play movie files. Others require a helper application, such as Windows Media Player (**Figure A.11**). See also **helper application**.

**newsgroup** A message group organized around a specific topic, such as using a particular graphics program, computer equipment for sale, and game playing. To read or post messages to a newsgroup, you must have a newsgroup reader such as Outlook Express.

**newsgroup reader** A program, such as Outlook Express, that is designed specifically to read and post messages to newsgroups. Most newsgroup readers also provide features for sorting, archiving, and otherwise handling messages.

**GLOSSARY**

**plug-in**　An add-on module that gives a Web browser a new capability, such as the ability to play certain types of audio or video data or to display 3D graphics. Netscape Navigator uses plug-ins; Internet Explorer uses ActiveX components. See also **ActiveX component**.

**RealPlayer**　A popular program that allows audio and video data, such as music and news reports, to be received and played over the Internet (**Figure A.12**).

**search engine**　A software tool that enables a search site to retrieve and index information from the Internet, such as Yahoo!, AltaVista, and HotBot (**Figure A.13**).

**self-extracting archive**　A compressed file that—when run—can automatically extract its contents. Unlike normal file archives, a self-extracting archive does not require a special extraction program. See also **compression, file** and **ZIP file**.

**shareware**　Software that you can "try before you buy." Shareware is distributed on the honor system. If you decide to keep it, you must send its author the requested fee. See also **freeware**.

**TCP/IP**　Abbreviation for *Transmission Control Protocol/Internet Protocol*; a network communications protocol that is used to connect computers over the Internet.

**thread**　A set of newsgroup messages, all relating to the same topic. Outlook Express calls them "conversations."

**upload**　To transmit a text, data, or program file to another person, BBS, information service, or location on the Internet. See also **download**.

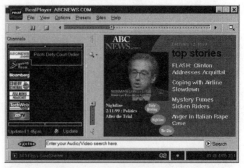

**Figure A.12** IE5's support for RealPlayer enables users to listen to music and radio show clips, as well as view movie clips over the Internet.

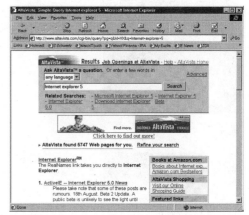

**Figure A.13** Every search site, such as AltaVista, employs one or more search engines to help you locate topics of interest on the Internet.

GLOSSARY

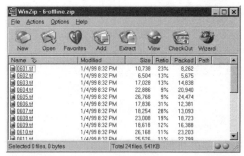

**Figure A.14** WinZip's simple interface makes it easy to extract compressed files from their archives.

**URL** Abbreviation for *Uniform Resource Locator*; an address for an item on the Internet, such as a Web page or a file. Different types of addresses have different prefixes. For example, Web addresses are preceded by **http://** and addresses of FTP sites start with **ftp://**. Sometimes URLs are shortened, as in www.peachpit.com.

**WAV file** A popular PC format for audio files.

**Web page** A page of information on the World Wide Web. Every Web page has a unique address that specifies the page's location. See also **URL**.

**Web site** A collection of Web pages created for a single company, organization, or individual.

**Webmaster/Webmistress** The person responsible for administering a given Web site.

**World Wide Web** An international system for linking text, graphics, and multimedia documents on the Internet; frequently shortened to *the Web*. CERN, the European Laboratory for Particle Physics, is considered the birthplace of the World Wide Web, and Tim Berners-Lee its creator. The World Wide Web Constortium (www.w3.org) is responsible for setting standards for the Web. A www in an address prefix (as in http://www) stands for World Wide Web.

**ZIP file** A compressed file or group of files, where the compression protocol is compatible with the algorithm used by PKZIP and WinZip, PC archiving programs (**Figure A.14**). See also **compression**, **file** and **self-extracting archive**.

# IE5 Keystroke Reference

You can perform common tasks in Internet Explorer 5 by pressing a single key or a combination of keys. These keyboard shortcuts can speed up your work and are often more convenient than searching for the associated menu command.

**Table B.1**

| Web Page Navigation Shortcuts | | |
| --- | --- | --- |
| **TASK** | **KEYBOARD SHORTCUT** | **MENU COMMAND** |
| Go to next page | Shift Bksp or Alt → | View › Goto › Forward |
| Go to previous page | Bksp or Alt ← | View › Goto › Back |
| Scroll the page up | ↑ | |
| Scroll the page down | ↓ | |
| Scroll the page up one screen | Pg Up or click blank area above the scroll box | |
| Scroll the page down one screen | Pg Dn or click blank area beneath the scroll box | |
| Scroll the page a specific distance | Drag the scroll box up or down | |
| Scroll to the beginning of the page | Home | |
| Scroll to the end of the page | End | |
| Scroll page to the left or right | Drag scroll box at bottom of page to the left or right | |
| Move to the next link on the page | Tab | |
| Move to the previous link on page | Shift Tab | |
| Move between frames | Ctrl Tab and Shift Ctrl Tab | |

**Table B.2**

| Text Editing Shortcuts | | |
| --- | --- | --- |
| TASK | KEYBOARD SHORTCUT | MENU COMMAND |
| Cut selected text | Ctrl X | Edit › Cut |
| Copy selected text | Ctrl C | Edit › Copy |
| Paste text from clipboard | Ctrl V | Edit › Paste |
| Undo last editing command | Ctrl Z | |
| Select all | Ctrl A | Edit › Select All |
| Find text on this page | Ctrl F | Edit › Find (on this page) |
| Move cursor to Address bar | Alt D | |
| Add http://www. and .com to the current URL in the Address box | Ctrl Enter | |

*Note*: In addition to editing URLs in the Address box or text that you type into Web page forms, you can select the body text of any Web page and copy it using the Copy command.

The Select All command selects all text on the current page, while ignoring graphics. Select All cannot be applied to text in the Address box, although the menu command can.

**Table B.3**

| Miscellaneous Shortcuts | | |
| --- | --- | --- |
| TASK | KEYBOARD SHORTCUT | MENU COMMAND |
| Open a new browser window | Ctrl N | File › New › Window |
| Open Web page, folder, or disk file | Ctrl O or Ctrl L | File › Open |
| Open link in new window | Shift-click the link | |
| Close current browser window | Ctrl W | File › Close |
| Print the current page or frame | Ctrl P | File › Print |
| Display a pop-up menu for a link | Shift F10 | right-click the hypertext link |
| Display a pop-up menu for a graphic or other object | Right-click graphic or object | |
| Go to the selected link | Enter | |
| Click the selected button | Spacebar or Enter | |
| Refresh the current page | F5 or Ctrl R | View › Refresh |
| Force a page refresh | Ctrl F5 | |
| Stop current page from loading | Esc | View › Stop |
| Switch between normal and full-screen mode | F11 | View › Full Screen |
| Display Favorites bar | Ctrl J | View › Explorer Bar › Favorites |
| Display History bar | Ctrl H | View › Explorer Bar › History |
| Display Search bar | Ctrl E | View › Explorer Bar › Search |
| Open multiple folders in History or Favorites bar | Ctrl-click the folders | |
| Add current page to Favorites | Ctrl D | Favorites › Add to Favorites |
| Organize Favorites | Ctrl B | Favorites › Organize Favorites |
| Display IE5 Help | F1 | Help › Contents and Index |
| Show URL history list for Address bar | F4 | |
| Move between displayed toolbars | F6 | |
| Manually select a menu | Alt or F10 | |

After you have selected a toolbar by pressing F6 one or more times, you can choose menu commands and buttons (such as your Links) by pressing the arrow keys. To execute a chosen command or to click a selected button, press Enter.

Press A or F10 to select the File menu. To choose a different menu, press the ← and → keys. To choose a command, use the arrow keys; execute the chosen command by pressing Enter

# EMAIL KEYSTROKE REFERENCE

The following Outlook Express email-related commands have keyboard shortcuts.

**Table C.1**

| General Shortcuts | | |
| --- | --- | --- |
| TASK | KEYBOARD SHORTCUT | MENU COMMAND |
| Go to the Inbox (default command) | Ctrl I | |
| Create a new message | Ctrl N | File > New > Mail Message or Message > New Message |
| Create new folder | Ctrl Shift E | File > New > Folder or File > Folder > New |
| Find a message | Ctrl Shift F | Edit > Find > Message |
| Find next message | F3 | Edit > Find > Next |
| Find people | Ctrl E | Edit > Find > People |
| Open a particular folder | Ctrl Y | View > Go to Folder |
| Go to next unread folder | Ctrl J | View > Next > Next Unread Folder |
| Go to next/previous message | Ctrl > / Ctrl < | View > Next > Next message and View > Previous message |
| Abort a send/receive | Esc | View > Stop |
| Send and receive mail | Ctrl M | Tools > Send and Receive > Send and Receive All |
| Open the Address Book | Ctrl Shift B | Tools > Address Book |
| Make the next/previous pane active | Tab / Shift Tab | |
| Help | F1 | Help > Contents and Index |

**Table C.2**

| Message List Shortcuts | | |
|---|---|---|
| TASK | KEYBOARD SHORTCUT | MENU COMMAND |
| Open the selected message | Ctrl O or Enter | File › Open |
| Print the selected message | Ctrl P | File › Print |
| View properties of a message | Alt Enter | File › Properties |
| Find message in this folder | F3 | Edit › Find › Message in this Folder |
| Select all messages | Ctrl A | Edit › Select All |
| Copy the selected message | Ctrl C | Edit › Copy |
| Delete the selected messages | Ctrl D or Del | Edit › Delete |
| Move selected messages to folder | Ctrl Shift V | Edit › Move to Folder |
| Mark selected messages as read | Ctrl Enter or Ctrl Q | Edit › Mark as Read |
| Mark selected messages as unread | Ctrl Shift Enter | Edit › Mark as Unread |
| Mark all messages as read | Ctrl Shift A | Edit › Mark all Read |
| View next message in list | Ctrl > or ↓ | View › Next › Next Message |
| View previous message in list | Ctrl < or ↑ | View › Previous Message |
| View next unread message | Ctrl U | View › Next › Next Unread Message |
| View first message in list | Home | |
| View last message in list | End | |
| Refresh the message list | F5 | View › Refresh |
| Reply to author of message | Ctrl R | Message › Reply to Sender |
| Reply to all | Ctrl Shift R | Message › Reply to All |
| Forward selected message | Ctrl F | Message › Forward |

These shortcuts assume that one or more messages are currently selected (highlighted) in the message list pane.

**Table C.3**

| Message Preview Pane Shortcuts | | |
|---|---|---|
| TASK | KEYBOARD SHORTCUT | MENU COMMAND |
| Open message in separate window | Ctrl O | File › Open |
| Print the current message | Ctrl P | File › Print |
| Delete current message | Ctrl D or Del | File › Delete |
| View properties of the message | Alt Enter | File › Properties |
| Copy selected text | Ctrl C | Edit › Copy |
| Select all text | Ctrl A | Edit › Select All |
| Move message to different folder | Ctrl Shift V | Edit › Move to Folder |
| Mark message as read | Ctrl Enter or Ctrl Q | Edit › Mark as Read |
| Mark message as unread | Ctrl Shift Enter | Edit › Mark as Unread |
| Go to beginning of message | Home | |
| Go to end of message | End | |
| Scroll up one screen | Pg Up | |
| Scroll down one screen | Pg Dn | |

Most of these shortcuts also apply to existing messages that you have opened for reading in a separate window.

**Table C.3** (continued)

### Message Preview Pane Shortcuts

| TASK | KEYBOARD SHORTCUT | MENU COMMAND |
|------|-------------------|--------------|
| View previous message | `Ctrl` `<` | View › Previous Message |
| View next message | `Ctrl` `>` | View › Next › Next Message |
| View next unread message | `Ctrl` `U` | View › Next › Next Unread Message |
| Reply to author of message | `Ctrl` `R` | Message › Reply to Sender |
| Reply to all | `Ctrl` `Shift` `R` | Message › Reply to All |
| Forward current message | `Ctrl` `F` | Message › Forward |

Most of these shortcuts also apply to existing messages that you have opened for reading in a separate window.

**Table C.4**

### Outgoing Message Shortcuts

| TASK | KEYBOARD SHORTCUT | MENU COMMAND |
|------|-------------------|--------------|
| Send current message | `Alt` `S` or `Ctrl` `Enter` | File › Send Message |
| Save current text as a draft | `Ctrl` `S` | File › Save |
| Close the message window | `Alt` `F4` or `Esc` | File › Close |
| View properties of the message | `Alt` `Enter` | File › Properties |
| Cut selected text | `Ctrl` `X` | Edit › Cut |
| Copy selected text | `Ctrl` `C` | Edit › Copy |
| Paste text from clipboard | `Ctrl` `V` | Edit › Paste |
| Undo last edit | `Ctrl` `Z` | Edit › Undo |
| Select all text | `Ctrl` `A` | Edit › Select All |
| Find text in this message | `F3` or `Ctrl` `Shift` `F` | Edit › Find › Text in this message |
| Go to beginning of message | `Ctrl` `Home` | |
| Go to end of message | `Ctrl` `End` | |
| Go to start of current line | `Home` | |
| Go to end of current line | `End` | |
| Scroll up one screen | `Pg Up` | |
| Scroll down one screen | `Pg Dn` | |
| Add signature to message | `Ctrl` `Shift` `S` | Insert › Signature |
| Check spelling of document | `F7` | Tools › Spelling |
| Check addressee names | `Ctrl` `K` or `Alt` `K` | Tools › Check Names |
| Check addressee names | `Ctrl` `Shift` `B` | Tools › Address Book |

These shortcuts apply to messages that you are composing, forwarding, or to which you are replying.

# News Keystroke Reference

The following Outlook Express newsgroup-related commands have keyboard shortcuts.

**Table D.1**

| General Shortcuts | | |
| --- | --- | --- |
| **TASK** | **KEYBOARD SHORTCUT** | **MENU COMMAND** |
| Create a new message | Ctrl N | File > New > News Message or Message > New Message |
| Find a message | Ctrl Shift F | Edit > Find > Message |
| Find people | Ctrl E | Edit > Find > People |
| Open a particular folder | Ctrl Y | View > Go to Folder |
| Go to next unread folder | Ctrl J | View > Next > Next Unread Folder |
| Abort a send/receive | Esc | View > Stop |
| Check all groups for new messages | Ctrl Shift M | Tools > Synchronize |
| Send and receive mail | Ctrl M | Tools > Send and Receive > Send and Receive All |
| Open the Address Book | Ctrl Shift B | Tools > Address Book |
| Make the next/previous pane active | Tab / Shift Tab | |
| Help | F1 | Help > Contents and Index |

**Table D.2**

| Message List Shortcuts | | |
| --- | --- | --- |
| TASK | KEYBOARD SHORTCUT | MENU COMMAND |
| Open the selected message | Ctrl O or Enter | File › Open |
| Print the selected message | Ctrl P | File › Print |
| View properties of message | Alt Enter | File › Properties |
| Mark message as read | Ctrl Enter Q | Edit › Mark as Read |
| Mark message as unread | Ctrl Shift Enter | Edit › Mark as Unread |
| Mark thread as read | Ctrl T | Edit › Mark Thread as Read |
| Mark all messages as read | Ctrl Shift A | Edit › Mark All as Read |
| Copy selected message | Ctrl C | Edit › Copy |
| Select all messages | Ctrl A | Edit › Select All |
| View previous message in list | Ctrl < or ↑ | View › Previous Message |
| View next message in list | Ctrl > or ↓ | View › Next › Next Message |
| View next unread message | Ctrl U | View › Next › Next Unread Message |
| View next unread thread | Ctrl Shift U | View › Next › Next Unread Thread |
| Expand a message thread | → | View › Expand |
| Collapse a message thread | ← | View › Collapse |
| Refresh headers and articles | F5 | View › Refresh |
| View first message in list | Home | |
| View last message in list | End | |
| Scroll down one screen | Pg Dn | |
| Scroll up one screen | Pg Up | |
| New message to newsgroup | Ctrl N | Message › New Message or File › New › News Message |
| Reply to newsgroup | Ctrl G | Message › Reply to Group |
| Reply to author of message | Ctrl R | Message › Reply to Sender |
| Reply to newsgroup and author | Ctrl Shift R | Message › Reply to All |
| Forward selected message | Ctrl F | Message › Forward |

These shortcuts assume that one or more messages are currently selected (highlighted) in the message list pane.

**Table D.3**

| Message Preview Pane Shortcuts | | |
| --- | --- | --- |
| TASK | KEYBOARD SHORTCUT | MENU COMMAND |
| Open the current message | Ctrl O or Enter | File › Open |
| Print the current message | Ctrl P | File › Print |
| View properties of message | Alt Enter | File › Properties |
| Copy selected text | Ctrl C | Edit › Copy |
| Select all text | Ctrl A | Edit › Select All |
| Mark message as read | Ctrl Enter Q | Edit › Mark as Read |
| Mark message as unread | Ctrl Shift Enter | Edit › Mark as Unread |
| Mark thread as read | Ctrl T | Edit › Mark Thread as Read |

Most of these shortcuts also apply to existing messages that you have opened for reading in a separate window.

**Table D.3** (continued)

### Message Preview Pane Shortcuts

| TASK | KEYBOARD SHORTCUT | MENU COMMAND |
|---|---|---|
| View previous message in list | Ctrl < | View › Previous Message |
| View next message in list | Ctrl > | View › Next Message |
| View next unread message | Ctrl U | View › Next › Next Unread Message |
| View next unread thread | Ctrl Shift U | View › Next › Next Unread Thread |
| Scroll down one screen | Pg Dn | |
| Scroll up one screen | Pg Up | |
| Go to start of message | Home | |
| Go to end of message | End | |
| New message to newsgroup | Ctrl N | Message › New Message or File › New › News Message |
| Reply to newsgroup | Ctrl G | Message › Reply to Group |
| Reply to author of message | Ctrl R | Message › Reply to Sender |
| Reply to newsgroup and author | Ctrl Shift R | Message › Reply to All |
| Forward current message | Ctrl F | Message › Forward |

Most of these shortcuts also apply to existing messages that you have opened for reading in a separate window.

**Table D.4**

### Outgoing Message Shortcuts

| TASK | KEYBOARD SHORTCUT | MENU COMMAND |
|---|---|---|
| Post or send message | Alt S | File › Send Message |
| Save current text as a draft | Ctrl S | File › Save |
| View properties of message | Alt Enter | File › Properties |
| Close the message window | Alt F4 or Esc | File › Close |
| Undo last edit | Ctrl Z | Edit › Undo |
| Cut selected text | Ctrl X | Edit › Cut |
| Copy selected text | Ctrl C | Edit › Copy |
| Paste text from clipboard | Ctrl V | Edit › Paste |
| Select all text | Ctrl A | Edit › Select All |
| Find text in this message | F3 or Ctrl Shift F | Edit › Find › Text in this message |
| Go to beginning of message | Ctrl Home | |
| Go to end of message | Ctrl End | |
| Go to start of current line | Home | |
| Go to end of current line | End | |
| Scroll down one screen | Pg Dn | |
| Scroll up one screen | Pg Up | |
| Insert default email signature | Ctrl Shift S | Insert › Signature › News Signature (Default) |
| Check spelling of message | F7 | Tools › Spelling |
| Check names in message | Ctrl K or Alt K | Tools › Check Names |

These shortcuts apply to messages that you are composing, forwarding, or to which you are replying.

# Installing and Updating IE5

Unlike previous versions of Internet Explorer, the IE5 installation procedure enables you to install just the Internet components you want. In this appendix, you will learn how to install IE5 by downloading it from the Internet. If you have IE5 on a CD-ROM, you should follow the instructions from the CD-ROM rather than the ones presented here.

In addition, Microsoft regularly issues updates to IE5; some add new features, and others correct problems with the program. To learn how you can add components to IE5 and install updates, read "Updating and Adding Components to IE5," later in this appendix.

# Installing IE5 from the Internet

As has been the case with previous versions of Internet Explorer, IE5 is free if you download it from the Internet. The instructions presented below assume that you are downloading it from Microsoft's Web site. (If you search the Web, you'll find that it is also available from several other major download sites, such as C/Net (http://www.cnet.com).

Note that if you want IE5 to be integrated into the operating system, you must have IE4 installed on your computer *before* installing IE5. (If you are running Windows 98, IE4 is already installed.) For details, see Chapter 1 ("Active Desktop").

## To install IE5:

1. Launch your current browser program and go to the Internet Explorer home page at:

   http://www.microsoft.com/windows/ie/

2. Click the Download Now button or the Download button in the menu on the left side of the screen (**Figure E.1**).

   The File Download dialog box appears (**Figure E.2**).

Download button                    Download Now button

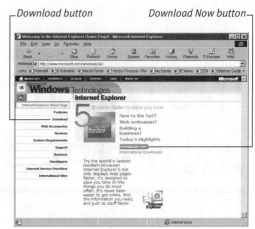

**Figure E.1** You can download IE5 from the Internet Explorer home page.

**Figure E.2** To begin the installation immediately after downloading the setup file, choose *Run this program from its current location*.

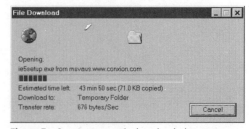

**Figure E.3** Setup program is downloaded to your computer.

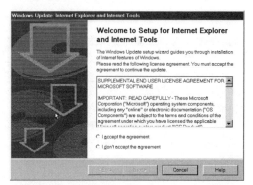

**Figure E.4** Before downloading IE5, you must agree to the terms presented in this screen.

*Typical installation*          *Custom installation*

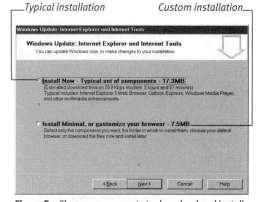

**Figure E.5** Choose components to download and install.

*Components list*          *Advanced options*

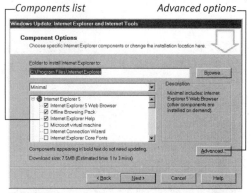

**Figure E.6** If you elect to perform a custom installation, the minimal components are pre-selected for you. Add or remove checkmarks to indicate the components you want to download and install.

**3.** Choose the option to *Run this program from its current locations* and click OK.

A small setup program is downloaded to your computer (**Figure E.3**) and then launches (**Figure E.4**).

**4.** Read the user agreement, click the radio button option that indicates *I accept the agreement*, and click the Next button.

**5.** Choose the components you want to install (**Figure E.5**) and click Next.

◆ *Install Now* will download all the essential components of IE5, as well as Outlook Express and the newest version of Windows Media Player.

◆ *Install Minimal, or customize your browser* lets you choose just the components you want (**Figure E.6**).

**6.** After a brief pause, a list of download sites appears (**Figure E.7**). Select a site in your country and click Next.

The selected software is downloaded to your computer (**Figure E.8**) and installed.

## ✔ Tips

- If the download is interrupted (either by you or excess network traffic), you will be given an opportunity to save a shortcut to your desktop. When you want to resume the download, click the shortcut.

- If you elect to perform the custom installation, be sure to click the Advanced button in the Component options dialog box (refer to **Figure E.6**). A new dialog box appears (**Figure E.9**) with the following useful options:

  - *Don't associate file types.* This prevents IE5 from changing some file associations you may have previously established.

  - *Compatibility.* This option leaves both IE4 and IE5 on your computer. If you develop Web pages, this will enable you to check their appearance in both versions of the program.

  - *Download only.* Rather than automatically install the selected components at the conclusion of the download, this option merely saves them to your hard disk so you can install IE5 later. This option is useful if you believe you may need to reinstall IE5 or want to move the components to a different computer.

- If you want to install additional components, see the instructions in the following section ("Updating and Adding Components to IE5").

*Site list*

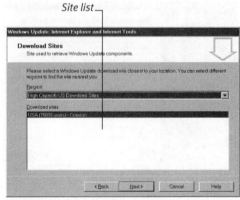

**Figure E.7** Select a region and site from which to download IE5.

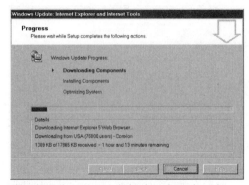

**Figure E.8** The Progress dialog box shows how the download/installation process is faring.

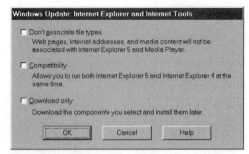

**Figure E.9** Advanced options for a custom download.

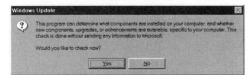

**Figure E.10** This dialog box appears each time you visit the Windows Update page. You must click Yes in order to continue.

*Show components that you have previously installed*— *Download button*—

**Figure E.11** The Windows Update page.

# Updating and Adding Components to IE5

If you installed IE5 by downloading it from the Internet, chances are good that you chose either the Typical or Minimal installation. In either case, there are additional IE5 components that you might want to install. Similarly, since Microsoft regularly adds to and updates IE5's components, you can use the same procedure (described below) to make sure that your installation is up to date.

## To update or add components to IE5:

1. Launch IE5, and choose Tools > Windows Update.

   The Windows Update page appears, followed shortly by the Windows Update dialog box (**Figure E.10**).

2. Click Yes to allow the Web site to check your system for installed IE5-related software components.

   The Windows Update page (**Figure E.11**) lists all available IE5 components that are not already installed.

3. Read the descriptions for the available components, entering a checkmark for each one you wish to install.

4. Click the Download button.

   The selected components are downloaded and then installed for you.

## ✔ Tips

■ It's a good idea to regularly check for new components and updates. If bug fixes or security patches for IE5 are released, this is where you'll find them.

■ You can also uninstall components from the same Web page. Click *Show Installed Updates* for a list of components that you can remove from your IE5 installation.

# INDEX

@ character, in email addresses, 170

## A

abbreviations, 273–279
Accessibility button/options, 124, 126
Active Channels, 109. *See also* channels.
Active Desktop
    and channels, 110, 113
    customization options, 13–15
    defined, 274
    and drag-and-drop, 19
    features and benefits, 3
    installation, 3, 7
    items, creating/managing, 16–21
    menu commands, 7–8
    and system crashes, 19
ActiveMovie controls, 95, 98
ActiveX controls, 95, 122, 123
Add Active Channel button, 111
Add Favorite dialog box, 51, 73, 99, 111
Add item to Active Desktop dialog box,
    16–17, 20, 113
Add Printer Wizard, 102
Address Book
    and business cards, 167–168, 210
    and digital IDs, 183
    importing/exporting data, 165–168
    major features, 156
    and Microsoft Wallet, 134
    opening, 157
    printing, 164
    purpose of, 155
    records
        creating, 158–159
        deleting, 159
        sorting, 164
    searching, 6
    setting display options, 163
    sharing data, 165, 166
Address Book Export Tool dialog box, 166
Address Book Import Tool dialog box, 165
Address box
    location/purpose of, 26, 36
    performing autosearch from, 61, 65
    using AutoComplete to type URLs in, 140
addresses
    email, 169–170, 179–180, 198
    in Microsoft Wallet, 134
    newsgroup message/article, 243–244
    Web page, 26
Advanced Dial-Up dialog box, 136
Advanced options, 119, 139–141
AltaVista, 61, 62, 67, 68, 278
America Online, 61, 68, 145, 154
anonymous user, FTP site, 91
AnyWho, 68
AOL. *See* America Online.
applets, Java, 122, 123, 277
archive, self-extracting, 275, 278
articles, newsgroup, 145, 219. *See also*
    newsgroups.
ASCII files, 175
ASF files, 96

INDEX